Acknowledgements

This book was completed thanks to the academic and personal generosity of a number of people. I would particularly like to thank Michael Morgan, whose continued efforts on my behalf have far exceeded what could fairly be expected of a PhD supervisor. Special thanks are also due to Mary Mander, who got me started in academia, and Sean Cubitt who was enormously helpful in attracting a publisher. I am also grateful to Nickianne Moody for creating the space for the final write up.

On a personal level, I am grateful to my father, David Ruddock, for not letting me join the Navy when I was 16 and making me go to University instead. Okay, you were right. Thanks also to Jo McWatt for the coffee and TV.

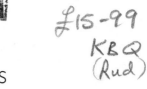
Understanding Audiences

Theory and Method

Andy Ruddock

SAGE Publications

London • Thousand Oaks • New Delhi   0761963448

To David Alexander Ruddock 1941–1999

 SAGE Publications Ltd
6 Bonhill Street
London EC2A 4PU

SAGE Publications Inc
2455 Teller Road
Thousand Oaks, California 91320

SAGE Publications India Pvt Ltd
32, M-Block Market
Greater Kailash – I
New Delhi 110 048

British Library Cataloguing in Publication data

A catalogue record for this book is available
from the British Library

ISBN 0 7619 6344 8
ISBN 0 7619 6345 6 (pbk)

Library of Congress catalog record available

Typeset by Mayhew Typesetting, Rhayader, Powys
Printed in Great Britain by Redwood Books,
Trowbridge, Wiltshire

Contents

Introduction: Science Wars and Cultural Studies

This is a book about audiences and how to study them – from a cultural studies perspective. Audience research must be placed, however, within the broader context of the truth claims made by social science and the position taken by critical media studies *vis-à-vis* these claims. What is it that cultural studies promises to tell us about the societies in which we live, and how does this knowledge differ in form and content from the 'truths' offered by other social and physical sciences? As will become clear, these are important questions to ask since, before we can set out to study any phenomenon, we must be very clear about what we want to know, and what it is possible to say about it within the confines of the methods and theories we use. Another way of putting this is to say that, although scholars from a variety of disciplines would agree that it is important to know how the mass media affect audiences, there is considerable disagreement over what we can know about these effects and how we can set out to measure them. Perhaps an anecdote will illustrate the point.

Physics versus cultural studies

For a time, in the summer of 1996, cultural studies was front-page news. No lesser source than the distinguished *New York Times* carried a story and, eventually, editorial pieces on what appeared to be little more than a storm in an academic tea cup. The story ran thus: MIT physics professor, Alan Sokal, had submitted an article to the journal *Social Text*, entitled 'Transgressing the boundaries: toward a transformative hermeneutics of quantum gravity' (1996). Now here was a very curious situation. Traditionally, cultural studies has been hostile to disciplines that claim to provide objective knowledge about the world through the application of tried-and-tested scientific methods, specifically the hard sciences, mainstream sociology and psychology (crudely those subjects believing that reality is simply out there to be measured and understood). For this reason, it was strange to see a physicist appearing in a cultural studies journal. It would have been laudable enough for Sokal simply to know that *Social Text* existed, let alone publish in it.

This incident was unusual since Andrew Ross and Stanley Aronowitz, both editors of *Social Text*, had begun to make apparently disparaging comments about the hard sciences. Following on from the work of Kuhn (1962), Ross and Aronowitz set out to re-contextualize science as a thoroughly social activity, a profession which responds as much to the ebb and flow of social norms as to the demands of objective codes of practice. Finally, in what amounted to an academic defrocking, Ross declared that you don't actually have to know very much about science to critique it: scientists are no better placed than the rest of us to comment on the social effects of things like nuclear power and genetic engineering. Against this history, Sokal's article appeared as a white flag. Here, apparently, was a physicist who was willing to defect. Mouths dropped as the emperor confessed to his nudity. Yes, said Sokal, physics was nothing more than a language-game. Reality, even physical reality, is a product of language rather than immutable natural force. *Social Text* published the piece, just as kings and queens of old publicly displayed the severed heads of vanquished foes. Victory was won!

But no, it was all a trap! Shortly after the publication of the essay, Sokal wrote to *Lingua Franca* denouncing the piece as an academic ruse. The whole episode had been designed to show that (a) publication in cultural studies journals was a matter of using the right jargon rather than adhering to tried-and-tested modes of inquiry; and (b) the editors of *Social Text* wouldn't recognize a decent critique of science if it slapped them in the face. Anyone who knew anything about physics would have trashed Sokal's piece; *Social Text* published it (Chapman, 1996).

Levitt (1995) had pre-empted Sokal in a response to Aronowitz (1995). Through a rather obscure baseball analogy, which probably doesn't work much past the Statue of Liberty, Levitt accused the *Social Text* crew of 'wannabe-ism'. They 'wannabe' real scientists but, lacking the talent and work ethic demanded of the physicist, chemist, mathematician and biologist, have settled for the pseudo-science that is cultural studies. For scholars such as Levitt and Sokal, the idea that science is a social practice, that it responds more to economic, political and linguistic influences than any determining physical laws of the universe, is absolute nonsense. Anyone who doubted this was invited to talk his or her way out of gravity by jumping out of Sokal's apartment window (Chapman, 1996). My old maths teacher once exclaimed in class 'Maths puts people on the moon, what the hell did history ever do?' Sokal would nod in agreement. Against the tangible triumphs of hard science – the planes we fly in, the buildings we live in, the medicines we take – the 'insights' offered by semiotic criticism of the mass media pale into insignificance.

What's the audience got to do with it?

The Sokal affair points to a serious division between the humanities and the hard sciences over how to approach academic work. It is based on a long-standing debate around things that are worth studying, and how we should study them. Relating this to the world of audiences, while cultural studies tends to see the mass-media effects as long term, diffuse and difficult to see, other schools of thought have argued that it is possible to measure them in fairly concrete terms. Others might argue that since these effects are indeed hard to measure with any precision, scholars should stick to studying things that *can* be measured accurately, or that can be used to provide useful knowledge, offering guides to future action. The latter position can be seen as motivating the push towards vocational degree programmes at the expense of the more 'esoteric' humanities. Aronowitz asks why the hard sciences have chosen this moment to mount such a concerted attack on a humanistic critique which has, in fairness, been around for several hundred years. His conclusion, that scientists' anxieties are prompted by the realization that the humanities are achieving some sort of institutional parity, might smack of present-minded self-aggrandizement or wishful thinking, but the image of oppositional fields facing each other with theoretical and methodological daggers drawn is largely accurate.

One can understand the disagreements between physicists and academics in the humanities, but the problem for media scholars is that they often work in areas that have internalized these sharp distinctions. For example, in the US people doing cultural studies are often billeted within departments of communication. Douglas Kellner (1995) sees this as an awkward housing arrangement. The discomfort is produced by the ambiguities contained in the word 'communication'. Boston and Donohew (1992) argue that communications departments typically define what they do in one of three ways: as scientific, hermeneutic or practical activity. That is, the study of communication is seen as consistent with the physical sciences (with all of the trappings of objectivism), interpretative sociology (including some of the trappings of relativism) or else it isn't seen as an academic area at all, being concerned principally with the acquisition of practical skills. Would-be cultural critics, journalists, film-makers and advertisers can all find themselves pursuing the same degree, at least in name. It is this situation that produces students entering academic media studies programmes in the misguided hope of acquiring skills which are immediately applicable to careers in media production.

On the other hand, the epistemological fog clouding the field can be cast in a positive light. Boston and Donohew's (1992) tripartite division, rather than being read as representative of a general confusion, can alternatively be seen as a necessary foregrounding of vital questions which are in and of themselves objects of inquiry. For instance, the question of whether communication involves the acquisition of practical knowledge raises larger issues. Is the communicative act a transparent practice that is, although it can be practised with greater or lesser degrees of sophistication (hence the need for public-speaking classes), basically common to us all? Or must communicative events be seen as related to issues of power in the sense that they involve attempts to convey culturally specific meanings across uneven discursive terrains?

This same question can be approached from a slightly different perspective. Boston and Donohew's (1992) tripartite distinction can be dichotomized. The 'science' and 'hermeneutics' categories are distinct from 'practice' in the sense that they see communications studies as relating to academic rather than practical knowledge. Whereas the latter focuses on the development of interpersonal skills, or the use of mass-media technologies, communications 'scientists' and 'hermeneuticists' reflect upon the social impact that these skills may have.

Throughout the twentieth century, this trend was best represented by those studies that addressed the impact of the mass media on the way people think and act in contemporary society. From the Payne Fund studies, beginning in the 1920s (Defleur and Lowery, 1988), through to the 'video nasty' controversies of the 1980s and 1990s, academics and non-academics alike have remained fascinated by the mass media's ability to manipulate the public mind. This common object of study, however, implies no theoretical or methodological conformity. The problem is that every concept we use to assess the impact of the mass media represents a maze of ambiguity. What do we mean by an effect? How is it brought about? How should we measure it? What on earth do we mean by 'the public mind'? This is where the science/hermeneutic division comes into play. Just because two researchers globally define their goal as being to assess the impact of the mass media does not mean that they are doing the same thing. Even if they use the same terminology, the meanings attached to key words such as 'communication', 'audience', 'public', 'effect', 'behaviour' and 'attitude' may be very different. Scholars working within communications departments thus find themselves confronting Sokal-like dilemmas everyday.

Traditionally, these differences are explained along the lines of the objectivist/relativist debate (Bernstein, 1988). That is, there is a division between those who argue that we can come to know the truth about the effects of the media on society because there *is* a truth that we can discover through the use of the right measuring tools, and those who would argue that our images of the media's impact on society depend upon the questions we ask and the methods we use to answer them. That is, our understanding of the media's role in contemporary culture is a product rather than a discovery of research projects with their own ideological axes to grind.

Within the communications discipline, the objectivist/relativist split is frequently equated with the distinction made between quantitative and qualitative methods of inquiry. As we shall see, much of the early work on the relationship between the media and audiences tended to use the former approach. This has been read by scholars such as Carey (1989) as suggesting a connection with the philosophy known as 'positivism'. Briefly, positivism forms the theoretical basis for the hard sciences in suggesting that the world has a fixed, observable structure which can be measured via the correct methodologies (Bernstein, 1988; Hammersley, 1989; Fay, 1996). Positivist media research thus suggests that the media's impact on the audience can be known with the same degree of certainty.

It is at this point that the gloves come off. Cultural studies has risen on the swell of a diverse yet steady campaign aimed at dislodging positivism from its sovereign position within the social sciences. Most scholars in the field would acknowledge that cultural studies is indebted to psychoanalysis, Marxism, feminism and postmodernity. Hall (1992) sees all of these paradigms as contributing to the dislodging of the Enlightenment project (the general attempt from the fifteenth century onwards to demonstrate how humans could tame the world through the development and application of medical, chemical, physical and biological science) that houses positivism. Taken together, these modes of thought cast doubt upon the reliability and even the validity of scientific research. Where science claims to show us the truth, we are presented with the argument that what we get is simply a version of truth that is the product of a priori definitions of what counts as a fact, definitions which are eminently contestable.

We can begin to see why cultural studies might unhappily share office space with media scholars using quantitative methods. This is nowhere more evident than within audience research. Audience research has emerged as an important part of cultural studies analysis of the social role of the mass media. This emergence has, however, assumed a distinctive form. If we confine ourselves to cultural studies, we could be excused for thinking that audience research began some time in the late 1970s, with the work of people such as Morley (1980) and Hall (1980). But taking the controversial step of situating cultural studies within the field of communication shows us that media audiences have been studied and publicly discussed from the beginning of the twentieth century. The reason why this contextualization is controversial is, as indicated above, that not everyone who has studied audiences has done so for the same reasons. Nor have the researchers used the same methods or reached the same conclusions about the relationship between the media and their audience. A comprehensive discussion of audiences and how to research them must therefore be sensitive to three points of antagonism. First, there are different motives for wanting to know about audiences. Secondly, these divergent motives lead to different methodologies – that is, ways of looking at, measuring and/or understanding audiences. Finally, the motives and methods driving a researcher are likely to influence or even determine the results he or she obtains or – more accurately – constructs.

Rating the audience

As Ien Ang (1991) notes, there are different reasons for being interested in media audiences. To be blunt, the nature of the questions one asks will be guided by the persons or institutions paying for or supervising the research. These initial motivations are likely to shape not only the questions you ask but also crucially the methods you use to gather your answers. In combination, the methods and their motivations will also exercise a determining influence over the way in which you view your data and the conclusions you will reach. This means that the question 'why study audiences' needs to be rewritten. Instead, what does it mean to study audiences critically?

For our purposes, critical audience research is best represented by what is now recognized as the discipline of cultural studies. But here, again, we encounter an annoying conundrum because cultural studies prides itself on *not* being an academic discipline, at least not in a traditional sense. Rather than presenting scholars with a fixed set of theoretical and methodological orthodoxies, cultural studies fancies itself as a sort of academic town hall meeting where anyone is welcome, as long as he or she is alert to issues of ideology and power. To this end, the field is marked by a seemingly endless tendency towards navel gazing, best summarized by the title of Johnson's 1987 essay 'What is cultural studies about anyway?' Not wanting to be left out of the game, I'll ask the question again. What is cultural studies about, and how does it influence how we approach audiences?

Perhaps we can begin by saying that cultural studies is involved with making the familiar strange. This is a theme crossing the various academic trajectories intersecting within the rubric. The American school of cultural studies has been highly influenced by interpretative sociology and anthropology represented by people such as Herbert Blumer and the Chicago School of sociology, Howard Becker and the anthropologist Clifford Geertz. Where Geertz (1973) has outlined the complexity of culture, Becker (1986) has followed in the tradition of the Chicago School in illustrating that even familiar, everyday patterns of human interaction involve intricate systems of symbolic exchange. The centrality of Raymond Williams, who invested the everyday activities of working people with the same depth, within British cultural studies speaks to the same concerns. Taken together, the American and British schools have established a need to interrogate the most taken-for-granted aspects of our culture – soap operas (Hobson, 1982; Ang, 1985; Buckingham, 1987; Katz and Liebes, 1990), clothes (Hebdige, 1979), shopping (Morris, 1990), the things that we never think about – and have turned these practices into semiotic puzzles in need of exploration and explanation.

This commitment has been strengthened through feminist and postcolonial scholarship. Critical of the class and male centredness of early cultural studies, scholars have emphasized the importance of gender analysis within media research (Radway, 1983; Press, 1991; McRobbie, 1994). Ethnicity and the problems of eurocentrism have been highlighted by Said (1978), Hall (1986a), Spivak (1988) and Amin (1989). Collectively, these scholars have questioned the apparently 'commonsense' patriarchal and eurocentric positions from which we are encouraged to speak and into which we are spoken.

If there is an end-point at all, it is to establish that life is much more complicated than we might think. The identities that we feel, which we experience every day in what might seem to be unproblematic ways, are presented as cultural constructs which have been made and not simply found. Cultural studies also suggests that life is much more interconnected than we think. We might experience everyday life as a series of fragmented episodes that don't necessarily fit together. But macro-levels of social organization are felt in the micro-contexts of living in some surprising ways (Johnson, 1987). Take, for example, watching television. For many people, watching is a private indulgence, a treat granted to oneself at the end of the day. Often we watch alone or with intimate friends and family, shutting out the rest of the world in the process. 'TV time' is the time when you stop being a bank clerk or a traffic warden or a plumber or a student. It is a personalized activity which has little or nothing to do with the rest of your day or life.

The insistence on interrogating the banal within cultural studies tells us that this view is unlikely to be supported. Media consumption is, even if you are by yourself, a social activity; consider, for example, the fact that when you are watching television, millions of people around the country are doing the same thing, establishing viewing as an activity with a common cultural currency. David Morley's *Family Television* (1989) and Janice Radway's *Reading the Romance* (1983) both illustrate how various modes of audiencehood can be used to regulate family relationships that in turn respond to broader social forms of identity, especially gender.

Already we can see, then, how audiencehood is more complex than first appears. As Ang's (1991) work goes on to illustrate, this complexity means that it is equally difficult to study media audiences. Audiences are hard to analyse because, in the first instance, they are difficult to define. From a common-sense perspective, it would be tempting to say that the audience is quite simply those people who attend to a particular text. If this is true, then matters of definition are straightforward. For instance, if we want to know who the audience for a showing of a movie in a local theatre is, we could toddle along to that cinema over the weekend and just count the number of people in front of the screen. Football audiences are particularly easy to measure in this way, as we can count the number of people coming through the turnstile. Turning to television, we would say that the television audience is comprised of those who watch. The audience for *Friends* is quite simply those people who bother to tune in to the show. This is the rationale behind the ratings.

Audiences are very important to the media industry. Canadian critic Dallas Smythe defined television's audience as a commodity waiting to be sold to advertisers (see Leiss et al., 1990). The cost of the commodity depends on its size and composition, which is in turn dependent on the television's ability to draw a crowd. So media industries want to know about who is watching. But what is it they want to know? To be crude, as far as the television industry is concerned, size matters. This is true regardless of whether we are talking about public or commercial television. Commercial television makes money through advertising, and attracts advertisers by pointing to the ability of shows to produce the right audience, both in terms of size and composition. Even the BBC has to prove its ability to serve large audiences because of the need to justify the licence fee. So institutional concerns want to know simply who is watching what when (Ang, 1991). This seems reasonable enough. It's the same thing as asking who goes to a football match. Or is it?

Ratings represent a form of institutional research. Critical audience scholars define themselves as standing in opposition to this sort of work (Ang, 1991). It follows that we need to understand some of the faults within the ratings industry to begin to understand why critical work is needed. A good place to begin is by asking whether it is possible to measure the television audience in the same way as one might count the crowd for a sporting event. And if it is, would this tell us everything we need to know about audiences?

The answer to both questions is no. At a fundamental methodological level, television audiences simply cannot be counted in the same way as a football crowd. Almost all of the time, the attempt to quantify involves dealing with numbers of people so vast that we couldn't possibly count them. Social science recognizes this, and has developed a variety of strategies to deal with the fact that the quantitative questions social scientists or pollsters ask are too complicated to be answered by a simple head count.

So how do we quantify? Social science has generated sampling methodologies that make it possible for us to make educated guesses about the behaviour of large numbers of people based on observations of a subsection of the population we want to know about. This sub-section is known as a 'sample' (Babbie, 1992). For example, when we see BBC ratings, we see the claim that 17–18 million people regularly tune in to the soap opera *EastEnders*. But this is a prediction based on observations of the viewing patterns in just a few hundred households. These households are systematically selected to represent a social microcosm, so that we can be fairly sure that the behaviours we see are representative of behaviours occurring among the population as a whole.

Such sampling can never be 100 per cent accurate. When you see the results of polls, these results will include a margin of error and a confidence interval, which tell us the degree to which the poll results are likely to vary from the true population (Babbie, 1992). These are best guesses. This does not mean that the results of surveys can be completely dismissed: pre-election polls tend to be fairly successful in predicting the outcomes of elections. But it does mean that social science bears in its core a necessary doubt, a recognition that its products are rough guides to reality, pictures that are partial, potentially distorting and potentially wrong.

It is this space between the represented and the actual that forms the basis for Ien Ang's (1991) deconstruction of ratings hegemony. Even accepting this disjunction as an unavoidable artefact of sampling procedure, one might defend ratings as being indicative of general trends, rather than attempts to quantify the audience precisely. They are just measures of relative audience size where ranking rather than exact size of audience is the key. Ang, however, suggests that the ratings rely on measuring devices that are prone not only to error, but also to outright fiction. Take the example of the diaries that ratings audiences use to keep track of their viewing activity. People simply fill in weekly diaries logging what they watch and when. The problem with this measuring device lies in the high level of motivation, participation and honesty demanded of the people taking part. In reality, these measures are likely to contain huge inaccuracies. People may forget to fill in the diaries. They may fill them in every few days, at which point they might forget what they have been watching. Or they might just ignore them. They might also deliberately censor diary entries. For instance, one can imagine a 45-year-old father of two who doesn't really want to admit that he religiously tunes in to *Baywatch*. This is the issue of social desirability. The father in question knows he isn't supposed to lust secretly after Pamela Anderson, and he certainly isn't going to tell media researchers that this is what he gets up to in his spare time. Generally speaking, we must be wary of surveys because of the tendency of respondents to give socially acceptable rather than truthful answers.

'Peoplemeters' were seen as an advance on this method as they require far less active participation. Viewers simply click a button when they are watching a specific programme. But again, because this involves active commitment on the part of the viewer, the results can be questionable: people may forget, or might deliberately ignore the button. Not to be outdone, the industry has devoted time and effort towards the development of the so-called 'passive peoplemeter'. This is simply a device which is activated every time the television is switched on. There are even efforts to develop a machine capable of recording and recognizing the faces of each family member in the room as a way of finding out exactly who is watching what (Ang, 1991). This technology would seem to overcome all of the problems of the diary and cruder peoplemeter forms. But does this mean that the peoplemeter will allow us to achieve perfect knowledge of audiences? In some ways, this is an unfair question. Despite the many differences dividing the humanities, the social and the physical sciences, it is generally acknowledged that one should apply a horses-for-courses approach to inquiry. That is, certain methods are suited to certain types of question (Jensen, 1991). So, for instance, semiotics might help you design a visually appealing car, but it won't make the car work. That's not what semiotics is about.

We might say the same thing about technologies used to measure audiences. These technologies might be very good at telling us some things, but not very good at telling us others. Think again about the motivation behind institutional research, the 'size matters' philosophy. Is size all that matters about audiences? Putting the question another way, does audience research only go as far as sorting the wheat from the chaff, the viewer/reader/listener from the non-viewer/reader/listener? If you're trying to shift advertising space, the answer might be yes. You just want to prove the existence of a large target audience for an advertiser. Once you have a number, your work is done.

But, for our purposes, the answer is no. Remember, cultural studies is involved in the task of making the familiar strange, the simple complicated. It follows that the institutional definition of audiencehood is an over-simplification. To illustrate why this is the case, take a look at the cartoon world. Recently, our screens have featured two programmes which very explicitly talk about the centrality of television in contemporary life. These programmes are *The Simpsons* and *Beavis and Butthead*. Both feature characters whose lives are, for the most part, ruled by the medium. Homer Simpson, patriarch of the Simpson clan, is hopelessly addicted to the tube, as are Beavis and Butthead, two teenage metal-head losers living somewhere in the USA on a diet of fast food and MTV. Yet it is in their interactions with television that we can come to appreciate how audiencehood can be much more complicated than we think, and involves asking a great many more questions, implying the use of a greater range of methods than those employed in ratings research.

One could plausibly read both shows as endorsements of the Frankfurt School's direst warnings about the impact of the mass media. Adorno and Horkheimer feared that the mass media function as narcotics on the audience, making them passive, child-like and easily manipulated (MacDonald, 1959). If the conclusions of the mass-society thesis are contestable, this should not obscure the importance of the Frankfurt School in introducing a political edge to audience research. What they indicate is that mass-media consumption concerns a range of political questions centring on social power relations. In other words, we need to know more about audiences than how big they are. We need to know how audiences are being politically influenced by media consumption.

Some very pessimistic predictions are made about this by both *The Simpsons* and *Beavis and Butthead*. Very often we find the characters absolutely transfixed by what they see on the screen, lured into the promises of fulfilment offered. The character of Homer, especially, is frequently shown swallowing televisual lies hook, line and sinker. Homer is, quite simply, the mass media-created Frankenstein predicted by the Frankfurt School. He constantly falls on his face because of his inability to stop consuming. And he can't stop consuming because he can't believe that television tells him lies. He even rebukes Bart for suggesting this. Beavis and Butthead are similarly entranced by the box. In one episode they join a religious cult, and are placed in a room with no television. They both have an *Exorcist*-like fit. They leave the cult, knowing that they cannot survive such deprivation. The boys' preferred texts are music videos. Again, this encourages us to see them as monsters created by hypodermic needles, morons with attention spans unable to deal with anything more complicated than a two-minute video clip. At the same time, Beavis and Butthead aren't entranced by everything they see. Sometimes they are highly critical of videos. Sometimes they get up and dance, sometimes they begin unconnected conversations. Sometimes fist-fights erupt, and the television just becomes the background noise for the conflicts that happen in their lives.

Beavis and Butthead suggest that audiencehood is an umbrella term used to describe a diverse range of activities. Ang (1991) illustrates this by deconstructing the common-sense wisdom of the ratings. The ratings are based on the belief that watching, being in the audience, is an uncomplicated matter of manifest behaviour. You are either watching television or you are not. This has come to be a widely accepted 'reality'. We often see this same logic reflected by anti-censorship activists, who claim that if you have a problem with television content, you can solve it by switching off. So one is either in the audience or out of it. Hence, the right yardstick will allow us to measure an audience which exists in a straightforward objective sense.

But is this true? Take a typical family scenario: mum, dad and two kids in the living room in front of the television. A cop show is on. Dad is watching, eyes glued to the screen. So is mum. One child is listening to a walkman while doing some ironing. The other is reading a magazine. By institutional measures, they are all in the audience. But are they? Counting them all as audience members implies that they are all doing the same thing. But they're not. What we see is a range of behaviours running from complete attention to partial inattention. One kid cannot see what's going on. The other can neither see nor hear. What this example shows is that television audiencehood can describe a range of activities which also reveal very different relationships between viewer and medium (Lull, 1990).

We might also wonder if it really makes any sense to talk about non-viewers in the contemporary media environment. Conrad Kottak (1990) says that we can only speak meaningfully of non-viewers in the very early stages of television's introduction into a society. After a period of time, because the medium adopts such a central position in our society, even people who never or seldom watch are still vulnerable to its influence. For instance, people who watch one or two hours of television per day are often considered to be light viewers. These are people who are too busy to be sucked into the box. But let's think about this in another way. Imagine how fit you would be if you spent an hour or two in the gym every day? At the other end of the health spectrum, what would you say about someone who spent two hours every night doing whisky shots? Gerbner et al. (1981) argue that in reality there is no such thing as a light viewer. People who consume one or two hours per day may watch less than others, but they still consume vast amounts of information, and television can be seen as making significant inroads into their leisure time. In short, our light viewer is every bit as dependent as any gym-rat or alcoholic.

At this juncture, it would seem that the case for positivism and quantitative research methods has been dismissed. How can we begin to measure audiences if we cannot even decide who they are, where they are and what they do? In general, quantitative methods are too methodologically rigid and theoretically naïve to be of much use to the kinds of question asked in cultural studies. For this reason, while intro-ductory anthologies feature a wide range of scholars and perspectives on the analysis of culture (for example, During, 1990; Grossberg et al., 1992), these selections never feature quantitative research. One can only conclude that such work is inextricably bound to positivism and insti-tutional research.

But even if this *is* the case, *need it be* the case? What I want to suggest is that the quantitative/qualitative split is largely representative of the confusion caused by the intersection of a number of key theoretical and methodological issues. Succinctly, the schism is based on a critique of the theoretical inadequacies of early communications research projects which tended to over-simplify the definition of what an effect could be. Because these works used quantitative methodologies, it was often argued that these flaws were inherent products of the measuring devices selected (Newcomb, 1978).

On further examination, however, it appears that, although theory and method are and should be closely related, many of the critiques underpinning the quantitative/qualitative debate do not necessarily imply the rejection of statistical analysis, even in interpretative-style projects. That is, although quantification is normally tied to the science/ knowing side of Boston and Donohew's (1992) typology, with all of its negative implications, a closer analysis of the sources for this division of the communications discipline reveals that this need not be so. Moreover, the problematization of what we mean by 'science', 'knowing' and 'interpretation' questions the tenability of such divisions.

Media studies students are accustomed to encountering the quantitative and the qualitative as either/or alternatives. Although there are many reasons for this, in catch-all terms it can be said that this schism is driven by the belief that each field asks essentially different questions because they see the communicative process as functioning in different ways. Cultural studies, for example, has typically argued that its central concerns can only be addressed through qualitative techniques, such as textual analysis and focus-group research. Quantitative surveys, which limit possible responses to the confines of multiple choice questions, may be able to do things such as gauge the depth of the factual knowledge that people have on a particular issue, but they are of little use, orthodoxy tells us, in inquiring into the semiotic process of meaning construction. Typically, cultural studies has concentrated on establishing the discursive dynamics producing subject positions that accept, reject or negotiate with centres of hegemonic power.

The inherently limited scale of qualitative inquiries means, however, that some important questions have not been addressed in sufficient detail. In reducing the forces of a social totality to the moment of watching television, for instance, cultural studies can do little more than take an educated stab at how media consumption relates to wider dynamics. This is especially troublesome for a discipline intent on exploring the spaces between the notions of culture and society, loosely defined in this instance as the patterns of meaningful actions executed within institutional limits (Jenks, 1993).

This problem is produced because the results of qualitative analysis cannot be reliably transposed on to a wider social spectrum. This, of course, is a distinct advantage of survey research. Can such data be used to fill in some of the gaps left by cultural studies work to date? We can ask this question because of recent work suggesting that there is a difference between positivism and empirical research. Empirical research refers to work which is in some way reliant on the observation of socially situated phenomena, rather than exclusively theoretical exegesis. We could be forgiven for thinking that Ang (1991) has dismissed the case for the former, especially in her conclusion that the problems of the ratings tells us that the notion of audience only ever exists as a product of discourse: the audiences we perceive in research are illusions conjured up by scientific methods.

But this does not necessarily mean that we must follow Allor (1988) into the conclusion that audiences do not exist. Of course they do, which is why Morley (1992) claims that whatever the problems with methods of observation, the question of audiences 'remains empirical'. Similarly, for all her postmodern musing, Ang (1996) concedes that differences between institutional and critical audience scholars are principally theoretical rather than methodological. That is, differences between researchers are best understood as being grounded in the way in which they conceptualize research problems, rather than the data-gathering methods they use. And data gathering, that is observational research, remains central to any move towards understanding audiences.

The division between quantitative and qualitative methods has evolved for a number of good reasons. But we are not duty bound to respect it. Scholarship matures in part through a willingness to transgress disciplinary orthodoxies, and cultural studies is no exception. Two conclusions follow for students within the field. First, if you wish to reject quantitative methods outright, then you should at least have a good reason. Secondly, if Ang is right in concluding that the real source of antagonism is theoretical rather than methodological, then are both qualitative and quantitative researchers faced with similar epistemological problems that can best be understood by recourse to the philosophy of social science?

In the light of these questions, the following chapters present a more catholic approach to audience research than is normally found in cultural studies texts. What follows is not an attempt to find the right way of looking at the audience, or to champion one approach over another, but rather an effort to think about how different methods produce different, but often complementary, forms of knowledge. The real points of difference are conceptual and practical rather than strictly methodological. What do we want to know about the audience? From this list, which questions are amenable to research (as we shall see, some questions are so broad as to be beyond the grasp of any one study)? What explains the success and failure of competing research programmes? What is the current state of play in audience research?

Chapter 1 begins by defining key terms and questions. These revolve around the relationship between theory and method. It is important to appreciate the interconnections between the two, especially given that students and academics alike are prone to complain that cultural studies is overly theoretical. This chapter argues that all research begins from a set of theory-laden suppositions. In short, theory is the foundation of methodological exploration of the material world.

Chapter 2 reviews the early period of mass-communication research, generally recognized as an hegemonic era for quantitative effects research (even if one could argue that we are still in this era). Chapter 3 reviews the history of public-opinion research, a major part of mainstream sociological audience research which nevertheless reflects a shift towards an interest in socialization over immediate effect, and which has recently offered some interesting examples of how one can study the dissemination of ideology via the mass media. Chapter 4 begins to de-couple quantitative methods and positivism by looking at cultivation analysis, which developed a more critical stance while still 'crunching numbers'. Chapter 5 outlines the general aims and assumptions of critical qualitative research, centring on the notion of ideology and the emergence of the encoding/decoding model, locating it as a key moment in the defence of empirical methods against the postmodern critique. In encoding/decoding, Stuart Hall and David Morley present us with a post-positivist way of thinking about media effects which nevertheless retains a notion of determination, allowing us to speak of actual, or perhaps more appropriately situated, audiences. We will also examine recent critiques of the encoding/decoding model, and ask how this suggests new avenues for future research. Picking up this theme, Chapter 6 introduces the concept of consumption as a topic through which we can explore the expansion of audiencehood into the realm of everyday life. The Conclusion asks what general questions on the politics of epistemology cross both quantitative and qualitative audience research, using the long-running debate on the media, sex and violence as a case study of the general pitfalls of social research.

1 Questions of Theory *and* Method

B efore discussing how to do study audiences, we need to establish criteria for judging the strengths and weaknesses of research. This framework will be developed through a discussion of conflicts that have arisen over the nature, goals and methods of social science. 'Normal' views of the scientist – the dispassionate viewer of the world, dependent on the accuracy of tried-and-tested observational methods – do not square with reality. Whatever the common-sense allure of value-free science, this chapter will describe the reasons why all social research is inevitably influenced by the academic, political and cultural context in which it is conducted. This does not mean that such research is futile, but it does mean that social research must be read with one eye on questions of 'who, where, when and why' before we get to the 'how'.

Cultural studies is often criticized for being overly theoretical. This criticism usually comes from academics in the applied natural and social sciences, and not infrequently from students who would prefer to be learning something useful, i.e. something that will get them a job. An exploration of controversies within the social sciences, however, reveals that theoretical issues are far from esoteric. Whether we acknowledge it or not, all social research begins from theory, from the set of assumptions that researchers use about the world in which they live and the nature of the work that they do. Theory and method are entwined, and the informed researcher must develop a way of accounting for this symbiosis.

The research context: what do we want to know?

What do media researchers want to say about the impact of the mass media on audiences? Anyone who embarks on an audience research project would like to think that he or she will generate insights that will tell us something about the way in which the media impact upon our lives. What criteria would such a project need to fulfil to make this claim? From a standard social science point of view, three terms come to mind. Two of these refer to the strength of the observational methods used. *Reliability* is the degree to which we can say that, if the same observational methods were applied to the same research site again, they would yield the same results. To choose a simple example, we could return to ways of measuring the attendance at a sporting event. Attendance is measured by simply counting heads, and we can be sure that anyone familiar with basic numeracy would measure the crowd in much the same way. *Validity* concerns the degree to which we can say that the thing we are measuring actually represents the concept we wish to discuss. Returning to our sporting crowd, suppose we wish to measure how liked and respected team A is: would counting the number of people who go to see the team play provide a valid measure? Quite possibly, the answer is no. Our crowd will inevitably include supporters of team B, who may neither like nor respect team A. Moreover, team A may be so detested by opposing fans that they show up in their droves in the hope of seeing team A falter. If this is the case, then counting the crowd, although it is undoubtedly a reliable form of measurement, is not valid since what you are observing are the numbers of people who both love and loathe team A (for discussions of reliability and validity, see Babbie, 1992).

Finally, *generalizability* is often regarded as a benchmark of solid research. In classic terms, generalizability refers to the degree to which we can transpose the observations made in a specific research setting on to a wider social context (Babbie, 1992). Not all projects set out to generate generalizable findings, especially within cultural studies. Having said this, much audience research does claim to inform us about general processes of mass communication through the observation of an audience sample. Whatever one's predisposition on the possibilities of objective social science, it follows that one should consider how various projects and approaches are positioned *vis-à-vis* this concept.

Taken together, these criteria, although they do not apply as stated in the terms above to all forms of audience research, provide useful ways for thinking about the 'truth' claims made by various theoretical and methodological branches of the social sciences. More specifically, they allow us to consider the cases for and against 'normal science'. These are fundamental questions in considering what it is that we want to – or can – know by studying audiences.

Why should we care about audiences?

Audience research is a complex process fraught with contradiction. So perhaps it is best to begin with a statement of what we can confidently proclaim about the mass media's impact. Anthropologist Conrad Kottak (1990) claims that, with reference to television, the medium has so permeated Western society that we can no longer meaningfully speak of non-viewers. Viewing estimates from many countries support his conclusions. In the UK, the British Audience Research Bureau estimates that the average viewer watches a staggering 29 hours of television per week. But, if anything, even as startling a figure as this underestimates the degree of our media exposure. Add in time spent listening to the radio, tapes and CDs, reading books, newspapers and magazines, glancing at billboards on our way to work and surfing the Internet, and it soon appears that we are all media audiences almost all of the time. These simple observations demonstrate that a concern with the media's social impact is no more than common sense. How can any student of society and culture afford to ignore such a time-devouring element of contemporary social life?

But what about the *nature* of the media's impact? Several examples of media influence spring readily to mind for anyone who pays even a fleeting attention to the news. We know, for example, that television has transformed a number of important social institutions. The murder trials of former American football star O. J. Simpson and British nanny Louise Woodward have raised questions about whether the trial by jury system, a system whose integrity relies upon the ability to sequester a jury from external influences, can survive media-saturated societies. Many claim that the quality of political campaigning is suffering a similar demise. In the 1992 US presidential election, the comedian Dennis Miller claimed that Ross Perot's campaign had suffered from his vice presidential candidate John Stockdale's poor performance in a televised debate. Unused to such a forum, and unable to hear properly (due to an ear-drum that had been perforated during a period as a prisoner of war), the otherwise erudite former naval admiral and then college professor came across as muddled and dull-witted. His true crime? Being bad on television.

Then, of course, we have long-standing concerns over the mass media's power to erode moral fibre, producing anti-social and even psychopathic behaviour. In the 1950s, comic books were blamed for juvenile delinquency (Wertham, 1955). More recently, the film *Natural Born Killers* has been connected with 14 murders worldwide, including a particularly gruesome killing frenzy performed by two Parisian students. The music industry has also been accused of provoking murder. The heavy metal group Judas Priest were sued by a teenager who had shot a friend and blown a substantial part of his own face off in a bungled suicide attempt. The shootings followed a day spent taking drugs and listening to a Priest song which, the plaintiff felt, encouraged his actions. The mass media are also blamed for provoking a host of other anti-social behaviours, such as assault, smoking, drinking, drug-taking and sexual promiscuity.

Still others point to a number of less observable, but equally important effects. British media researchers from the Birmingham School of sociology and the Glasgow Media Group (Eldridge, 1993) have devoted a great deal of time to outlining how the media can influence the shape of social policy by dictating the terms in which political issues are debated. The group claimed that negative press coverage played a key role in undermining the power of trade unions. They also argued that a jingoistic news industry accelerated Britain's entry into the Falklands War. The Gulf War of 1991 also provoked a number of concerns about the media's ability to mould public opinion (Mowlana et al., 1992).

We can say for sure, then, that there are many reasons why we need to examine and understand the relationship between media and audiences. But it is also at this point that we encounter a fundamental problem. You might have noticed a distinct difference between the reasons provided for a concern about audiences in the first paragraph of this section, and the subsequent justifications offered. If we want to justify audience research on the grounds of sheer media saturation, no reasonable person could raise an objection. Media saturation is an empirical fact. When considering the nature of the concerns that emerge from this fact, however, we move on to shakier ground. Whereas we can simply describe the amount of media exposure we receive, assessing the effects of this saturation requires acts of interpretation and evaluation. This implies several problems relating to validity and reliability. In some of the examples stated above, we can already see a number of potential controversies about the nature of media power. We can also see how media criticism is necessarily provoked by the political position of the researcher. Some people are more concerned than others, for example, about the apparent erosion of conservative sexual mores. The Glasgow Media Group also took an explicitly leftist stance in its complaints about the role that television played in undermining British trade unionism.

All of us have seen optical illusions involving drawings that resemble two things at once. A famous example is a drawing of what appears to be, from one perspective, a beautiful young woman dressed in Victorian fashion and, from another, an evil, wart-ridden crone. What we see depends on how we look at the picture. Krippendorf (1995) argues that media research can be thought about in the same way. The things that we see in the media, and in the effects on the audience, depend on the position we adopt before we even begin our research. *All* researchers approach their topic armed with a set of assumptions and tools which influence the nature of the things they see (Krippendorf, 1995). Think about the picture again. What is its reality? Does it depict a beautiful woman or a crone? The answer is both, both realities are present, but your ability to see one or the other depends on how you approach the object. It also follows that neither version of what the picture is provides the definitive answer; they represent equally valid approaches to the same reality. This alerts us to the clash between validity and reliability. Both interpretations of the picture reflect a portion of reality, but neither way of viewing it can claim objectivity: we cannot be sure that two people will look at the picture and see the same thing. Generalizability issues follow: we cannot be sure how far our way of seeing the picture is representative of what a wider audience sees.

In practice, it is very difficult, if not impossible, to adopt an entirely similar approach to media research. Having spent some time reading about the topic, you may well conclude that certain approaches to audiences offer few answers with reference to your own interests. But thinking about audience studies, it is best to start by acknowledging that all research involves limiting one's view, the things that one can say about audiences, by selecting a set of ideas and tools that allows us to see some things but not others. It remains for this chapter to chart what these tools are and how they are connected.

The standard view of the scientist

The popular, common-sense view of the scientist can be described in terms of the way that he or she is supposed to *think*, and the way that he or she is supposed to *proceed*. In terms of thinking, the scientist is supposed to remove him or herself from potentially biasing elements to view the world and interpret data in an objective manner. The basis for this view can be found in the work of French philosopher René Descartes. Descartes was a seminal figure in the Enlightenment, the period when an explosive growth in scientific knowledge created a new confidence concerning the ability of humans to control the natural world and their own destiny. For this reason, his work is also vital for an understanding of traditional views of what represents proper science.

Descartes' thinking is normally summarized by a quote taken from his *Discourse on Method*: 'I think, therefore I am' (Flew, 1971). This deceptively simple statement disguises a range of important suppositions regarding the relationship between the thinker in question and the world in which he or she lives. The sort of thinking Descartes is concerned with is thinking that generates true knowledge, knowledge that we can rely on, knowledge that has nothing to do with custom, tradition or prejudice. This could only be attained through the following process:

> I thought that I must reject as if it were absolutely false everything about which I could suppose there was the least doubt, in order to see if after that there remained anything which I believed which was entirely indisputable. So, on the grounds that our senses sometimes deceive us, I wanted to suppose that there was not anything corresponding to what they make us imagine. And, because some men make mistakes in reasoning – even with regard to the simplest matters of geometry – and fall into fallacies, I judged that I was as much subject to error as anyone else, and I rejected as unsound all the reasonings which I had hitherto taken for demonstrations. (Descartes, cited in Flew, 1971: 280)

Scientific thinking, then, is conducted by people who are able to remove themselves from potentially biasing elements of cultural values. This concept grounds the notion of objectivity or value neutrality. The true scientist serves no political master, but produces value-free knowledge for the good of all.

Having established how the scientist is supposed to think, it remains to describe how he or she is supposed to act. Descartes' theory of knowledge can be seen as operationalized by the tenets of a philosophical position known as 'positivism'. Not coincidentally, positivism emerges during the same period, being associated at first with the work of Auguste Comte (Kolakowski, 1992). Positivism can be seen as related to the Cartesian belief that true knowledge is based on things that we can be sure are true. One way of interpreting this is to say that science is based on the gathering of physical evidence that cannot be doubted. This is the founding principle of positivism. Believing that we live in a world with a fixed and knowable physical structure, positivist science is based on the development of observational methods which allow us to see that reality for what it is (Fay, 1996). Kolakowski (1992) sees positivism as being defined by four rules:

1   'The rule of phenomenalism' (1992: 3), which holds that the nature or truth of an object of study is manifest in its physical, observable (and hence knowable) features.

2 'The rule of nominalism' (1992: 4), which holds that scientific observations must be based on the presence of a tangible object.
3 The rule of value-neutrality, which as the name suggests holds that values cannot be classified as knowledge, nor can they be scientifically examined (since they lack a physical referent).
4 The rule of scientific unity, the idea that there is a single scientific method that is equally applicable to all fields of study whose goal it is to produce true knowledge.

Taken together, the Cartesian view of scientific thought and the positivist prescription for scientific action provide what looks like a sensible course for potential researchers. Knowledge grows through a neutral process of observation that, by confining itself to a physical world that is objectively measurable, remains aloof from political positions based upon value judgements that can be classified as neither true nor false.

Attractive as this view might be, it is hopelessly divorced from the reality of conducting social research. In fairness, few if any social scientists believe in this pure form of positivism, but the model does serve a useful role as a touchstone for many of the problems that we encounter when trying to research social issues such as the impact of the mass media. If, then, Descartes and the positivists outline a widely accepted common-sense view of scientific activity, what is wrong with this picture?

Can we have a science of the social?

As we have seen, positivism defines science as a means of seeing clearly. Scientific methodology is thus based on methods which allow us to see things for what they actually are. Take, as an example, advances in the health field. Suppose you suspect that you are overweight. How would you confirm that your suspicions were true? One way would be to ask friends or partners if they think you are overweight. The answers you get are not likely to be objective; no partner with an interest in maintaining a harmonious relationship is going to say yes, even if he or she thinks that this is the case. The reply that you get to this question, then, does not reflect the perceptions of the partner, but instead reflects your partner's idea of what it is you want to hear.

So, we turn to science in the form of a set of scales. Scales have no concern for your feelings, or for current fashions in body types. They simply objectively measure your weight. They will tell you, in no uncertain terms, whether or not your body has grown larger. But scales do not necessarily tell us how fat we are. With the growth of fitness culture, it has become clear that, under certain conditions, gaining weight can be a good thing. If you start going to a gym, your body may get larger as fat is replaced by heavier lean muscle tissue. This invalidates traditional ways of defining what being overweight is. You have probably all seen charts in diet books which define 'normal' bodies in terms of a ratio between height and weight. The increasing popularity of weight training has substantially invalidated these charts, since according to them the Schwarzennegeresque behemoths that we envy at the gym are fat.

Scientifically speaking, we would say that these charts and scales now provide us with an incomplete picture of reality. An additional methodology has emerged in the form of bodyfat testing, which offers more accurate measures in terms of comparing the fat to muscle ratio in the body – literally telling us how fat we are. This provides a classic example of how science improves our knowledge about ourselves through providing more complete ways of seeing. The notion of 'complete' seeing is central to the inductivist thinking on which positivism is based. Inductivism refers to the belief that knowledge grows from accurate observation of the world (Popper, 1974). Again, the idea has a lot of common-sense purchase, as the example above shows. But is this philosophy applicable to the analysis of society or culture? Silverman's (1993) discussion of what represents a researchable social problem suggests that, for many reasons, inductivism, and thus *certain elements* of positivism, do not fit squarely into social science. Silverman points out that the world is such a complex place that its reality always exceeds the methodological limits. He also suggests that values inevitably intrude upon research. Social scientists have to live with the fact that the views we have of cultural problems will always be partial.

Consider again the weight issue. So, we now have ways of measuring not only our weight but also the percentage of that weight represented by fat as compared to muscle. A person can say, for example, that he or she is 5 feet 9 inches tall, weighs 160 lbs and carries 14 per cent bodyfat. These facts stand independent of dominant cultural perceptions of what is or is not fat. Or do they? The 14 per cent figure means absolutely nothing in isolation. To interpret its meaning we need an expert to tell us what our bodyfat percentage is supposed to be. There are many books available to the public that will give us this information, but how do the so-called experts decide what it should be? Part of the decision is surely based on medical information, such as rates of heart disease among people within a certain range, but it might also be influenced by culture. The figure for what is desirable may be under-estimated, given the current taste for *svelte* figures for both women and men. On the other hand, the figure may be too high, based on the recognition that cultures of eating in many parts of the world make lower bodyfat percentages practically unattainable – Europeans and North Americans are just not going to give up red meat, cheese and fried food. Either way, it is difficult to argue that the 'science' of health and fitness is isolated from cultural norms.

The dangers of such intrusions are evidently greater in social research, which does not deal in quantifiable structures. Silverman (1993) does not argue that this should be used either as an excuse to abandon such work or an invitation to say anything we like about the world in which we live, regardless of evidence. Rather, he suggests two things. First, we have to accept that theory has a legitimate role to play in the practical appli-cations of research methodologies: observation is always based on pre-sumptions about what is desirable or how something works. Secondly, there are certain strategies for dealing with the fact that social science does not deal in quantifiable phenomena that remain unsullied by values or political beliefs. Silverman contends that the best strategy for the social researcher is to 'limit the damage' of this reality by carefully thinking through what represents a researchable social problem.

This is harder than it sounds. Thinking about the media, one cannot deny that something like the issue of negative effects on the audience, in the form of inappropriate behaviour or 'dumbing down', is a social problem. Concerns about the potentially damaging aspects of media content are virtually as old as communication – even the ancient Greek philosopher Plato expressed his fears over the effect that storytelling, in its various forms, had on its audience:

> Then shall we simply allow our children to listen to any stories that anyone happens to make up, and so to receive into their minds ideas often the very opposite of those we shall think they ought to have when they grow up?
>   No, certainly not.
>   It seems, then, our first business will be to supervise the makings off fables and legends, rejecting all which are unsatisfactory; and we shall induce nurses and mothers to tell their children only those which we have approved, and to think more of the moulding of their souls. (Plato, 1989: 45)

Here Plato echoes contemporary fears. But these views are unreliable since they are based on non-systematic observation. They are also based on processes of communication that are so complex that they become virtually impossible to see with any clarity. Returning to the example of the Judas Priest trial, as details of the crime and the victims emerged it became clear that the murder/suicide attempt had taken place within the context of a taste for drugs as well as heavy metal music, and a lifetime of abuse and disappointment. The case was dismissed with the recognition that it was impossible to see where the impact of the music could be distinguished from the effects of the youths' environment.

This brings us to an important distinction that Silverman (1993) makes between research problems and general issues of concern. The latter, such as public fears about media effects, tend to be broad ranging and unfocused. While many politicians, commentators and members of the public believe that the media play a damaging role in contemporary life, they are unclear about how the process works, or how we could gather solid empirical data to support their case. Researchers must divorce their work from these general concerns. Definitions of social problems emerging from public debates must be questioned. For example, instead of setting out to ask *how* it is that the media corrupt audiences (an assumption now routinely made in governmental circles), the researcher should ask *whether* this is the case. Alternatively, he or she may wish to ask if the sorts of effects that are the content of public concerns are the most important sorts of effects to measure. The British cultural studies branch of audience research has, accordingly, functioned along the belief that fears over sex and violence miss much deeper influences which the media have on the way we think and behave. Additionally, researchers should limit their ambitions concerning the sorts of problems that are within their grasp. Silverman's suggestion that we should aim to 'say a lot about a little, rather than a little about a lot' (1993: 3) warns us against trying to take on an issue that we have neither the time nor the resources to address fully. The task of the audience researcher thus appears to be quite humble in the face of the bombastic claims of Cartesianism and positivism. We must accept that we will never entirely master the intricacies of the relationship between the media and their audiences, and that the knowledge we have of them will be coloured by the strengths and limitations of the theories and methods used. Honesty is required about the realities of the research process, qualifying normative (positivist) views of the scientist through a recognition of the role that theory plays in the formation of observations.

Beyond simple positivism: the notion of the paradigm

Once the idea that research is conducted in a cultural vacuum is dismissed, what replaces the image of science propagated by straightforward positivism? This is a question that has been vigorously pursued by philosophers of scientific method, most notably by Karl Popper and Thomas Kuhn. To understand the significance of their work, we must first appreciate that dismissing positivism also dispels any hope of discovering a unifying scientific methodology. A number of competing research paradigms fill the resultant void. A paradigm is a self-contained academic universe, defined by an exclusive, internally consistent set of beliefs and methods. In the previous discussion of the different directions taken by media research, for example, it was clear that the Glasgow Media Group was motivated by a very different view of how media power works than those who are concerned with the media's ability to produce anti-social behaviours. This in turn implies an alternative methodology.

Guba and Lincoln (1994) explain paradigms as being defined by three interconnected criteria: ontology, epistemology and methodology. Ontology and epistemology are significant in that they illustrate how research begins by outlining theoretical suppositions that are taken as given by the researcher. Ontology refers to how we understand the nature of reality. Positivism is premised on realist ontology; that is, the knowable world consists of tangible phenomena, things we can see, feel and measure. Epistemology refers to a theory of knowledge. It is related to ontology in that the nature of the reality you set out to explore influences the sort of knowledge that you can have of it. Epistemology, then, also refers to a specific way of thinking about the relationship between the researcher and the researched. Returning once more to positivism, the ontological belief in a world of fixed structures standing independently of human will is the cornerstone of the epistemological belief in the possibility of objective science. If reality exists independently of our will, then our only choice as scientists is systematically to abandon those elements in our culture and in our heads that prevent us from seeing the world as it is.

The ambiguous drawing of the young/old woman can be used to explain how competing paradigms emerge. Positivism, as an ontological and epistemological position, cannot account for the fact that the diagram contains two realities. To understand the picture, one must ontologically accept that reality is a complex phenomenon that must be interpreted, not seen. Epistemologically, the reality of the picture is produced through interaction with the researcher; its meaning depends on the position of the observer. Methodological implications follow. Observation, measurement and interpretation depend on the understanding of the ontological and epistemological nature of the work at hand. Some people believe that media effects are distinct, observable and hence measurable, prompting certain forms of quantitative research. Others, believing that effects are less obvious, disguising themselves by mingling with other sources of social influence, have tended to pursue qualitative, interpretative means.

The path of social research is shaped not only by real problems that demand attention, but also by intellectual heritage. The sorts of issues studied, and the way in which they are studied, depend on the range of ideas and research tools that have been introduced to us in the course of our education. It is this heritage that defines what Kuhn (1962) calls a paradigm. Such a view of 'scientific' activity alerts us to the role that theory plays in research. Far from being the esoteric preserve of ivory tower academics who are largely unwilling to get their hands dirty with everyday concerns, it is, instead, the unacknowledged bedrock of all research.

Silverman (1998) elucidates via a six-part typology of the research process. He agrees with Kuhn in stating that scholarship begins with the researcher's understanding of his or her location within a paradigm that determines the sorts of questions that he or she will ask. He provides an example that is useful with regard to media research. Locating behaviourism as a research paradigm, stimulus-response is a concept that develops from this. Behaviourism sets out to examine how specific elements of the environment function as stimuli to human actions. Much of the debate around the issue of television violence is premised on this concept, the idea that violent television images can prompt viewers to imitate what they see on the screen.

Next comes theory. A theory is a 'set of concepts used to define and/ or explain some phenomenon' (Silverman, 1998: 103). 'Agenda-setting' is one of the theories we will encounter later on. This theory suggests the interconnection of two concepts: media content and public opinion. The theory holds that the focus of public opinion will be determined by media definitions of importance. That is, we tend to be concerned about issues that gain a lot of media coverage (McCombs and Shaw, 1993). This brings us to the practical part of the research process. Having defined key concepts, theories and questions, the next task for the social researcher is to operationalize these concerns. The first part of this operationalization is, in Silverman's terms, the formation of hypotheses. Hypotheses are testable propositions; statements whose truth can by examined empirically. If we are using stimulus-response theory, then we can hypothesize that the power of a media image, the stimulus, will reveal itself in audience behaviour. As a crude example, an incredibly violent film such as Mel Gibson's *Braveheart* should encourage at least some of its viewers to beat each other around the head. If this does not happen, then we can say that the hypothesis is not supported. Of course,

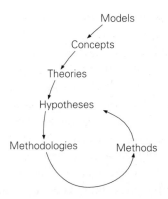

Figure 1.1 *Silverman's research model (1998: 104)*

the researcher needs not only to define what ideas to test, but he or she must also decide how they can be tested. This question is answered through methodologies and methods. Methodology refers to a general practical approach. A researcher may specialize in projects that generally favour quantitative methodology, such as the social survey. There are, within this broad methodology, a variety of sorts of surveys (or methods). Different sorts of questions will, as we shall see, demand different sampling and questioning procedures.

Silverman leaves us with a research model that forms a sort of figure of six (Figure 1.1). One problem with this model is that it suggests a certain procedural unity in social research that does not exist in practice. Some might argue that the top part of the figure could be simply conflated into the term 'theory'. As for practical matters, as Silverman admits, qualitative researchers tend not to use hypotheses, preferring to be guided by less specific questions. Approaching *Braveheart*, we could focus on meanings instead of behaviours: why do audiences enjoy battle scenes?

Yet Figure 1.1 is still useful in that it demonstrates the impossibility of value-free science. Certain elements of the process remain immune from criticism. While hypotheses, or research questions, may be modified according to empirical evidence, models, concepts and theories remain constant. The implication of this is that if one is not satisfied with the results of research projects suggested by specific research paradigms, the only recourse for the researcher is to abandon the paradigm. This once again makes a dent in the positivist belief in the unity of the scientific method. It does not, however, cast us adrift in a sea of relativism. Relativism, the idea that truth is only ever a product of the values that shape culture, is the spectre that haunts researchers following the demise of crude positivism (Bernstein, 1988). If, as Silverman's work implies, scientific knowledge is largely shaped by preconceptions and the ideas that shape scientific cultures, then it could be concluded that knowledge is a mere reflex of prejudice. If this is so, the researcher need not think too deeply about theoretical and methodological issues, since one statement about the world is just as good as another.

The dangers of this position are obvious. It quite simply makes studying and research a complete waste of time. Yet evidence of scientific progress is all around us: we live longer than our ancestors, thanks in part to medical science. It takes hours rather than months to circumnavigate the globe. And progress is not limited to the physical sciences. Turning to media research, it would be fair to say that there are huge disagreements between paradigms on the nature of media power. Nevertheless, we can say that at least the discourse on this power is far richer than it was 40 years ago; we are better informed about the range of effects likely to occur. In this sense, we can say that media studies has grown more robust as a field. But how can we speak of progress, once crude positivism has been dismissed as a viable guide? The answer is provided by the debate between Thomas Kuhn and Karl Popper on the nature and prospects for scientific growth.

Popper, Kuhn and scientific progress

Karl Popper is often viewed as an apologist for traditional views of science, especially in comparison with Thomas Kuhn. Nevertheless, Popper's rejection of inductivism makes his thinking consistent with post-positivism. His is a more sophisticated empirical view which retains a belief in the utility and integrity of scientific methods rather than method (singular). Juxtapositions of Popper and Kuhn (see Lazar, 1998) ignore commonalities that Kuhn (1974) sees in their work. The collection of essays found in *The Philosophy of Karl Popper* (1974) lends weight to this conclusion. What we find in this collection is disagreement not on whether science improves, but how and how rapidly it does so.

However the process occurs, it does not do so through observation alone. Responding to a number of essays on his work, Popper begins by outlining his fundamental beliefs. While he rejects inductivism, Popper remains, in his own words, 'an empiricist of sorts', the significance of this being that he addresses the interconnections between theory and method.

I was . . . certainly not a naïve empiricist who believes that all knowledge stems from our perceptions of sense data. My empiricism consisted in the view that, though all experience was theory impregnated, it was experience which in the end could decide the fate of a theory, by knocking it out; and also in the view that only such theories which in principle were capable of being thus refuted merited to be counted among the theories of empirical science. (Popper, 1974: 971)

Popper dismisses inductivism since he believes that observation is guided by the sorts of beliefs and concepts that are found in theories. He argues that positivism makes the error of ignoring 'metaphysics', by which he means concepts that are difficult if not impossible to observe, and hence prove or disprove. There are no human activities, including research, that can completely dispel metaphysical concerns. This is especially true of social research, since values and beliefs are the very substance of culture. We have seen, for example, how many concerns about media effects are premised upon valid, yet contestable, moral commitments.

Popper replaces inductivism with 'hypothetico-deduction' (Lazar, 1998). Knowledge grows not through simple observation, but through the imaginative formulation of hypotheses, possible explanations of the things that go on around us. Popper remains a realist, in the sense that he believes in a world of observable forms, but he also believes that this reality is multi-layered. Theories and hypotheses are tools that allow us to dig into these multiple layers. 'There is a reality behind the world as it appears to us, possibly a many layered reality, of which the appearances are the utmost layers. What the great scientist does is boldly to guess, daringly to conjecture, what these inner realities are like' (Popper, 1974: 980). Yet the first quote shows that observation, and thus method, remain an important part of research. Despite his 'metaphysical' sympathies, Popper does not believe that theory alone constitutes knowledge. Theory can only become the basis for true knowledge if, in the spirit of empiricism, it can be tested against observation. Falsification emerges as the point of demarcation between science and non-science. Only theories that can be empirically tested get to play a role in the development of knowledge. Although Popper clashes with 'verificationists' in stating that no theory can ever be proved beyond doubt (since there is always the chance that a new test will arise that can falsify it), he nevertheless feels that the more tests a theory stands up to, the more useful it is as a guide to reality. His notion of falsifiability is important to a post-positivist view of scientific activity. Since no theory can ever be proved, only disproved, the scientist moves from the world of the true and the false to a more complex one, filled with theories that are more or less useful. Hence, while we should be cautious about looking for Truth with a capital 'T', we can still speak of progress, and of a scientific community that is committed to this progress.

Enter Thomas Kuhn. Kuhn caused something of a controversy in academic circles with his book *The Structure of Scientific Revolutions* (1962). Some years later, Kuhn restated his views on Popper's work in the essay 'Logic of discovery or psychology of research?' (1974). While agreeing that some researchers follow Popper's model, Kuhn argues that such people are the exception rather than the rule within scientific communities. We can see what he means by referring to Silverman's (1998) research typology. Popper would draw a different model, one in which the empirical data gathered by methods would *routinely* inform not only the development of hypotheses but the core concepts and theories informing a paradigm. Kuhn counters that such a circuit is only completed under extraordinary circumstances. Most of the time, scientists are the guardians, not the interrogators, of paradigms. As they are trained in ideas and procedures that only make sense within a specific paradigm, attempts to subvert that paradigm also threaten to usurp researchers' authority. Research is primarily driven by a professional survival instinct. Paradigmatic equilibrium can only be disturbed by an overwhelming tide of falsifying data. Scientists, in this sense, resemble religious zealots, jealously guarding their compounds against enemy raids. Even though Kuhn concedes that paradigms can fall, being replaced by different models, this process is more akin to a religious conversion than a logical progression. New positions do not grow on a foundation of existing knowledge, but instead we see a war between different regimes of truth. Kuhn's ideas resonate with the history of audience research. Morris (1996) complains that, by the late 1980s, critical media studies had lapsed into a repetitive tendency to celebrate the audience's ability imaginatively to 'play' with media texts. Nothing new was being said, as researchers endlessly sought empirical justification for what they already 'knew'. This is the very same criticism that Hall (1982) directed at the North American mass-communication research discussed in Chapter 2.

Popper responds to Kuhn by conceding that his views are accurate in many ways: 'I do admit that at any moment we are prisoners caught in the framework of our theories; our expectations; our past experiences; our language.' But the fact that this is often the case is not to say that it should be the case:

> if we try, we can break out of our framework, but it will be a better and roomier one; and we can at any moment break out of it again. The central point is that a critical discussion and a comparison of the various

frameworks are always possible. It is just a dogma – a dangerous dogma – that the different frameworks are like mutually untranslatable languages. The myth of the framework is, in our time, the central bulwark of irrationalism. My counter thesis is that it simply exaggerates a difficulty into an impossibility. (Popper, 1974: 1152)

Popper provides us with a pragmatic approach to growth within the social sciences. Research is never innocent of social forces, but, in knowing this, we can allow for our own shortcomings, and thus be willing to listen to the insights offered from different perspectives.

Guba and Lincoln (1994) use Popper to differentiate between positivist and post-positivist views on social research. Guba and Lincoln define each paradigm as being guided by different ontological, epistemological and methodological orientations. Positivism is guided by crude realism, where the world is seen as a physical structure created by physical laws of cause and effect. The task of the observer is to figure these laws out. This suggests an epistemology that posits a distinction between the observer and the observed. The scientist is an observer, not a participant in the object of study. Creating an analogy, the positivist researcher is like a policeman/woman observing the interrogation of a suspect through a two-way mirror. He or she can see but cannot be seen. His or her presence has no influence on the things that happen in the interview. The focus on laws and physical processes produces experimental, manipulative methodologies whose aim is to prove hypotheses.

Post-positivist researchers such as Popper operate from different assumptions. While they retain a commitment to a form of realism – the belief that there is a physical world that forms the basis for human perceptions of reality – the nature of this reality is so complex that we can never know it completely. Nor can we develop a single method that will tell us everything we want to know. This is all the more so given that, epistemologically, the researcher is a participant in the culture that he or she wishes to study. This being the case, methodological triangulation is the best approach. That is, researchers should be open to a variety of ways of analysing reality, since multiple methods give us a more complex, although never complete, view.

Popper, Kuhn and cultural studies

The conclusion to this discussion is that interdisciplinarity is important if we want to develop a sophisticated debate about social phenomena such as media audiences. Yet research remains coloured by paradigmatic concerns. Before going any further, then, it is necessary to map the paradigmatic origins of this book, making it clear how this foundation influences the following chapters. To do this, we must ask the following question. What does the Popper/Kuhn debate have to do with cultural studies?

Grossberg (1996a) acknowledges cultural studies as a paradigm defined by ontological and epistemological beliefs. Many of these beliefs are commensurate with Popper's ideas on the nature of reality and our attempts to understand it. The first of these beliefs is *materialism*, which can be seen as being *related* to realism. Materialism views culture as the product of tangible human practices. This is a point that can get lost in discussions of ideology which often dominate cultural studies. Ideology will be discussed at greater length later on, but at the moment we should point out that, although ideology can be defined as a network of values and beliefs, ideological power only comes about when these beliefs become tangible in the form of cultural practice. That is, however contestable ideologies might be, they are nevertheless real in the sense that they form the basis for human activity. Like realism, then, materialist analysis believes that ideology gives birth to a world of real structures and processes.

Despite this belief, it is also true for cultural studies that even if we live in a world of real processes and structures, the forms, functions, meanings and effects of social phenomena are complex. As such, cultural studies adopts an *anti-reductionist* and *anti-essentialist* approach. That is, the paradigm does not believe that it is possible to discover simple historical 'causes' leading to 'effects'. Take the history of media technologies as an example. Winston (1990) criticizes what he calls 'technologically determinist' historical accounts which see new media technologies as emerging from a scientific research process that has nothing to do with other social forces. So the radio, patented in England at the turn of the century, comes about as a result of Guglielmo Marconi's electronic genius. But why would an Italian choose to come to Britain to further his work? The reason is that the British shipping industry offered the best support (Winston, 1998). This tells us that historical change, in this case the advent of the radio, cannot be explained by simple causes. For Marconi, electronic genius was not enough. To succeed, Marconi had to work in a society that valued his work. Only in such a situation could his invention become a social force. This alerts us to what Winston calls *cultural determinism*. This concept sees historical change as an interactive process encompassing many factors, some of which are more obvious than others.

The task of the anti-essentialist, anti-reductionist cultural historian is to seek out ever more complex patterns of social development, to enrich our understanding of society by adding more and more pieces to the puzzle of how and why cultures develop in the manner that they do. This is similar to Popper's notion of falsifiability, where scientific knowledge grows from a continuing effort to destabilize established factual and theoretical regimes.

The commensurability of Popper and Grossberg's idea is perhaps less straightforward than I have suggested. Grossberg, together with many others within cultural studies, would be a great deal more cautious about, if not contemptuous of, the possibility of scientific progress. We can see this in the way that critical audience research has ignored the theories and methods that will be discussed in chapters 2 and 3. Nevertheless, the notion that critical research should be aimed at the deconstruction of contestable cultural 'truths' is consistent with Popper's – and for that matter even Descartes' – view of the research process. This being the case, perhaps it is wise to heed Popper's call for interdisciplinarity. Recent books on critical audience research (Lewis, 1991; Morley, 1992; Moores, 1993; Ang, 1996; Nightingale, 1996; Abercrombie and Longhurst, 1998) tend to focus on the qualitative audience research of the 1980s and 1990s, paying relatively little attention to the theories and methods of other paradigms. The implication is that the pre-1980 era has little to tell us about media audiences and the nature of media effects. Perhaps this is an error. If understanding social phenomena depends on building complex pictures of reality using the many tools available to the researcher, and if all research traditions are paradigms, endowed with strengths but also plagued by weaknesses, then perhaps we should consider how so-called non-critical research traditions have informed our understanding of audiences.

Conclusion

This chapter has contextualized the pursuit of knowledge within a rejection of objectivist views of social science. However comforting it might be to believe that 'the truth is out there', waiting to be discovered by the right methodology, the reality that we live in is far too complex to be conquered by any single mode of research. Social research is just that, a *social* process influenced by a variety of factors other than the relentless pursuit of truth. This means that in evaluating such research, we need to be sensitive to the way in which 'findings' are influenced by paradigmatic factors in the researcher's background. These will include both theoretical and methodological concerns.

Exercises

1 Select a popular, frequently discussed topic relating to the social role or impact of the mass media. What does this topic assume about the nature of reality (is reality simply 'out there' to be seen, measured and understood, or is reality something which we, as a society, create for ourselves)? What does this topic assume about the nature of the relationship between media and society? How are these effects or impacts assumed to work?

2 Pick a topic that you would be interested in researching. What assumptions have you made before you begin?

2 Media Effects

The rapid escalation in the scale of mass communication from the 1920s to the 1950s was accompanied by a growing academic interest in media effects. Much of this work was conducted in the United States, although many of those involved were refugees from Nazi Germany. Most of this research also had positivist tendencies. Certainly by the Second World War, quantitative and experimental methods were the norm, a situation that remains to the present day in the US.

Cultural studies tends to ignore early mass-communication research because of the latter's positivist associations. Certainly many of the concepts and methods used at this time are difficult to reconcile with those used in critical audience studies. Nevertheless, there are several reasons why it is useful to look at the 'effects tradition'. On a very basic level, it is important to identify the paradigmatic differences between effects researchers and cultural studies. How, for example, does the concept of 'attitude' differ from that of 'ideology'? What are the differences between media-related 'behaviours' and 'cultural practices'? This is to say that the effects tradition provides a case study which demonstrates the themes encountered in the discussion of positivism and the debate between Kuhn and Popper (see Chapter 1).

Yet simply to use effects researchers as straw targets to set the scene for the advent of cultural studies is to underestimate the complexity of the period. A review of media research in the United States in the 1930s and 1940s shows that the quantitative, positivist hegemony was contested, and its victory was a result of historical exigency as well as academic debate. Moreover, these positivist tendencies were relative, not absolute, meaning that the theoretical and methodological schisms between the effects tradition and cultural studies have been exaggerated. So what is, or was, the effects tradition, why did it develop in the way that it did, and what exactly are its ontological and epistemological roots?

The view from cultural studies: mad scientists and
statistical lies

Think of the story of Frankenstein. A common theme in film versions
of the story concerns Victor Frankenstein's descent into madness.
Possessed by his work, Dr Frankenstein loses his grip on reality, failing
to see that the monster he has created has little to do with the original
goals of his research. Now think of Mark Twain's adage concerning the
existence of 'lies, damn lies and statistics'. Twain's quote attacks the
blind faith that we place in efforts to 'measure' social processes. We are
warned that skillful statisticians can manipulate figures to produce any
reality they please. This leaves us with a vision of a positivist paradigm
staffed by mad scientists and numerical charlatans. Many scholars in
cultural studies view their effects tradition peers from one or both of
these positions.

Brian Winston (1986) favours the 'nutty professor' version in his
review of Albert Bandura's behaviourist research on children and media
violence:

> This deeply flawed tradition begins with a bobo doll [a children's punching
> bag] in the applied psychology lab of Stanford University in the early fifties
> . . . Having missed their vocation as *Candid Camera* stunt organizers, the
> Stanford researchers dreamed up the following exercise: 'An experimenter
> brought the children, one by one, into the test room. In one corner the child
> found a set of play materials; in another corner he saw an adult sitting
> quietly with a large inflated plastic bobo doll and a mallet.' A second group
> saw the same drama on a TV monitor. A third group saw the adult, now
> dressed as a cartoon cat, also beat up the doll. The last group (the control)
> were not exposed to the maniac with the mallet. 'The results', the
> researchers wrote, 'leave little doubt that exposure to violence heightens
> aggressive tendencies in children.' One must demur. (Winston, 1986: 9)

Winston is suggesting here that Bandura's myopic allegiance to experimental methodologies produces research which is hopelessly divorced
from the reality of the audience's experience.

David Gauntlett (1998: 120) makes the same charge, stating that
'media effects research has quite consistently taken the wrong approach
to the mass media, its audiences and society in general'. Gauntlett goes
on to provide ten reasons why effects researchers are unable to grasp the
true impact of the mass media. These objections are related to the
previous discussion of the connections between ontology and epistemology (see Chapter 1). The fundamental flaw of effects research, such as
the Bandura experiment, is that ontologically speaking it misunderstands

the relationship between the media and society. Taking Winston's account of the Stanford research as an example, we can see that the focus of this work lies in measuring what the media do to people. The danger of phrasing the question in this way is that it can suggest that the media stand apart from other social institutions, trends and forces. That is, such an approach does not allow for the fact that the media affect but are also affected by the rest of society.

Lewis (1991) argues that experiments are flawed because they assume that the world is driven by distinct forces that can be identified, separated and examined in isolation from one another. They also assume that people can be cleansed of their social backgrounds so that the effects the media have upon them can be clearly identified. Ontologically, experiments are aligned with cruder forms of positivism; the world, even the social world, is there to be measured. Epistemologically, this results in inflexible methods that are incapable of dealing with the subtleties of media meanings.

Gauntlett (1998) concurs. Experimental media violence research focuses on behaviours, ignoring how violent media imagery can influence reasoning. Added to this is the problem that what researchers consider to be violent may not be seen as such by the audience. This last point is indicative of a wider problem concerning the relationship between effects researchers and the people they study. The former regard the latter in much the same way as a physicist might regard iron filings lying on a piece of paper waiting to be ionized by a magnet: playthings to be manipulated. Here again we can see echoes of positivism, where the scientist regards him or herself as a dispassionate observer. This means that the scientist is not disposed towards formulating the problem of effects taking into account what audiences themselves say about what they see; for example, objecting to the definitions of media violence suggested by researchers. This arrogance means that researchers can miss a good deal of the audience's experience. According to Gauntlett, a *Titanic*-like effects tradition steamed into an iceberg of failure due to a dogmatic epistemological faith in the wrong methods. Yet Gauntlett (1998: 120) also recognizes that his selective history of mass-communication research misleadingly tars all who worked within it with the same brush: 'I will impose an unwarranted coherence upon the claims of all those who argue or purport to have found that the mass media will commonly have direct and reasonably predictable effects upon the behavior of their fellow human beings, calling this body of work simply the Effects model.'

In applying this critique to all of the efforts that have been made to quantify media effects, through experiments or surveys, Gauntlett corrals all such work into the 'hypodermic needle' or 'magic bullet' model. The assumption of this model is that the media are so powerful that they can directly inject their ideas into the audience's heads (McQuail, 1987). Yet, as the author himself admits, this collectivization of all quantitative work is 'unwarranted'. To paraphrase Raymond Williams (1960), there is no such thing as the effects tradition, only ways of seeing methodologically and conceptually disparate works as being a unified effects tradition. This is not to say that Gauntlett is entirely wrong: his essay valuably charts many of the things that can and have gone wrong in quantitative media research, and it is certainly possible to find many projects that are guilty of some of his accusations. But it is misleading to suggest that all researchers using quantitative methods in the early period of audience research fell into the same traps.

To begin with, some quantitative research is more positivist than others. While experiments were and still are an important feature of mainstream audience research, the 1930s to the 1950s also saw extensive use and development of surveys, often in forms that were amenable to more qualitative critical insights. Indeed, the 1930s and 1940s were characterized by the considerable use of quantitative and qualitative research in conjunction, as well as theorizing about communication that prefigured many of the concepts that would emerge in cultural studies. Reviewing the literature of the time, very few researchers thought of media effects in 'hypodermic' terms, or if they did the evidence they gathered on audiences soon led them to dismiss the idea. Robert Park and Herbert Blumer opposed what they saw as the positivist bias of communication research. But even those researchers who placed their faith in traditional scientific methods realized as early as the 1930s that media effects were difficult to define and measure. Contra Gauntlett, the era did see a degree of methodological flexibility. This is underlined by the fact that in 1960, Joseph Klapper, who produced an important summary of audience research called *The Effects of Mass Communication*, called for a phenomenistic approach to communication. Klapper's suggestion was: 'in essence a shift away from the tendency to regard mass communication as a necessary and sufficient cause of audience effects, toward a view of media as influences, working amid other influences, in a total situation' (1960: 5). Klapper voiced many concerns that would later arise in critical work on audiences. To begin, he warned that media research had sometimes been guilty of taking institutional definitions of media-related problems at face value. Much of the research that had focused on violence, for example, responded more to governmental concerns than empirical evidence. Klapper was unafraid to state that, at this juncture, there was still much that was not understood about the social influence of the mass media. Hence the search for new questions and ways of studying audiences. The importance of interpreting the general thrust of effects research in this way is that later paradigms can be seen as building upon rather than ignoring this body of work.

Which is not to say that mainstream social science and cultural studies think of media power in the same way. Conceptual and methodological schisms remain, and must be understood. The two approaches function from a different theoretical heritage, and quantitative research methods are ill equipped to account for some of the ways in which audiences relate to media fare. The task, then, is carefully to map out what exactly it was that early effects researchers set out to do. How did they think about communication? Why did they choose quantitative methods? How did they interpret the information gathered by these methods? What did they learn?

Before proceeding, readers should note that this book divides the so-called effects tradition into two camps. This chapter considers work that tried to measure the media's impact on behaviours, whereas Chapter 3 on public opinion includes much of the work that studied the power of the media to influence they way people think. The reason for this is that behaviourist research is the closest fit one can find in communication research to positivism. Having said this, there are problems in dividing the concepts of thought and behaviour. As we shall see, for many researchers altering thought was a vital step towards altering behaviour. Indeed, Chapter 3 will feature many projects with behaviourist components. In general, however, this chapter will focus on research for which the material behaviours or the immediate emotional responses of audiences to media stimuli are the principal 'effects' sought.

Early models of communication

The early hegemony enjoyed by traditional social science methods in communication research did not emerge naturally. The 1920s and 1930s saw diverging views of the nature of mass-communication effects, producing different ways of looking at audiences. This period was crucial to positivism's early triumph.

The 'hypodermic needle' model suggests a very simplistic view of the mass-communication process. Initial fears about media power reflected this simplicity. This was because much of this research concentrated on the concept of propaganda. It is easy to see why propaganda should have been such a concern during the 1920s and 1930s. There was little time to dwell on hidden forms of persuasion, concentrated on by more recent scholars, at a time when governments and industry were engaged in blatant efforts to induce certain behaviours among gullible viewers, readers and listeners. To many, the First World War demonstrated just how susceptible media audiences were to mass persuasion. Both the allies and the Germans remained convinced that propaganda had played a vital role in sustaining the war effort, despite the crippling casualties endured by all combatants.

This concern found academic expression in Harold Lasswell's *Propaganda Technique and the World War* (1927). Although this book pursued the effectiveness of propaganda through the method of content analysis (Lasswell, 1927/1953), Lasswell's thinking on the way in which propaganda functions represents one of the clearest articulations of 'hypodermic needle' style thinking. As he was later to state, propaganda is the attempt to produce a specific behaviour among a target audience using a media stimulus (Lasswell, 1927/1953). This way of thinking about communication was picked up by Carl Hovland, a seminal figure in the development of experimental methods of measuring media effects. In the late 1940s, Hovland defined communication as 'the process by which an individual transmits stimuli to modify the behavior of other individuals' (1948/1953: 182).

Hovland and Lasswell shared what James Carey (1989) calls a 'transmission' idea of how communication works. This means that, for them, communication (and the power of communication) concerns 'the transmission of messages over distance for purposes of control' (1989: 15). Carey sees this as a primarily physical way of understanding communication, harking back to pre-electronic days when messages had to be literally carried from sender to receiver. This focus on physicality dovetails with positivist themes. Just as the positivist believes that true knowledge derives from the observation of material processes, so too the transmission view of communication sees media effects as things that we can 'see'.

Epistemological consequences were to follow. Lasswell and Hovland strongly advocated the use of positivist methodologies. Lasswell championed quantitative methods due to weaknesses he saw in his first area of expertise, the study of First World War propaganda. In an essay entitled 'Why be quantitative?' (1944/1953), he complained that much of this work had been highly impressionistic. At this time, communication and/or media studies did not exist as a discipline, meaning that media researchers were unbounded (or unguided) by established research methodologies. For Lasswell, this resulted in a lack of scientific rigour. Analyses of German and allied propaganda presented readers with anecdotes and case studies concerning specific messages or campaigns, but gave no indication of how representative the reported messages were of propaganda as a whole. Referring to the criteria for judging the usefulness of social research, what Lasswell was saying was that impressionistic analyses of propaganda might have been valid, but they were also unreliable. In using some of the quantitative techniques discussed later, researchers could at least ensure that the case studies they picked were representative.

Hovland (1948/1953) strode even more boldly into the positivist camp. For him, the goal of the communication researcher was to discover the 'rules' of persuasion, the conditions under which it is possible to shape the thoughts and behaviours of media audiences. His reasons for arguing this were unashamedly practical. The purpose of communication research was to allow for better communication between different groups in society, especially between workers and management, and government and its citizens. In this sense, studying communication was not about pointing to variations in social meaning, but was about learning how to make yourself understood. This assumed that there is a right and a wrong way to communicate, according to a set of objective laws – the laws Hovland set out to discover via experimental methods.

Hovland and Lasswell were united by a preoccupation with communication structures and effects that could be measured. They were positivist in the sense that they felt that communications as a discipline could only be built on reliable scientific procedures that could establish physical phenomena, in the form of message structures and tangible effects upon audiences. This was to have a major influence on effects researchers as the two scholars, together with like-minded colleagues, were to dominate audience research in the 1940s and 1950s. But this is not to say that qualitative methods and interpretative concepts were immediately driven from the emerging discipline. Hovland saw the study of communication as an interdisciplinary concern. Although heavily influenced by the quantitative modes of psychological research, he also saw a role for the more qualitative strands of anthropology and sociology. In this sense he was not entirely opposed to the path being forged by Robert Park and Herbert Blumer. Park (1939/1953) provided a different view of the role that communication played in society. He felt that instead of looking at the power of messages to *change* thoughts and behaviours, researchers should examine the role that communication plays in *sustaining* the thoughts and behaviours that shape society. Blumer (1948) provided methodological accompaniment, claiming that quantitative research methods were not suited to the analysis of culture, which required more interpretative techniques. Hovland was sympathetic to the last point at least, seeing focus-group research as a promising complement to traditional survey analysis. But if interdisciplinarity was the theory, it was only sporadically the practice. Some work in the 1930s and 1940s used a combination of quantitative and qualitative methods, but by the Second World War most researchers chose one approach or the other. Cmiel (1996), Gary (1996) and Peters (1996a, b) see this as emerging from institutional pressures that were brought to bear on researchers as a result of the war.

The Second World War, the Cold War and the consolidation of positivism

Following a counterfactual historical tack, it could be argued that effects research in the United States would have pursued a more interdisciplinary path had it not been for the intervention of the Second World War, closely followed by the Soviet challenge. Experimental projects were certainly a notable feature of the pre-war period, represented most famously by the Payne Fund studies. These were a series of projects designed to measure, under controlled experimental conditions, the power that film had to mould children's attitudes (Charters, 1933/1953; Defleur and Lowery, 1988).

But at the same time, other scholars were producing work suggesting that communicative effects were so complex that they could be neither measured nor comprehended via experiment alone. Blumer was also interested in the impact of films on audiences, but studied these effects using a variety of non-experimental methods. Drawing samples from a wider population, including not only children but also workers and college students, Blumer and Thrasher used a number of techniques to gather data. Participants were interviewed, completed surveys and also wrote autobiographical accounts of their film experiences, describing how they saw films as having influenced them (Charters, 1933/1953). In moving beyond the relatively narrow question of how films changed attitudes, Blumer and Thrasher began to indicate how media consumption can only be understood within the context of audiences' social location.

This theme was elaborated by Hadley Cantril's *The Invasion from Mars: a Study in the Psychology of Panic* (1940). In 1938 Orson Welles broadcast a radio play based on H. G. Wells's novel *The War of the Worlds*. The radio production placed an innovative spin on the original piece by transposing the scene from Victorian England to (then) modern-day America. As an additional twist, the play was written in the style of a news broadcast, the narrative driven by a journalist's eye-witness report. Welles enhanced the news feel of the piece by having the journalist interview a number of actors who played the sorts of public officials that one often finds in news reports: politicians, policemen and high-ranking soldiers. The broadcast began with an announcement warning listeners that what they were about to hear was a radio play. But for a number of reasons that Cantril describes, a significant propor-tion of the audience thought that the invasion was real. For a media researcher, this was a godsend. Here at last was a chance to examine just how 'magic' the media 'bullet' was under non-experimental condi-tions. Cantril leapt upon the opportunity in a way that shows greater sophistication than is normally granted to effects researchers.

Methodologically, Cantril was to teach a number of important lessons. Initially, he demonstrated how official statistics could be used to justify the importance of audience research. Six weeks after the broad-cast, the American Institute of Public Opinion conducted a poll estimating that 6 million people had listened in, of whom 1.2 million admitted to being frightened. Cantril supplemented these figures with phone records from the American Telephone Company, listing a massive increase in the number of calls to the police and radio stations during the broadcast. Radio station managers also reported an upsurge in correspondence from listeners regarding the play. All of these sources provided empirical proof that *The War of the Worlds* had had a significant impact on American life.

Cantril's research was certainly guided by many positivist themes. He understood his work to be important since it tested key hypotheses behind the 'hypodermic needle' view of media effects: 'the radio audience consists essentially of thousands of small, congregate groups united in time and experiencing a common stimulus, altogether making possible the largest grouping of people ever known' (1940: xii). This vision of huge numbers of people all having the same experience resonates with the idea of direct and predictable effects that concerned propaganda theorists.

Unsurprisingly, Cantril opted for standardized surveys (described later in this chapter) as a major research tool. Over 1,000 questionnaires were sent to school administrators to report upon perceived effects of the broadcasts on children. But Cantril also used a number of qualitative, open-ended interviews that allowed listeners to explore their responses to the play in their own terms: 135 people who had reported being frightened by the broadcast were asked about their experiences. It was in these interviews that Cantril found evidence for a holistic approach to audience research that understood media reception as interacting with other factors in the listeners' social make-up. Cantril found that there were different reasons why some people had been frightened: some were persuaded by the fact that the play sounded so much like the news, especially in its use of authority figures as information sources. Others were disturbed because they were expecting an attack of this sort on the United States; after months of listening to reports of the escalating military crisis in Europe, some listeners believed that either the Germans or the Japanese had launched an invasion, enhancing the terror by adopting an alien guise. In the context of the later attack on Pearl Harbor, these were not perhaps outlandish reactions.

Personal characteristics of the listeners also conditioned responses. In one of the most interesting case studies, a highly religious middle-aged woman, generally disgusted at the moral state of US society, became convinced that she was listening to reports of divine retribution. Others were more or less persuadable according to certain aspects of their personality and social background. These tendencies did not always correspond to the indicators that one might expect. A wealthy Yale undergraduate was convinced that the invasion was real, again due to the play's use of (fictional) authority figures. Cantril interpreted this as reflecting the fact that the man in question was a solid part of the American establishment. Having enjoyed privilege his entire life, the man had the utmost faith in all social institutions, including the media, and simply could not conceive of the fact that any one of these institutions would lie to him.

Putting this information together, Cantril concluded that media effects could only be understood as a component part of a total social experience. The experimental method suggested by the 'hypodermic needle' model: 'puts a false emphasis on the problem by assuming that a social stimulus is essentially a series of discrete elements to which people have somehow learned to react. The enormously important possibility which our approach has so far overlooked is that social stimulus situations have their own characteristic and unique qualities' (Cantril, 1940: 74). Here Cantril argues that propaganda research functioned along an inadequate notion of media effects. The idea that the mass media could simply impose their will upon a docile audience was dismissed, as in many ways was the utility of experimental approaches to the media. The subtext of *The Invasion from Mars* was a further call for interdisciplinarity, and a warning that the positivist ontology and epistemology offered by experimental research could not adequately explain the material effects of the media.

But history intervened. Very soon after *The War of the Worlds* research was conducted, it became clear that the United States was being drawn into the Second World War. Preparation and execution of the war effort required the mobilization of national resources, including academia. While scholars such as Cantril and Blumer were calling for a general exploration of the social uses of communication, with no particular end result in mind, certain developments in the early 1940s saw the bulk of communication research being directly harnessed to the goals of the state. This produced a re-emphasis on propaganda. The reason for this development was simple. The Roosevelt administration knew that it faced a difficult task in persuading the American people of the need to confront the Axis powers. This was all the more so given the numbers of Americans of German and Italian descent, who faced the prospect of fighting relatives. What was called for was a quick and effective means of changing attitudes. If some researchers were arguing that direct effects, capable of overturning years of socialization, could not be brought about via existing media form and content, the institutional response to this conclusion was to send researchers back to their desks and laboratories to find out how these effects could be achieved. Like it or not, the success of the war effort depended on the government's ability to persuade citizens to become embroiled in European affairs, even if this ran against their normal political instinct.

So the early 1940s witnessed a re-emphasis on Hovland's search for the laws of persuasion. Communication emerged as a central concern for the nation-state, as a means of moulding national resolve (Peters, 1996a). The Rockefeller Foundation, which commissioned the most notable pieces of communication research in the 1940s, played a crucial role in the merger of state and academe. Gary (1996) provides a fascinating account of how political and economic pressures influence academic work in his analysis of the Foundation's activities immediately prior to the US entry into the Second World War. While officially holding neutral status, the Roosevelt administration could not be seen as overtly sponsoring research into propaganda. Enter the Rockefeller Foundation, which, Gary claims, functioned as a pseudo state agency in commissioning effects research. John Marshall, officer in charge of the humanities division of the Foundation, was responsible for setting up research schools at a number of America's most prestigious universities: the Princeton Radio Projects and Public Opinion Research Center, Columbia's Office of Radio Research, and the New School for Social Research's Experimental Division for the Study of Wartime Communication. The names of the scholars who worked in these institutions is a who's who of effects research: Lazarsfeld, Cantril, Lasswell, Stanton, not to mention Hovland who was drafted into the army (Schramm, 1963). This period, then, saw the compulsory articulation of communication research with the goals of the state, goals that were explicitly positivist. Marshall suggested that research should focus on how the media could be used to expand knowledge, change attitudes and strengthen democracy. Since he controlled the purse strings of research funding at this time, his 'suggestions' were influential.

This marriage of scholarship and nationalism did not end on VJ day. Almost immediately the Axis threat was replaced by the Soviet one, so the problem remained as to how communication could be used to brace the public for the Cold War. Perhaps the goals of communication researchers were less overt; instead of whipping up an anti-Soviet frenzy, researchers examined how better to inform the public about affairs of state, new health practices, and how to keep lines of communication open in the event of a nuclear attack. Nevertheless, the focus remained on a positivist search for the laws of communication. And so, a decade after conscription into the war effort, the emerging discipline of mass communication had yet to be demobbed.

This explains the predominance of quantitative research in US effects research. Having said this, it is also true to say that, during the 1950s, researchers began once again to tug at the thread first identified by Cantril. But before we can assess the exact methods and findings of effects research in the 1940s and 1950s, we need a rudimentary understanding of the logic and goals of quantitative research.

The logic of quantitative methods

In order to understand what the effects tradition set out to do, we must be able to understand the logic of quantitative research. This will enable us critically to assess the truth claims made by specific research projects, and will also reveal why this work is accused of positivist ontologies and epistemologies. Readers should be warned that what follows is merely a brief introduction to the area.

The fundamental goals of quantitative research are entirely compatible with the analysis of culture. Consider Grossberg's (1996a) description of materialist cultural studies. Grossberg argues that culture evolves in a specific form due to the intersection of a range of forces: politics, the economy, social organizations and so on. Add to this an idea proposed by Howard Becker (1986). Becker, a qualitative anthropologist, defines culture as the phenomenon that explains how it is that people 'do things together'. A quantitative social scientist would agree with both of these points. Taken together, the task is to identify the social phenomena that explain the development of common modes of thought and behaviour. Quantitative concepts and methods are designed to allow us to do this in an organized, valid and reliable way.

Units of analysis and variables

This begins with the identification of units of analysis and variables (Seale and Filmer, 1998). The unit of analysis is the social phenomenon the researcher is charged with investigating. In audience research, viewers, readers and listeners are the units of analysis. Seale and Filmer define variables as things 'on which units of analysis vary' (1998: 129). Audiences will vary on a number of factors such as sex, education and age. These represent three different types of variable. Sex is a nominal variable. This means that although two different units of analysis may vary in terms of their sex, this variation implies no rank ordering. A man is worth no more than a woman is. This is not true of the idea of education, where a rank ordering is implied: we would say that someone with a degree is more educated than someone who did not attend a university or college. Education is an example of an ordinal variable. However, exactly how much more educated is someone with a degree than someone without? This is difficult to quantify. Not so with ages. We know that a 45-year-old is 20 years older that a 25-year-old. Variables where it is possible to specify the exact distance between different units of analysis are called interval variables (Babbie, 1992). The distinction between different sorts of variable is important since this influences the sorts of analysis which the researcher can perform. It is not possible, for example, to calculate the mean of a nominal variable.

Another important distinction is that made between independent and dependent variables. The distinction is analogous to that made between the concepts of 'cause' and 'effect'. Independent variables are things that impinge upon units of analysis producing certain effects, or dependent variables. In research on media violence, many researchers have asked if media images (independent variables) have the power to produce violent behaviour (the dependent variable) among audience members (the units of analysis). Variables, then, are ontological devices which allow researchers to divide situations into component parts. In media research, they let us classify different types of audience members, define the sorts of effects we are looking for, and also identify possible sources of those effects. The goal is to examine how these factors interact to produce a determinate social situation.

Sampling

If the goal of the researcher is to explain to us 'how we do things together', or to tell us how our cultural practices and experiences are organized, it follows that he or she must find a way of relating the results of a research project to society in general. The specific units of analysis observed must resemble a wider population. Take, for example, the television ratings. We often see charts in newspapers enumerating the numbers of people who have watched certain shows. These figures normally run into millions. Yet we also know that these numbers are estimates, best guesses about the behaviours of millions based on the observation of hundreds or perhaps a few thousand. To make these claims, researchers must be reasonably sure that the people they are observing are similar in viewing habits to millions of others. To do so, they must attend to the problem of sampling.

Random sampling methods are used to select people who are representative of the wider population for whom one is trying to generalize. The term 'random' is a little misleading since there is nothing casual about these procedures. We should note that different projects involve different levels of generalizability. Some want to develop knowledge about the audience in general, while some might wish to focus on a certain subset of the audience.

Take the ratings as a case study. Researchers are charged with estimating the numbers of people actually watching television based on the observation of a subsection of that audience. To do this, they must be confident that the subsection is broadly similar to the wider population from which it is drawn. In order to achieve this confidence, researchers must ensure that all members of this wider population have an equal chance of being selected for the sample (Hansen et al., 1998). The first thing the researcher needs in order to do this is a list of the target population. Subjects are then picked from this list. This will often involve starting selection at a randomly specified location on the list. The goal is to eliminate any form of systematic bias from the sample selection. That is, the structure of the list of the universal population must not systematically exclude any portion of the population that the researcher wishes to address. Suppose, for example, that we decide to use the telephone book or a list of registered voters. Such lists exclude households without a telephone or those who are not registered to vote. This does not mean that such resources must not be used; the point is that the researcher must be clear about just who the sample is representative of. So, if ratings were based on electoral rolls or telephone directories, results would be representative of television viewers who are also voters or who own a telephone.

It may not always be desirable to say something about the audience in general. Sometimes researchers are particularly interested in a subsection of the audience or in comparing subsections. In this case, a *stratified sampling* procedure may be more appropriate. As the name suggests, this refers to a technique which 'stratifies' the universal list according to criteria such as sex, race or age. If we have a list of possible participants which includes this information (electoral roles do, telephone listings don't), then we order it in a manner allowing us to select, for example, equal numbers of men and women. Illustrating the difference, suppose we had a list of 10,000 television viewers from which a sample of 1,000 were to be randomly drawn. Using non-stratified sampling, we would select every tenth name on the list, beginning from a starting-point chosen at random. Such a procedure gives us no control over the type of people in the sample – there may be more women than men, younger people than older people, white people than black people and so on, according to the way the list is structured. We can overcome this problem by stratifying the list. Stratification is a way of enhancing the representativeness of a sample (Babbie, 1992; Hansen et al., 1998).

As with many things in the social sciences, sampling theory does not perfectly relate to sampling practice. As Babbie (1992) states, it is virtually impossible to find a list of potential participants that does not include some form of systematic error. The problem is exacerbated by the fact that it is often impossible to find a universal list of potential participants. Researchers are always limited by factors of time, money and geography. These practical realities mean that, while media researchers might want to say something about a national media audience, their comments will be based on the observation of a sample that is drawn from a spatially limited subset of the total audience. A survey, for example, is likely to be administered in a specific city. Representativeness might be ensured by selecting participants from different parts of that city, so that the sample reflects the demographic diversity of the national population. This is known as *cluster sampling*.

This does not exhaust sampling possibilities. Qualitative research uses different methods that have a different relationship to the idea of generalizability. But the quantitative projects that made up much of the effects tradition used random sampling as a basis for the statistical analysis that was the foundation of their conclusions about media effects. Having selected participants for projects, the next stage is to decide how one is to treat them. Effects researchers used either experimental or survey methods.

Experiments

We have already encountered experiments in Winston's disparaging remarks directed at Bandura's behaviourist research. Experiments are designed to examine the relationship between independent and dependent variables by controlling the environment in which the two meet. In Chapter 1, I discussed the Judas Priest trial as being representative of the difficulties of trying to establish a connection between media texts and violent behaviour. This difficulty arises because the social context of the murder/suicide was 'contaminated' by a number of other factors. Alcohol and drugs were other independent variables that may have explained the event; or perhaps they interacted with the music to produce a powerful overall effect. But which was the most important: the drugs or the music or the pre-existing psychological condition of the murderer/victim?

Experiments are designed to solve these problems. In observing the power of an independent variable to produce a specific effect on the audience, the experimenter must systematically exclude all other variables that could produce the same effect. The great objection made to this approach is that it is less feasible in social science than it is in biology, chemistry and physics. If we want to know about the effect that a virus has on a blood cell, we can create a vacuum around that cell before introducing the virus to it. In this way, we can be sure that any changes in the cell are the product of the virus. This is not the case with media effects. What is more, even behavioural psychologists acknowledge this. Behaviourism suggests that human beings learn to respond to external stimuli through conditioning; that is, they learn through experience to attach certain behavioural responses to certain cues (Flanagan, 1995). The cell's reaction to the virus is purely biological, being governed by a physical, necessary relationship. But a human's reaction to a stimulus, while it can be just as involuntary, is governed by psychological factors shaped by socialization. Consequently, the experimental social scientist must remember that he or she cannot treat subjects as the biologist treats the cell, since it is impossible to strip people of their socialization. This means that the behaviours observed in experimental projects on media effects are always influenced by external social forces.

But it is still possible to argue that a media stimulus can produce a distinct effect that can be observed under experimental conditions. Social scientists get around the problem of socialization by varying experimental designs. The biologist described above has used a very simple before-and-after design, where the dependent variable, the cell, is examined before and after the introduction of the virus. Since the only difference between the two conditions is the presence of the virus, then we can be sure that this is what explains any changes.

Not so with human subjects. It is not possible to seal human beings from external influences beyond the realm of the experiment. Suppose a researcher sets out to examine the effectiveness of a politician's televised speech on enhancing the perceived trustworthiness of the speaker. The researcher decides to use a before-and-after design. After selecting a sample, he or she administers a survey to sample members, measuring their perceptions of the politician. He or she then shows them the speech, and re-administers the test. Any changes in credibility ratings are interpreted as effects of the speech. But remember, human beings cannot be isolated from an environment supplying them with constant information that has the power to change perceptions. Suppose that it takes the researcher some time to set up the second survey. The sample, having viewed the speech, is asked to return the next day. That morning, the newspapers feature photographs of the politician emerging from an adult store, laden down with magazines and videos. This is strange, since the politician publicly favors strong anti-pornography legislation. Later, the researcher is intrigued to discover that respondents seem to have reacted negatively to the speech; the politician's credibility ratings have gone down. He or she hypothesizes that this is explained by a distaste for overt propaganda. Perhaps the audience was annoyed by such an obvious attempt to persuade them. The researcher is wrong. The difference is produced by changes in the sample's informational environment between survey one and survey two.

Experimenters deal with this problem by introducing what are known as *control groups* (Stouffer, 1950/1953). In the previous example, the researcher could have drawn another sample and administered the same surveys at the same times. The only difference would be that the second group would not see the speech. If the negative response from the experimental group was the product of news revelations about the politician, not the speech, then a similar dynamic should be viewed in the control group. Hence the researcher can be reasonably sure that as long as the experimental and control groups are relatively homogeneous, differences between the two are the product of media exposure. As we shall see, this before-and-after test using control groups was typical of much of the effects tradition.

Surveys

As the above example illustrates, surveys have a part to play in experiments. But they also have a stand-alone role in quantitative research into media effects. Surveys are often used to ask people about their reactions to the media in general, or their response to a certain media event or show. They have the advantage over experiments in having access to natural reception sites: they ask people about real-life situations. A survey is a method of interviewing a large number of people and standardizing their responses, making them amenable to statistical analysis. This is normally done through the use of multiple choice questions. These are questions which the respondent must answer using a range of responses provided by the interviewer. Imagine you are given the task of comparing attitudes towards television violence between light and heavy television users. Your first problem would be delineating the groups. When asked how much television they watched per day, a sample of 400 viewers could conceivably give 400 different answers. The researcher can overcome this by asking viewers to classify their viewing in terms of a limited number of categories. He or she could ask, for example, if respondents watch television for less than 1 hour per day, 2–3 hours per day or more than 3 hours per day. Asking the question in this form means that the survey automatically sorts the sample into subgroups of light, medium and heavy viewers.

A survey, then, is an organized and standardized conversation that aims to achieve not only validity, but also reliability. Suppose you were given the task of researching the above question. Talking to a colleague, you mention how struck you were by a recent conversation you had with someone who watches 5 hours of television every night. You were stunned by how animated this person became when talking about images of violence he or she had seen. You also noticed just how many instances of on-screen aggression the person seemed to remember. Your colleague nods, having had very similar conversations with other people who watch a lot of television. It seems that you have uncovered a common vein. But you are also aware that you cannot reliably compare these conversations, whatever their surface similarities. Because the structure of these conversations was not identical, you are unsure to what extent the responses of your violence fans are indicative of the same thing. Perhaps your conversation was more antagonistic: your respondent had objected to your condescending approach to his or her media habits, and had deliberately exaggerated his or her taste for violence to shock you. This compares with your colleague's conversation, which had been congenial and in which the respondent had expressed genuine preferences. Or perhaps you had weighted your questions more heavily towards extreme forms of media violence than your colleague had. For all of these reasons, you would have little basis upon which to make a systematic comparison between these conversations.

Surveys develop a number of methods to standardize hundreds and thousands of conversations so that such comparisons can be made. The main tool is to provide respondents with sets of identical questions to be answered in codified form. Designing such a survey is difficult, since researchers need to ensure that the form of the questionnaire does not influence the answers given. The phrasing of a question can influence a respondent. Returning to our fictional scenario, suppose you and your colleague decide to measure the degree to which light and heavy viewers differ not only in their preferences for on-screen violence, but also the degree to which they are concerned about this violence. You decide to assess this concern through the following question:

Many people think that there is too much violence on television. Do you:
(a) Agree (b) Disagree?

There are many biasing elements in this question. Respondents are given information about what other people think; they are told that many are concerned by violent television content. This might create a desire to be part of the crowd; the respondent might agree with the statement simply because he or she thinks that this is the socially acceptable thing to do. Suppose another respondent agrees with the statement because he or she genuinely believes that there is too much violence on television. Does this then represent a true picture of his or her media concerns? Not necessarily. Perhaps this person is concerned about media violence, but is far more concerned about the effect of advertising. His or her answer, then, misrepresents his or her level of anxiety about violence: yes, violence is an issue, but not the most pressing one. The question is flawed, in this case because of the limited scope it offers to voice concerns.

The goals of the survey are to allow people to express their true feelings, as far as this is possible within the multiple choice format. Perhaps a better way of phrasing the question would be:

Which of the following issues about television content concerns you the most?

(a) Sexual content?
(b) Violence?
(c) Advertising?
(d) Images of women?
(e) Images of different ethnic groups?
(f) Images of different class groups?

This question diminishes problems of directing respondents' attention towards the violence issue at the expense of all other concerns.

The order in which questions are asked can also influence responses. Imagine the preceding question was placed after the following items:

Do you (a) agree or (b) disagree with the following statements?

1 Television monopolizes too much of our time.
2 Television distracts children from their schoolwork.
3 Television distracts children from participating in sports and hobbies.
4 Television provides children with a number of negative role models.
5 Television encourages children to use violence to resolve conflicts.

Many people are aware that concerns about television's anti-social power are often focused on children. They are also aware that these concerns are heavily weighted towards the violence question. If these five questions were asked before the item on respondents' primary concern regarding media effects, the danger is that the violence issue would be pushed to the fore.

However careful the researcher is, it remains true that surveys using multiple choice questions suffer from validity problems. The limitation on permissible responses creates the danger that the answer given reflects the bias of the survey as much as, if not more than, the thoughts of respondents. The only real way of dealing with this is to consider the merits of surveys by asking how the form and content of the questions used may have influenced the results gained.

Methods of analysis

Surveys and experiments are designed to quantify variables and to establish statistical connections between them. In the example we have been working with so far, the researcher would be interested in establishing a connection between amount of television exposure and concern over media violence. More specifically, he or she would want to know the strength of the relationship between viewing and concern. The researcher would also want to know how confident he or she could be that the differences observed in the sample would also be present in the general population. But few relationships in social science are ever direct. It is not that there might not be a relationship between these variables, but the relationship will be mediated through a number of other factors. Surveys and experiments are designed to account for as many of these interactions as possible.

If the question about media violence were administered to a representative sample of television viewers, the easiest way of reporting results would be to publish the percentage of people who were concerned about the issue. This is an example of *univariate analysis*. Such statistics are a familiar part of news reporting, as journalists increasingly use opinion polls to create stories about political events. However, such statistics are descriptive, rather than analytical. Media researchers are not only interested in what people think, but also why they think what they do. They also want to explain why different groups of people think different things. The danger of focusing on only two variables, such as amount of television viewing and concern about on-screen violence, is that any perceived relationship between the two might be spurious; that is, caused by the presence of other variables. It could be, for example, that both viewing and concern are influenced by living environment. People living in high-crime areas might watch more television because they spend more time at home. Hence their viewing levels and their concerns about violence are both dependent variables, caused by the independent variable of the crime rate in their area. If this is true, then there should be no difference between levels of concern between light and heavy viewers who live in high-crime areas.

Another possibility is that effects might be present only in certain parts of the population, or may be especially powerful among certain groups. That is, the correlation between viewing and concern over violence might be especially strong in high-crime areas or might only hold true in these places. If this were true, then the correlation between viewing and concern would be stronger or would only be found among those viewers living in high-crime areas. This is called a *specification*.

The statistical analysis of the relationship between variables is a way of recognizing that apparent media effects can be the product of inter-acting forces. In other words, they acknowledge the impossibility of examining people under strictly experimental conditions. Survey analysis can deal with this issue in several ways. Subgroup analysis provides one example of what is called a *multivariate approach*, which takes into account several independent variables in the explanation of a dependent one. In addition to dividing the sample among light and heavy viewers, we could also subdivide these groups still further, looking for differences according to demographic variables. As an example, consider Table 2.1, taken from Ruddock (1998a), which examines the way in which attitudes towards foreign policy alter according to levels of interest in two sorts of news – news in general and international news – among American television viewers. Respondents to this survey were asked whether they approved or disapproved of four foreign actions taken by President George Bush. They were asked to rate each action on a scale of 1–3, with higher values signalling approval. This produced an overall scale ranging from 4 to 12, again with higher scores indicating greater approval of Bush's actions. The numbers beneath the table show the grand mean for the sample as a whole. The mean score on the index is 9.5. Given that the median point of the approval scale is 8, this shows a general tendency towards approval.

The global mean, however, is of limited significance in a study which aims to examine how interest and exposure to the news media might influence foreign policy opinions. For this reason, responses are sub-divided according to a number of potential independent variables. The vertical axis of the table divides the sample on both news indices into three groups: low, medium and high interest. These groups are then further subdivided on the horizontal axis according to levels of educa-tion, sex, race, and political ideology. Each cell then represents the mean score of people falling within specific media and demographic groups. The top left-hand cell, showing a figure of 9.0, represents the mean score for people with low levels of education who also have low levels of interest in news in general. The bottom right cell's figure of 9.9 represents the mean score for people of a liberal political interest who express a high level of interest in international news. Dividing mean scores in this manner allows us to examine different levels of approval for different sorts of people. It also allows us to see if the media have a significant effect above and beyond any that might be the product of social differences, or if these media effects are acutely felt among certain sectors of the population.

Additionally, Table 2.1 allows us to see the significance of any such differences. The data were analysed using a computer package called SPSS-X. This program calculates subgroup mean scores and also cal-culates the probability that any differences observed are the product of chance or sample error. There are many sorts of tests for statistical significance, formulated for application to different sorts of variables,

Table 2.1 Approval of George Bush's foreign policy, 1990

News ideology	Education			Sex		Race			Political ideology		
	Low	Medium	High	Male	Female	White	Black	Other	Con.	Mod.	Lib.
General news											
Low	9.0	9.3	9.3	9.3	9.2	9.3	9.0	9.2	9.3	9.3	9.1
Medium	9.5	9.7	9.6	9.6	9.7	9.6	10.0	9.1	9.6	9.6	9.9
High	9.5	9.8*	9.7*	9.8*	9.7*	9.7*	10.0*	8.5	9.6	9.8*	9.9*
International news											
Low	8.8	9.4	9.4	9.2	9.3	9.3	9.2	8.5	9.4	9.3	9.1
Medium	9.4	9.6	9.5	9.6	9.5	9.6	9.5	8.8	9.5	9.5	9.7
High	9.9*	9.9*	9.6	9.8*	9.8*	9.7*	10.3*	9.8	9.6	9.9*	9.9*

Con., conservative; Mod., moderate; Lib., liberal.

Grand mean = 9.5.

Standard deviation = 1.7.

* represent a significant difference between subgroups where p = <.05

but they have in common the fact that they are expressed in the form of a *P* value. Where the *P* value is 0.05 or less, social scientists agree that differences between subgroups are highly likely to reflect similar differences among the population as a whole (this figure means there is only a 5 per cent chance that this is not the case). Moving back to Table 2.1, asterisks next to figures represent significant differences within the demographic subgroups listed on the horizontal axis according to the media variables. The bottom left-hand cell shows a figure of 9.9 with an asterisk. Three cells above, we see a figure of 8.8. This means that different levels of attention to international news produces a significantly higher approval for George Bush's foreign policy among people with low levels of education. Scanning the whole table, we see that this is true of eight of the eleven subgroups listed on *both* news indices. We can be confident, then, that people who were more attentive to the news also tended to be more approving of Bush's foreign policy.

It is impossible to do any sort of justice to the complexity of statistical analysis in this section. There are many other methods to examine the role that independent variables play in the production of an overall social effect. *Multiple regression*, for example, can show the significance and strength of the influences that a number of factors play in the production of something such as attitudes towards foreign policy (Seale, 1998). The point is that all of the various methods used by statisticians to analyse data produced by experiments and surveys are designed to answer the same question: the role that a certain cultural practice, experience or position has in influencing the way people think and behave. It is also clear that social scientists face a number of practical difficulties which mean that we must attend to the differences between theory and practice. While the social scientist might yearn for the clean precision of the biologist, physicist or chemist, the fact is that he or she is dealing with social rather than physical substances which respond to no clear laws. If we drop an object out of a window, we can be sure it will fall to the ground. But if we expose people to the media, we cannot be sure that they will react in the same way, since these reactions are not governed by any universal law such as the law of gravity. This is exacerbated by the fact that the way in which data are collected can have an effect in itself. All of this means that the numbers produced by experiments and surveys cannot be seen as speaking for themselves. In interpreting the significance of data, it is important to take into account the way in which samples were drawn, the tools that were used to generate the data, and the way in which the data are analysed before we decide if a project provides information that is both valid and reliable. Bearing this in mind, it is now possible to consider the main body of effects research. What methods has it used, what conclusions has it drawn, and how trustworthy and useful are these conclusions?

Effects: violence, fright, arousal

We left the history of effects research at a time when media research was harnessed to state goals. This represents an official interest in media research focusing on pro-social (from the state's perspective) effects. But this does not exhaust the scope of official interest. There were also concerns, in governmental and non-governmental circles, about the mass media's anti-social potential. During the 1960s, the surgeon general and the National Institute of Mental Health commissioned research into the effects of media violence in the United States (Gunter, 1994). Such actions demonstrate the behavioural concerns about the effects of the media that were common in the post-war period, concerns that created a tradition of experimental research into the ability of media images to provoke aggressive actions.

Albert Bandura's research provides the most famous example, and the most derided in critical circles. Bandura (1978) contends that television not only teaches children how to act aggressively, but also erodes the power of social restraints on violent behaviour, in part by de-sensitizing viewers to the effects of this violence. Phrased in this form, Bandura's work seems perfectly at home within positivism. The most troubling part of these conclusions is the way that they suggest that children's reactions to the media are every bit as involuntary as the response of a dropped object to gravity. Yet other parts of Bandura's 'social learning theory of aggression' suggest a more complex view of media effects. Parts of his theory indicate a desire to move beyond narrow behavioural concerns towards less visible, cognitive effects. He speaks, for example, of different interpretations that can be made of media violence performed by the police or military: 'People vary markedly in their perceptions of aggression for social control and even social change. The more advantaged citizenry tend to view even extreme levels of violence for control as lawful discharges of duty, whereas disadvantaged members regard such practices as expressions of institutional aggression' (Bandura, 1978: 1). At times, Bandura even seems to dismiss the effects direction that his very own work had encouraged many to take:

> The critical question for social scientists to answer is not why some people who are subjected to aversive conditions aggress, but rather why a sizable

majority of them acquiesce to dismal living conditions in the midst of affluent styles of life. To invoke the frustration-aggression hypothesis, as is commonly done, is to disregard the more striking evidence that severe privation generally produces feelings of hopelessness and massive apathy. (Bandura, 1978: 19)

This is a hugely significant statement. It suggests that Bandura is more than aware that there is far more to media effects than their immediate behavioural consequences. The main danger of media saturation, Bandura concludes, is not that it makes audiences do violent things, but that it stops them from doing anything at all – a curious statement to come from a behaviourist. Yet Bandura's conclusion intersects with key theories used by cultivation analysis and critical cultural studies.

But if Bandura's work indicates a growing theoretical compatibility between different research traditions, methodological gaps remain. Despite public and official hysteria about media violence, the 'hypodermic needle' effects model never had a foothold in post-war research. Behaviourists maintained that the media could evoke violent behaviours, but also became convinced that other variables had to enter the frame to produce these effects. Yet effects researchers remained divided from colleagues in other paradigms in the way in which they conceptualized these other factors.

Consider Table 2.1, on attitudes towards foreign policy, once more. The sample is divided into demographic subgroups in order to see if media effects are influenced in any way by social identity. The idea is that different identities produce different experiences and ways of looking at the world. Differences between subjects are therefore defined in terms of the deep-seated products of socialization. Many who have approached the issue of media violence experimentally produce other ideas on the differences between viewers. These differences are related to often short-term psychological states. Earlier, Bandura mentioned an 'aggressive cue' hypothesis. This refers to the idea that audiences are more likely to respond to violent content with violent behaviour if they are somehow agitated. This idea led several researchers to experiment with the relationship between anger and violent media content.

At the same time as Bandura was rethinking his theories of aggression, Sebastien and colleagues (1978) were trying to get beyond the limitations of the 'bobo doll' studies by conducting a 'natural experiment' at a young offenders' institution. Sebastien et al. echoed Milgram and Shotland (1973) in objecting to the unreality of the 'bobo' experiments. First, the text used was not an actual television programme; it was unlike anything that viewers were likely to encounter. Secondly, the setting for the viewing was unlike real places where people watch television. Thirdly, the indicators of violence used in the study, hitting a doll that was designed to be hit, did not resemble real-life situations that might tempt people to use violence. Finally, there was the importance of dealing with intervening variables.

Sebastien et al. (1978) set out to rectify these problems by showing a series of films to young offenders. The young men in question were housed in 'cottages', sleeping four inmates. Each cottage was equipped with a recreation room, featuring a television and video recorder. This represented the 'natural' viewing environment. The researchers used this environment to study the connections between violent media content, non-media-related levels of frustration and the tendency towards real-life aggression. The latter was measured as the likelihood that the sample would, when given the opportunity, be verbally aggressive. The question was: were those who saw violent films more likely to be abusive than those viewing non-violent content? Verbal aggression was used as a more realistic indicator of real-world violence than, as in the 'bobo' study, the tendency to hit a punchbag (after all, what else are you going to do with it?).

The study was constructed in the following way. The sample was divided into four, two experimental and two control groups. One sample of boys watched one violent film each night, Monday to Friday, while another viewed five non-violent films. Another group watched a violent film on Friday evening only, while the second control group watched a non-violent film on Friday only. For the duration of the experiment, the youths were prevented from watching all other television to ensure that the selected films were not contaminated by other programmes. The boys were then exposed to different levels of frustration. They were asked to complete a puzzle, while being either encouraged or insulted by a 'confederate' of the researchers. They were then given the opportunity to respond verbally to the confederate. Not surprisingly, those who were the most insulted were also the most likely to be rude to this person. Through subgroup analysis, the researchers found that the most aggressive group was those who had viewed the Friday night violent film only, and had been exposed to the highest levels of insult. This, it was concluded, provided evidence that media violence can cause aggressive behaviour among agitated people.

Several objections can be made to this study. Several of them are ethical. It is generally accepted that subjects should take part in experiments of their own free will; there is some question as to how 'voluntary' the participation of prison inmates can be. This is made worse by the fact that in return for being deprived of a week's television viewing, excepting videos selected by the researchers, the youths were paid the princely sum of $1, hardly generous even at the time. Also we must ask how typical of the general population the sample was. One could argue that the sample was already disposed towards violence, if only by the fact that they may have felt resentful at being captive subjects for the researchers. Hence the parameters of the aggression observed might only hold true for people who suffer additional frustration on top of already pressured environments. However reliable the methods used, questions of validity remain.

Despite these problems, this type of study design is very common in violence research. It has also been used by those interested in connections between violence and pornography (Harris, 1994). Diener and Woody (1981) suggested that media violence had the most impact among people who find pleasure in the pain of others. This is a troubling proposition when violence is connected with sexuality in aggressive pornography. Could exposure to different types of pornography combine with frustration to provoke violent behaviour under experimental conditions? Harris (1994) reviews notable work in this field, such as Donnerstein et al. (1975), Donnerstein and Hallam (1978) and Donnerstein (1980). All conducted experiments where sample audiences were shown pornography of varying levels of intensity (in terms of explicitness and levels of violence) to examine the behavioural impact of such material. Subjects were exposed to either positive or negative treatment by a confederate; some were treated rudely during the course of the screening, others were insulted while performing a problem-solving exercise. They were all then given chances to exact revenge by administering electric shocks to the confederate. It was generally found that those exposed to more explicit forms of pornography were significantly more likely to deliver longer and more frequent electric shocks to the confederate. The shocks were fake, but the sample subjects were not told this. Validity emerges again. Sample subjects for this research were often drawn from students at the universities that the researchers worked at, raising the same ethical and methodological problems encountered in the young offenders' study. As an indicator of potential real-world violence, we must also question the validity of the electric-shock treatment.

Milgram and Shotland (1973) tried to overcome these validity problems in their own research on television violence. Even though the young offenders' study was conducted in the sample's actual living environment, one could still object to the artificiality of the study. The puzzle-solving section, for example, was probably unlike anything that the youths had encountered before or would encounter again. All of us have had to perform tests, but very few of us have been systematically insulted while doing so. Milgram and Shotland (1973) tried to overcome this problem by studying reactions to apparently natural stimuli. Their rationale was as follows:

> We expose the viewer, under a naturalistic set of circumstances, to a television program depicting antisocial behaviour. The viewer is then presented with temptations in real life similar to those faced by the television character. The question is whether the television character's depicted actions influence the real life behaviour of the viewers. And of course, we run a control, parallel condition featuring a television drama in which antisocial behaviour was not an element. (1973: 3)

The programme selected as the media stimulus was a hospital drama. The episode shown featured the story of a young man who loses his job at the hospital. At the same time, the hospital is conducting a televised fund-raising drive to which people can contribute by leaving money in collection boxes distributed around the city where the drama takes place. Desperate for money and angry at the way the hospital has treated him, the young man is shown smashing and robbing five of the boxes.

The sample population was drawn via newspaper advertisements and leaflets distributed in the streets. Quota sampling was used to ensure the presence of many young men and 'disadvantaged minorities', which federal crime statistics of the time showed to be the most frequent perpetrators of crimes. Respondents were promised a transistor radio in return for their participation, which they were told involved giving their assessment of a television programme. The real purpose of the research was disguised to avoid prompting responses. The advertisements and leaflets attracted 607 people to the screenings of the test and control (non-violent) programmes.

After the screenings, viewers were told to go to an office to collect their prizes. When they got to the office, however, they were confronted with a curt sign informing them that the company running the test had run out of radios. This created the impression that the viewers had been tricked. The room also contained a poster advertising a hospital fund-raising drive and a collection box, containing some money. The idea was that the viewers now found themselves in a real-life situation that was much like the fictional one they had just watched. Would they respond in kind, either smashing the box or leaving it (the control group)? The results were less than spectacular. Although about 23 per cent of the total sample tried to break into the box, or stole something else from the room, those who had seen the anti-social version of the programme were no more likely than were members of the control group to behave in this way.

In many ways, this study is representative of the broad thrust of direct effects research. Its results are typical of the 'some do, some don't' ambivalence that Klapper had identified in 1960. Comstock et al. (1974) argue that the more that researchers allowed the real world to permeate the laboratory, the less dramatic their results became. We can illustrate this argument by comparing Sebastien et al.'s (1978) and Milgram and Shotland's (1973) work with experiments carried out to examine the physiological effects of media exposure. Reeves and Thorson (1986) subjected viewers to ECG tests to determine the way in which different sorts of media content provoke different levels of brainwave activity. Pornography research can follow a similar physiological route; subjects may, for example, be attached to devices measuring perspiration or heart rate to show how erotic images influence the body (Harris, 1994). But what does this research tell us? Of course, as Bandura points out, although the responses noted might be involuntary, they are nevertheless the products of learned behaviour. Our culture teaches us what is violent and what is erotic. So this sort of work might tell us interesting things about what we find acceptable and unacceptable. But it offers little beyond this descriptive point. One of the problems is that the arousal measured is an ambiguous state. If we observe that an image has made a subject's pulse race, we do not know if this is because he or she finds it exciting, erotic or repulsive. The physical reaction fits all three states.

What we really want to know is what these reactions mean. Once we move towards the translation of physical and mental reactions into material behaviours, things become complicated. Under conditions where experimenters are able to antagonize subjects and then provide them with really obvious opportunities to respond to the person that has caused the antagonism, positive results are shown. When, as in the case of the Milgram and Shotland (1973) study, the connections between media text, frustration and source of that frustration are attenuated, the results are less dramatic.

This leaves the question of how far it is possible to replicate the everyday experience people have with the media under experimental conditions. Because a person who is subjected to highly explicit pornography shows a willingness to deliver electric shocks to a person who has annoyed him during the course of an experiment, does this mean that he or she is likely to assault a partner if the same or similar material is viewed in the home?

The conclusion from all of this is that violent media content cannot transform normally peaceful people into thugs. This does not mean that we should not be concerned. It is possible that media violence has a number of less direct, but equally disturbing influences on society. Cantor (1994) argues that the main power of violence is the power to shock and frighten. If this is not a particularly 'shocking' discovery, what is of use is Cantor, Wilson and Hoffner's (1986) survey research on what kinds of things frighten what kinds of children. Surveys were distributed to parents of schoolchildren in the US following the screening of the television movie *The Day After*, the story of a nuclear attack on the US. The interesting thing about this research is that the parents reported that teenage viewers were more likely to be frightened or disturbed than were younger viewers. The researchers explained this as reflecting the fact that only older children were able to differentiate between this and other horror/science fiction programmes in recognizing the plausibility of the scenario. The indicators of fright reported were things such as general unease at the time of viewing and disturbed sleep.

Some quantitative survey and experimental investigations of media violence were turning away from behaviourism. Instead of asking what people did in response to media violence, some scholars began to ask how such images had a cognitive and emotional impact. Barry Gunter (1985) showed how some of the techniques discussed in this chapter could be used to construct a more nuanced view of the relationship between audiences and media violence. Gunter was interested in what people make of this violence, since any behavioural effects must be based on an understanding of the stimulus. He exposed panels of viewers to a series of clips from violent shows, and asked them via multiple choice questions to rate how shocking, enjoyable and realistic these clips were. He then studied correlations between these perceptions and demographic features of the respondents. If this all sounds pretty conventional, Gunter took an unusual approach to demographics, especially gender. Instead of dividing the sample into male and female, Gunter asked each respondent to rank him or herself on a number of questions relating to male, female and androgynous tendencies. Respondents were thus distributed along a gender continuum, where biological females could identify with masculine tendencies and vice versa. One of the interesting things that Gunter discovered was that reactions to violence were determined by gender traits rather than sex as a biological category. Women who identified with masculine traits were less concerned and frightened by media violence than were men who identified with feminine characteristics. Perceptions of violence were therefore affected by the socialization of the individual.

Still other possibilities emerge. Cultivation analysis, discussed in Chapter 4, interprets media violence as demonstrations of social power.

Barker and Petley (1997) find debates on violence more interesting than violence itself. They echo Klapper (1960) in concluding that these debates really reflect elite social concerns. Experimental research has fulfilled a useful function in the sense that it has clearly demonstrated the problems of trying to establish causal connections between on-screen and real-world violence, and has largely dismissed the notion of the direct effect. This can be seen as setting the stage for those paradigms that have looked for more subtle but no less powerful influences wielded by the media.

Other sorts of behaviours

As post-war research set about solidifying the limited effects position, so too some scholars cast their theoretical and methodological nets wider to assess other forms of behaviour surrounding media use. Berelson (1949), Hertzog (1950/1953) and Wolf and Fiske (1949) examined the social uses of newspapers, radio listening and comic book reading respectively. Berelson (1949), seizing the opportunity created by a newspaper strike in New York, used a quantitative survey to measure the 'meaning' of missing the newspaper. Newspapers were significant not for their ability to change behaviours and thoughts, but for the role they played in structuring the day and connecting the individual to society. In a similar vein, Lazarsfeld and Dinerman (1949) used the same methodology to inquire why some people did *not* listen to the radio during certain times of the day. There were times, he discovered, when listening to the radio was conducive to social needs and times when it was not. Meanwhile, Wolf and Fiske (1949) used qualitative, open-ended interviews to assess the role that comic books played in the lives of young male readers. They did not find a moronic, uniform sample seduced into a life of sin by these lurid rags, but instead found readers displaying different preferences and levels of media literacy who derived a range of pleasures from comics.

These studies are significant since they established a path for *uses and gratifications research*, notably discussed by Blumler et al. (1974) and McQuail (1998). A common theme in these studies concerned the functionalist role that media played in people's lives. Communication research had begun with a focus on the media's power to persuade, with a special concentration on the ability of specific messages to produce predictable behaviours. By the 1950s, however, there was a shift towards the analysis of the role that the media in general played in everyday life. Berelson (1949) and Lazarsfeld and Dinerman (1949) suggested that reading the paper and listening to the radio were activities that were interwoven with other daily rituals. Moreover, media usage was directed towards the fulfillment of social needs. Katz made this turn explicit, writing:

> Less attention [should be paid] to what media do to people and more to what people do to the media. Such an approach assumes that even the most potent of mass media content cannot ordinarily influence an individual who has no use for it in the social and psychological context in which he lives. The uses approach assumes that people's values, their interests, their associations, their social roles, are pre-potent, and that people selectively fashion what they see and hear to these interests. (cited in McQuail, 1998: 152)

McQuail sees this as the founding principle of uses and gratifications research. Behaviourists had largely concluded that, for the majority of people, the mass media could not make people do anything they did not want to do. At the same time, public opinion research (discussed in Chapter 3) added that, under normal circumstances, the public could not be persuaded to think anything they did not want to think. Cumulatively, a picture emerged of a public steeped in habits of thought and deed that, in 'pre-potent' fashion, guided media usage. Far from being omnipotent, Katz suggested that the media could be manipulated to serve the public. Viewers, readers and listeners had a range of social and psychological needs that they satisfied through media consumption.

This became the focus of uses and gratifications research. A paradigmatic shift was signalled by a redefinition of variables. Where the psychology of the audience had been seen as a dependent effect of media use, it now emerged as the independent variable determining the actual use and therefore social impact of the mass media. Through quantitative surveys and statistical analysis, uses and gratifications researchers set out to discover what these psychological needs were, and how they were satisfied through media consumption. A different picture of the audience emerged in the process: where once had been the passive dupe, there now stood a new, confident breed who knew what they wanted and how to get it. The focus had also shifted from message to medium; if researchers had been interested in the power of specific texts, they were now more interested in the role of the media in general. However valid concerns about the media's power to influence society were, at the same time they did help people to relax, unwind, exorcise tensions that might otherwise cause aggressive behaviour and keep in touch with the world.

Critical scholars are unsure of how far this can be hailed as a development. Some argue that uses and gratifications research began asking questions that were to be taken up by cultural studies, while others feel that paradigmatic differences between the two negate such connections (Morley, 1992). While the focus on individual psychological needs and the use of mainstream sociological methods suggest a proximity to positivism, Blumler et al. (1974) argue that uses and gratifications research does not believe that audiences hold sovereignty over the media. While it is true that viewers have the power to use the media in a conscious attempt to serve social and psychological needs, it is also true that they have little power to shape media structures. The reason why this issue was largely ignored by early uses and gratifications research was that the model was initially engaged in overthrowing the idea of audience passivity that lay at the heart of direct effects.

Uses and gratifications research supports the argument that the early era of communication studies did not function as 'ordinary science' in the Kuhnian sense. It is true that the theories and methods used by many European media scholars have been largely ignored by North American mass-communication research. But it is quite another thing to state that this tradition has consistently used the same methods and conceptualizations of society. The 1930s to the 1950s were decades when these scholars wrestled with a number of key methodological problems and theoretical models. The 'hypodermic needle' hypothesis was rejected, not defended, by the use of multiple methods. Even if quantitative methodologies were the norm, there is considerable evidence of reflexivity on the part of the people who used them. Effects researchers did think about the problems of trying to study audiences experimentally, and developed survey methodologies designed to overcome these issues. They were also, in some cases, open to the use of qualitative methods. Valuable lessons were learned in this time. By the late 1950s it was clear that the effects of the mass media could only be understood as interactive products of text and context. The focus, then, shifted away from short-term effects towards the overall issue of the role that the media played in socialization. This theme is common to a variety of post-1960s' paradigms.

Exercises

---

1   A famous brewery has been stung by complaints that its television commercials are sexist. The brewery hires you to

conduct an experiment to determine if indeed its commercials contribute to sexist attitudes.

(a) What population do you sample from (among what type of people are you most likely to find these sexist attitudes)?

(b) What are the independent and dependent variables you will be dealing with?

(c) What form will your experiment take? Will you use a control group?

(d) What method will you use to measure changes in attitudes towards gender brought on by exposure to the commercial?

(e) Suppose you find that, according to your measures, the commercial is indeed effective in eliciting sexist responses. Can you think of any other variables that might render this relationship spurious?

2 This topic is clearly related to the wider issue of the role played by the media in the construction of gender. Is the experiment the best way to approach such an issue? Is this a researchable problem?

3 Media and Public Opinion

Polls and opinions

As Walter Lippman (1922) realized, analyses of public opinion and media power often go hand in hand. Lippman argued that modern democracies require their citizens to hold opinions on situations and people beyond the reach of everyday experience. The only possible sources of information for these opinions are the mass media, who are thus granted considerable power to manipulate society. Lippman is widely cited in mainstream communication research, but also encapsulates many issues of concern to critical media scholars who would not normally see themselves as interested in public opinion. As such, he signifies a desire to chart connections between media content, audience reactions and social policy that transcends paradigmatic boundaries.

The history of public opinion research runs parallel to the previous account of effects studies (see Chapter 2). Much of the work discussed here centres on very similar concerns and methods. Having said this, those scholars who were more interested in what people thought about media content than how they physically or physiologically reacted to it established a distinct path leading towards the concept of socialization. While many academics were interested in immediate and therefore short-term responses to stimuli, others began to ask how media content realized cumulative effects over long periods of time. By the 1960s, those working within the public opinion tradition were asking questions that were clearly related to the emerging critical trend in media studies.

This is a strange argument to make given the scorn that qualitative researchers have poured upon public opinion polls. The pollsters' 'weapon of choice' is normally the large sample survey, although academic opinion research also uses experimental techniques (for example, Iyengar and Kinder, 1987). However much these pollsters might pride themselves on their ability accurately to predict the outcome of elections campaigns (the 1948 US presidential and 1992 UK general elections being the only notable exceptions), many have cast doubt on both the reliability and the validity of this sort of work.

A 1996 televised debate on the future of the British monarchy provides a case study of the objections that can be raised to polling methods. The debate, broadcast on ITV, one of the UK's national broadcast networks, was followed by a telephone vote. Viewers were asked if they wished the monarchy to continue: 70 per cent of the voters said yes. Was this a clear public endorsement? Methodologically speaking, the answer was no, since the results were highly unreliable. They represented the responses not of the British public, but of that section of the public who was watching the debate, who was interested enough to make a telephone call, and whose patience was not exhausted as the vote registration system struggled to log incoming data. In the face of such enormous sampling and data entry problems, the results were technically worthless. Of course, the debate was about producing good television, not good science. Polling has become an important part of the news media (Mann and Orren, 1992), and as such has been influenced by the blurring of distinctions between information and entertainment.

Unfortunately, academic polling is often criticized for making the same sorts of mistakes. Herbert Blumer and Pierre Bourdieu provide articulate and detailed accounts of these accusations. As we know, Blumer's was one of the first voices raised against the positivist hegemony in social research. His general distaste for quantitative methods was turned toward polls in his 1948 article 'Public opinion and public opinion polling'. Blumer's chief objection to opinion polls lay in their conceptual poverty: vast amounts of time were devoted to developing ever more sophisticated measurement techniques, but little attention was paid to the far more important question of what it is that these techniques were supposed to be measuring. Just as positivist effects researchers had been criticized for having a poor grasp of the nature of the connections between media and society, so too Blumer accused pollsters of having no real sense of what public opinion was, how it developed or how it influenced social policy.

Bourdieu (1990: 170–1) picks up this critique, depicting pollsters as statistical magicians who use surveys to conjure up images of opinions that exist only in their research:

[a survey] will measure nothing but the effect exercised by the measuring instrument. This is the case every time the pollster imposes upon those polled a problematic which isn't theirs . . . thus eliminating the only interesting problem, the question of the economic and cultural determinants of the capacity for broaching the problem as such.

In other words, however careful pollsters are to avoid the methodological errors that riddled the monarchy debate, their data tell us little about what is going on in a culture. Bourdieu's response is useful, since while we could object to the monarchy debate on the grounds of reliability, what he and Blumer are objecting to is the *validity* of public opinion research. This is significant since it provides access to a similar debate that occurs *within* the polling community on the problems of survey research.

Polling concepts and methods: key problems

Even those who use surveys would agree that Bourdieu and Blumer have a point. Brady and colleagues (1992) acknowledge post-positivism since the public opinion poll sets out to measure an intangible object. While we could use this argument to dismiss surveys in general, perhaps it is more profitable to consider how pollsters use it to enhance the validity of their work.

Literature within the corpus of the polling industry indeed reflects sensitivity towards methodological pitfalls. Moreover, some of this debate centres on conceptual rather than strictly methodological issues. Added to the problem of the intangibility of public opinion is the realization that many people will offer an opinion on any subject, if asked to do so (Brady et al., 1992). Unwilling to appear ignorant, people will adopt positions on subjects of which they know little or nothing. This is the crux of Bourdieu's complaint: people express feelings towards issues which in reality they care very little about. When this happens, polls can significantly misrepresent the shape of public concerns.

The validity problem is clear: the pollster must question the extent to which the answers given in response to his or her questions reflect the shape of public concerns that exist independently of his or her measuring tools. While it is impossible to gain unmediated access to this sphere of concern, it is possible to be sensitive to the issues involved. In this regard, survey researchers must often ask how well informed and stable the opinions they are measuring actually are. Zaller (1994) points out that, since the 1950s, surveys have shown that the majority of voters possess very little political knowledge. If this is true, then the opinions that people hold can often be based on a flimsy informational foundation. As such, public opinion can be suspect in respect of its intensity (Lane and Sears, 1975) and stability (Converse, 1975). People are unlikely to feel passionately about opinions that they have spent little time considering, and it may be easy to sway them from these positions for the same reason.

Although there is little the pollster can do about levels of public knowledge, he or she can at least be aware of the potential for measurement error produced by this situation. Measurement error refers to the degree to which Bourdieu is correct in stating that responses to questions are influenced by the form and content of these very questions (Maccoby and Holt, 1946/1953). Brady et al. (1992: 70) give an illustration of how this can happen:

> in June 1978 . . . [a] Harris poll asked a nation-wide sample of Americans, 'Do you favor or oppose détente – that is, the United Sates and Russia seeking out areas of agreement and cooperation?' Seventy-one percent said they favored détente and only 15 percent reported they opposed it. The same month *The New York Times* and CBS News asked, 'Should the United States try harder to relax tension with the Soviet Union or should it get tougher in its dealings with the Russians? Thirty percent said that they thought the United States should relax tensions; fifty-three percent favored getting tougher.

The responses to these questions suggest very different things. The first depicts a peace-loving American public eager to move beyond the Cold War; the second a majority in favour of its continuation. Let us assume that these two surveys used correct sampling procedure so that those surveyed were indeed representative of the population in general. What could account for the different results gathered? It is possible that the differences can be explained by the structure of the questions. The Harris survey did not provide respondents with the option of getting tougher with the Soviets, presenting *détente* as the only reasonable option. Hence the way in which questions limit or extend the information and positions offered to respondents can influence the opinions they articulate. Responsible polling necessitates a sensitivity towards the constant threat of this sort of measurement error. Yet as Kagay (1992) points out, even carefully designed polls can produce very different views of public opinion. One explanation for this is that, like culture, public opinion is fluid. Logically, social advancement can only happen if people constantly amend their opinions in reaction to new information. In this sense, public opinion is supposed to be, if not unstable, then at least flexible. Thus a range of external social factors influences polls.

One key factor is the time at which one decides to question the public. Timing is important since most opinion surveys are cross-sectional: they measure public opinion at a specific place and time. However well informed and stable the opinions found might be at this time, there is no guarantee that the same survey conducted at a later time would yield the same result. It is this issue which led Lazarsfeld et al. (1949) to study the media's impact on the US presidential election of 1940 via a panel study. Instead of asking voters for their preferences at one point in time, respondents were interviewed repeatedly over a period of months to chart not only their opinions but also trends in their opinion changes. This panel study approach reflects the realization that public opinion is a process, not a thing.

A final methodological issue to consider at this stage are the relative merits of 'surface' and 'depth' answers provided by multiple choice and open-ended questions. The problems of multiple choice questions have been detailed in Chapter 2, and we can see that Blumer's and Bourdieu's objections to polls are based on the assumption that they exclusively use this sort of tool. Paul Lazarsfeld (1950) is again instructive in this area, since although he was a key player in the positivist tradition of communication research, he was also responsible for outlining the contributions that qualitative methods could make. Lazarsfeld acknowledged the validity of complaints about the technical focus of surveys. Opinion polls were ill equipped to describe the processes of opinion formation. Pollsters were also slaves to client interests. Corporate and governmental issues monopolized their time, preventing them from the academic exploration of wider cultural climates and trends. Lazarsfeld felt that polls could be used to record a sense of history, of the values and feeling defining an historic moment. Although he doubted their reliability, fields such as interpretative anthropology and sociology had a role to play in this pursuit. Scholars needed to understand not only the shape of public opinion, but also the processes through which that shape had been formed. Interviewing could clarify what respondents meant by certain answers, how it is they had reached their conclusions and what factors had influenced them. Interviews could also identify key moments in the crystallization of opinions, locate motivations behind opinions and allow the tracing of connections between different opinions.

Further methodological and conceptual discussion will follow, but already it appears that many researchers who believe in the value of opinion polls nevertheless concur with key themes in the Bourdieu/ Blumer critique. Public opinion is not simply a thing to be measured, but it is a complex social phenomenon whose form and function must be interpreted and debated. For this reason, the history of this research as it has evolved within communication studies has featured a continuing conceptual and methodological debate on what public opinion is and how it can be described and interpreted.

What is public opinion?

One of the reasons for the conceptual poverty that Blumer saw in much survey research is that public opinion is a notoriously vague term. Palmer (1936/1953) traces the idea back to the ancient Greeks, and also shows its importance to European political philosophy during the industrial revolution. Wilson (1975) describes a similarly vigorous debate on the nature and role of public opinion in the nascent United States of America. Yet much of this intellectual energy derived from the fact that those involved were not entirely sure what public opinion was or what its role in democracy should be, either in a pragmatic or normative sense.

Let us begin with the problem of definition. Herbst (1993) offers five versions of what public opinion is. Since the eighteenth century, public opinion has been variously defined as;

1 'The general will of a political community'. (Shafritz, cited in Herbst, 1993: 438)
2 'Opinions assigned to an ignorant public by the media'. (as above)
3 'The beliefs of different publics'. (Plano and Greenberg, cited in Herbst, 1993: 438)
4 'Majority opinion'. (Garrison, cited in Herbst, 1993: 438)
5 'The result of elections, referenda and polls'. (Smith and Zurcher, cited in Herbst, 1993: 438)

Herbst's list gives us some idea of the complexities of defining public opinion. The items on the list cannot be viewed as alternatives from which we may pick and choose, since none of them is exhaustive or mutually exclusive. That is, while all five definitions contain at least a grain of validity, none grasps all the forms and functions that public opinion can assume. Moreover, there is a good deal of ontological antagonism between some of the elements: while some reflect functionalist visions of symbiosis between public opinion and democratic ideals, others display cynicism towards such utopianism. The most sensible course of action is to describe the differences between normative and critical positions, showing how each has exerted an influence on the direction of communication research.

As European democracy began to flower following the French Revolution, so it was believed that the freedom to develop and express opinions was central to political growth. All public policy was to be heavily publicized so that citizens could debate the actions of political elites and communicate their feelings to this group (Palmer, 1936/1953). It is this view that underpins liberal-pluralist views of what public opinion should be and how it should work. These same views provide the ontological basis for definitions 1, 3 and 4 in Herbst's list. So, from a normative position free from doubts raised by theories of ideology, hegemony and media manipulation, public opinion is quite simply what the public think, either as individuals or as members of social groups characterized by a particular worldview.

The problem with this approach is that, while it might describe an ideal, it often does not reflect the materialities of public opinion. Utopian views are built upon faith in human rationality. Political actions can only be presented for public consent if one assumes that the public can be trusted to approve the best course of action. However, doubts about the public's capacity to behave this way emerged simultaneously with the drive towards universal enfranchisement. De Tocqueville's fears about the 'tyranny of the masses' were echoed in the American political thought of the early post-colonial period. Concerns were raised that majority rule could be inimical to the inalienability of certain human rights; the wishes of the masses might damage the structure of democracy or impinge on the rights of minority groups. In such cases, early political theorists envisioned situations wherein it was the government's task to *ignore* ill-considered majority opinion (Wilson, 1975).

The very same concerns can be found in contemporary political science. Because commentators cannot agree on how rational public opinion is, they also disagree on ideal relationships between opinion and policy. Geer (1991) sees public opinion as important since it ensures against extremism: anxious to maintain the goodwill of the majority, politicians shun divisive partisan policies. In this view, policy is led by opinion. But this may not always be the case. Using foreign policy as a case study, Powlick (1991) argues that since people often know little of the issues involved, it is the job of politicians to do what must be done, persuading the public on the justification for their actions after the fact. NATO's air strikes against Serbian forces in March 1999 provided an example. British Prime Minister Tony Blair and US President Bill Clinton appeared on television to explain the reasons for the raids after they had been launched. The rationale for this was that since many people knew very little about the political turmoil in the former Yugoslavian federation their opinions did not provide a reliable basis for policy.

Utopian beliefs in pubic rationality are thus problematized, since there are many occasions when the public is simply unwilling or unable to be rational. For this reason, public opinion is not a thing existing in our heads, but is instead an area of hegemonic political struggle where various interest groups compete for our attention. Politicians endeavour to mould our opinions to fit policies, rather than letting themselves be guided by the will of the people. This directs our attention to two things: distopian or critical views of public opinion, and the media's role in the formation and expression of political sentiments. Since debates about the quality of public opinion circulate around the issue of communication between politicians and citizens, the mass media have been important sites for research. Although from a utopian perspective the development of the mass media promised to oil the wheels of democracy, others argued that the electronic media in particular did more harm than good.

This distopian tendency focuses on the absence of reciprocity in mediated debates. Angus (1994) points out that modern views on how democracy should work are premised on ancient models of society. The idea that the public had the right to hear and speak made sense in oral societies, but does not apply today. Although we might be in an unprecedented situation in terms of our ability to receive information, avenues for responding to that information are very limited. The reality of today's media environment is that, despite the rise of cable access stations and forums such as radio and television phone-in programmes, most of us listen without speaking.

James Curran (1991) and Peter Dahlgren (1991) have detailed the consequences of this in their analyses of Jurgen Habermas's notion of the public sphere. Habermas locates his democratic ideal in the European coffee-house culture of the eighteenth century. Democracy flourished as great men of letters thrashed out the issues of the day through energetic argumentation. This sort of public opinion was rational since everyone had access to the same information, and had the right to express an opinion on that information. Habermas contrasted this with the sort of public opinion that existed in pre-modern times. Here, the ignorant subjects of European monarchs were simply given symbols, in the forms of icons of kings and queens, to which they were told they owed allegiance.

The problem with today's public sphere is that, while it is ostensibly aimed at empowering the public, the mass media have created citizens who have more in common with the medieval serf than with Voltaire. Overloaded with fragmented information, voters can do little else but watch in awe and confusion as the world is paraded before them. They say nothing in response because they are confused by what they see, hear and read. It is this sort of work that explains critical perspectives on public opinion research. The idea that public opinion is the media's version of what people think alerts us to issues of power and manipulation in political debates, as well as structural inequalities in communication (Curran, 1991).

If the debate on what public opinion is and how it is or should be connected to policy is marked by both utopian and critical perspectives, then so too is research into the role played by the media in shaping the discussion of public affairs. As we have seen, public opinion can be seen as the product of informed, rational minds, or it can be seen as the product of politically motivated manipulation by political elites, the mass media or both. Audience research on the subject reflects both perspectives. Much of the work from North America in the 1940s and 1950s evidenced a desire to find how democracy could be enhanced by improving methods of communication, in this sense reflecting the positivism of effects research. But, at the same time, there was a consistent and growing trend towards analysing those elements of mediated communication that degraded rather than enhanced the quality of the public sphere. Hence, despite Blumer's and Bourdieu's protestation, public opinion research has shown a growing interest in critical positions.

Mass communication research: positivists and utopians

In Chapter 3 I suggested that media researchers in the United States were explicitly recruited to serve the needs of the state during the Second World War, with this period of service extending into the 1950s. This means that much of the American public opinion research of the post-war period reflects normative, utopian philosophies dovetailing with positivist methodologies. Key figures of the period adopted an openly partisan position in their work. For some, the purpose of public opinion research was to enhance the efficiency of American politics. Bernard Berelson (1948/1953: 448) saw the analysis of public sentiments as central to 'the defense of peace and prosperity'. As reasonable a statement as this might seem, we must remember that the question was *whose* peace and prosperity was to be defended? Lasswell (1941/1953: 469) was in no doubt about this, stating that 'among all who share the traditions of America, the problem is not whether democracy ought to live, but how.' The preservation of the American way of life was partly dependent upon 'the discovery of popular and consistent measures of public opinion'. Given that researchers of the time saw their work as vital for national survival, it is perhaps understandable that they sought rigorous methods of investigation. Lazarsfeld (1952/1975) felt it was important to avoid 'impressionistic' (read interpretative) methods given the reliability problems involved. It is this feeling that explains the dominance of various forms of survey research in the field.

Building on these concerns, Berelson (1952/1975) located the roots of public opinion research within psychology, a location which influenced the concepts and methods that would be used for investigation. The overall project was an overt attempt at social engineering. Political science had mapped out the role that opinion should play in democracy. It was the goal of media researchers to show how the media could be used to make these models a reality. Berelson saw this task involving two questions: finding the personality types that are conducive to democracy, and discovering how different forms of communication can influence opinion. An interesting element of Berelson's thinking at this juncture was his refusal to differentiate between mass and interpersonal communication. Indeed, as we shall see, conversations were often seen as being more powerful influences of opinion than media content. This means that Berelson, and the research tradition that he represented, would not have been sensitive to Angus's (1994) argument that normative views on democracy ignore important differences between oral and electronic communication, with the latter tending to erode the reciprocity that is vital to a functional public sphere.

Mass communications research: central concepts and methods

As the above comments indicate, Berelson was at this time interested in studying interactions between different sorts of communication in the formation of public opinion. The question to be pursued by media researchers was how 'some kinds of *communication* on some kinds of *issues*, brought to the attention of some kinds of *people* under some kinds of *conditions*, have some kinds of *effects*' (Berelson, 1948/1953: 451). What sorts of problems were suggested by the italicized concepts?

The kinds of communication Berelson and his contemporaries were interested in were mass and interpersonal and, crucially, the interaction between the two. How did the media influence the sorts of things that people talked about? Reversing polarity, how did everyday face-to-face communications affect the reception of mass-media content? Much of this early research focused on the sorts of mass communication that were vital to the functioning of American society: Lazarsfeld et al.'s *The People's Choice* (1949) looked at the effects of political campaigning;

Hovland et al.'s *Experiments in Mass Communication* (1949) examined various issues in the areas of propaganda, campaigning, marketing and public information. The common theme in these and many other works was how the media could be used to sell people, ideas and goods. It was found that success in this regard depended on the sorts of people being communicated to and the context in which they received information; to this end, researchers began to look for those people who were particularly receptive or resistive to media messages, according to their individual psychology and/or their social position. They also asked how these factors could multiply the sorts of effects produced by mass communication.

Positivist-style social engineering lay at the heart of much of this work. Some projects were directed at solving very real and potentially catastrophic problems facing the US at this time. 'Project Revere', for example, sought to measure the effectiveness of airborne leafleting campaigns in maintaining communication links in the event of a nuclear strike (Defleur and Lowery, 1988). As with other parts of the effects tradition, these early efforts to study public opinion can be seen as searching for the laws governing its formation via quantitative experimental and survey methods. What were the most effective methods of persuasion? How quickly could ideas be spread?

To this end, a great deal of attention was paid to the issue of how media messages could be manipulated to become more or less effective. Project Revere, which involved bombarding a mid-western town with propaganda leaflets, experimented with the quantity of per capita leaflets dropped in an attempt to discover the optimum ratio for the diffusion of messages. Janis and Feshbach experimented with the use of fear appeals in public health campaigns (Janis, 1963). In one study, groups of school children were encouraged to brush their teeth via various messages about the consequences of tooth decay. It was found that campaigns focusing on relatively mild health problems were more effective than others that made alarming connections between poor dental hygiene and cancer. Other questions followed. Were persuasive messages that presented many sides of an argument more effective than one-sided messages because they were seen as more objective? How did the credibility of the speaker influence audience perceptions (Maccoby, 1963)? Irving Janis (1963) also felt that the power of mass communication depended on the weakness of the audience. Through applying psychometric tests to the people who were exposed to persuasive messages, Janis argued that some people were more persuadable than others: aggressive males tended to be the least suggestible, whereas anxious people, unsure of their position in society, were more open to having their opinions changed.

Yet if change began as an important issue in public opinion research, it did not stay there for long. A significant difference between this research and the 'hypodermic needle' effects model is that studies such as Project Revere did not assume that the audience was comprised of anomic individuals. Diffusion studies such as these, studies which set out to find how quickly mediated information could spread throughout a community, saw people as living within closely integrated networks bound by interpersonal communication. Moreover, these interpersonal networks were far more influential in shaping thoughts and behaviours than were the mass media.

These ideas were articulated by Katz (1963) who had developed the concept of the 'opinion leader' in his work with Paul Lazarsfeld. Katz argued that the effects of mass communication were filtered through respected figures in local communities. Most people, he felt, were more reliant on other people than the mass media for cues as to how they should feel about social and political issues. On a range of issues from consumer choices and film preferences to voting decisions, Katz and Lazarsfeld found that, if the media had any power at all, it was filtered through these opinion leaders.

Following on from the conclusion drawn in Lazarsfeld et al.'s *The People's Choice* (1949), it was also found that most people tended to use mass-media information primarily to reinforce opinions they already held and decisions they had already made. Leo Festinger (1963) suggested in his theory of cognitive dissonance that people sought to harmonize the relationship between their behaviours and the information they received from the mass media. Festinger hypothesized that people found it distressing to find their beliefs and behaviours contradicted by mass-media information. Such occasions produced 'cognitive dissonance', a situation in which actions and thoughts contradict one another. People try to remedy this situation by changing either the way they think or the things they do – to bring beliefs and actions back into alignment. However, Festinger also discovered that people often select information from the media that reinforces decisions they have already made. Consumers, for example, often seek out positive reviews of high-cost products, such as cars, *after* purchasing. In this situation, cognitive dissonance is avoided by using media content to reassure.

Public opinion researchers were thus in agreement with their behaviourist colleagues about the nature of media effects. This was summarized by Janis (1963: 55):

> In general, our results bear out the work of many other social psychologists and sociologists in indicating that the net effect of mass media

communications tends to be very limited, often consisting only of reinforcing pre-existing beliefs and attitudes. Attempts at producing major changes
in social prejudices and political stereotypes generally meet with an
extraordinarily high degree of psychological resistance.

Janis's conclusions were a little more focused than the 'some do, some
don't' position of violence researchers. People were likely to be influenced by the media if they were highly interested in the political topic
being debated, were susceptible to the structure of the argument being
presented, or were of the personality type that is open to persuasion. But
these effects were mitigated by social setting.

Issues of media manipulation that are central to critical views of
public opinion were thus largely absent from this research. The notion
of selective perception suggested that people made up their minds *before*
exposure to media content. The more pessimistic researchers of the time
suggested that another reason why the media were relatively unsuccess-
ful in manipulating popular consciousness was that people were not
interested enough in current affairs to pay any attention to news programming. In the work of Hovland, Janis, Katz, Lazarsfeld and their
contemporaries, we find a public who is not powerless in the face of
marketing and public health campaigns. If we look back to Herbst's five
definitions of public opinion, the one that best fits this situation is 'the
general will of the political community', since it appeared that there was
very little the media could do to influence this will.

Mass communication research: critical elements

Although it is tempting to argue that, by the early 1960s, mass-
communication research had reached an impasse wherein questions of
media power had been dismissed, it is also true to say that key
researchers were aware of continuing conceptual problems in the relationship between the media and public opinion. Some were troubled by
their own relationship with the government, the media and the public.
At the dawn of the Cold War, Robert Merton warned against the
dangers of adopting a narrowly technical, positivist stance. Merton
acknowledged that social scientists could not claim neutrality in political debates since 'the initial formulation of the scientific investigation
[is] conditioned by the implied value of the scientist' (1947/1953: 467).
There was an obvious problem, then, if research agendas were set by the
relatively short-term needs of the Cold War:

when effective mass persuasion is sought, and when effectiveness is measured solely by the number of people who can be brought to a desired action or the desired frame of mind, then the choice of techniques of persuasion will be governed by a narrowly technical and amoral criterion. And this criterion exacts a price of the prevailing morality, for it expresses a manipulative attitude toward man and society. It inevitably pushes toward the use of whatever technique works. (1947/1953: 465)

In other words, the research demanded and paid for in the United States during the 1950s was not necessarily the only sort of research that was possible, or even desirable for anyone interested in 'morals'. Merton's opinion was surprisingly echoed by Lasswell, who called on scientists to resist the lure of government and corporate funding to develop a disinterested 'third' voice. This call was produced by the realization that mass communication was a resource of power that could be used to accentuate rather than ameliorate divisions between the 'haves' and 'have-nots':

There is little doubt of the crucial importance of a third voice during the next few years. The Computer Revolution has produced an instrument that can be employed by centralized elite structures to consolidate their position. It is no news that knowledge is power, especially knowledge that is promptly available and includes information about individuals and groups that lays open their vulnerabilities to blackmail or tactics of positive inducement. A question is whether those who organize a third voice can act quickly enough to join with leaders of pluralistic groups who are demanding access to available systems of storage and retrieval, and who are willing to assist in policing the use of information in ways that guard against the abuse of power. (Lasswell, 1972/1975: 611)

Here Lasswell implored his colleagues to switch sides, serving the public rather than the state by exposing the mechanisms of mass persuasion. In Merton's opinion, this was to be achieved by a shift in emphasis from short-term to long-term media effects; instead of looking at the persuasive appeal of specific texts or campaigns, researchers should examine the cumulative effects of long-term exposure to a range of persuasive appeals. This switch necessitated conceptual as well as methodological refinement. As we have seen, by the late 1950s it was not possible to categorize mainstream communication research as nakedly quantitative or positivist, since a range of research techniques, including qualitative tools, was available for use. The real question was: to what end were these tools to be put? What is it that researchers should be looking for – if not short-term attitudinal shifts?

The 'founding fathers' were less than explicit on this point, but two conceptual developments should be noted. The first is a recognition that perceptions and opinions are collectively formed. As Lasswell stated, 'what we come to think and feel is intimately bound up with the collective processes in which we find ourselves' (1941/1953: 471). This statement indicates a shift away from looking at people as atomistic units made up of psychological predispositions formed in isolation from external influences.

The second important development leads on from this interest in collective human experience. Lazarsfeld suggested that public opinion was the manifestation of deeper cultural processes: 'the problem was always to place public opinion somewhere between the rather permanent and subconscious value system of society and the fleeting reactions of a people to the passing events of the day' (1957/1975: 621). Public opinion, then, is not just an expression of an attitude towards a particular event, object or issue, but it is also an expression of a general moral and political orientation.

Far from being the end of mainstream mass-communication research, the late 1950s represented, to Paul Lazarsfeld at least, a welcome new beginning where the methodological advances of the previous decades could be augmented and operationalized by a more sophisticated conceptualization of the issues surrounding communication and persuasion. Combining his work with insights offered by Merton and Lasswell, the focus seemed to be shifting away from narrow interests in persuasion towards the analysis of connections between communication and social power. In expressing an interest in relations between public opinion and underlying value systems, Lazarsfeld was at the same time questioning the use of 'change' as an indicator of influence. He was in effect asking how public opinion could bolster established modes of political thought. Merton and Lasswell suggested that this was a question best directed at the state and the media, rather than the public. What was emerging was an interest less in how communication could be used to make people buy, vote or adopt certain health practices, and more in how long-term exposure to political and commercial communication could develop deep-seated orientations towards people, issues, objects and, crucially, institutions.

Hence, while many in the emerging European schools of media research abandoned quantitative-based research methods, others set about using these tools to answer new questions. In 1975, *Political Communication: Issues and Strategies for Research*, edited by Steven Chafee, evidenced the conceptual reinvigoration of the effects tradition. The collection made clear that the limited effects model had been largely invalidated by structural changes in political communication. Rothschild (1975) argued that the decrease in party loyalty, combined with a massive increase in campaigning expenditure, had rendered voters in America more open to manipulation. On a more general level, by the 1960s media saturation had eclipsed the power and importance of personal communication: people were now often entirely reliant on the media for information.

In short, the scale and complexity of political communication had increased, requiring more sophisticated research efforts. Blumler and Gurevitch (1975) warned that a blind faith in methodology would not be enough; the atheoretical examination of relationships between variables revealed little. This was all the more so, according to O'Keefe (1975), since it was no longer possible to treat media content as an independent variable. To do so is to assume that such content is homogeneous, consistent and distinct from other possible sources of influence. None of this is true with regard to political information provided by the media: conflicting viewpoints are broadcast; programming other than news and campaign propaganda can contain information and commentary; and the media are themselves subject to external influences. In O'Keefe's (1975) view, despite a continued faith in the power of quantitative techniques, the normal rules of positivist science no longer applied to the study of political communication.

The collection, *Political Communication*, witnesses an evolution rather than a revolution, a paradigm shift, not a paradigm change. How could established methods be used from a different conceptual basis? Chafee (1975) provides an example in his discussion of diffusion studies. Classically, diffusion studies examined the speed at which information, often provided by media campaigns, travels through a society. Through repeated surveys or panel studies, researchers keep track of how long information takes to 'diffuse'. Results can then be illustrated in graph form, with the number of people informed plotted on the y axis, and the time-scale for the diffusion on the x axis. Results typically take the form of an 'S' curve: at the beginning of an information campaign few people are informed, but these numbers accelerate in the middle stages of the campaign, tailing off again towards the end as the campaign tries to reach those having little contact with the media or other people (Chafee, 1975).

Chafee points to a key conceptual problem with this sort of research as it was carried out during the 1940s and 1950s. Early diffusion studies often assumed that powerful social and political institutions *wanted* information to diffuse through a society. Much of this research centred on political campaigning, or public information initiatives, in which institutional goals were directed towards the rapid dissemination of information. But what if there were situations where the same institutions did not wish the public to become more informed? This is the question that interested Chafee. Early diffusion studies had naïvely assumed situations in which information could be gathered and shared without restraint. Yet the American experience of the 1960s and 1970s showed that, in politics, the reverse was often true. The Vietnam War provided copious examples of what Chafee called 'information hoarding', wherein the US military and government did their best to prevent news coverage of certain events such as the Mai Lai massacre. The Watergate scandal also alerted the American public to the fact that it was often in the interests of the political elite to keep the electorate in the dark.

This raised a distinctly new research agenda: how could the media be used to obscure and distort public knowledge? What could explain such distortions? In contrast to earlier work, new effects research viewed the media as being significantly dysfunctional rather than functional. The issue of power was introduced in a new sense: communication was often used to enhance the gap between the powerful and the powerless, rather than being used for the general good. Blumler and Gurevitch saw this new orientation as being defined by the following question: 'How does the articulation of a country's mass media institutions to its political institutions affect the processing of political communication content and the impact of such content on the orientations to politics of audience members?' (1975: 169).

Agenda-setting

Agenda-setting research provides a notable example of the application of this new question. McCombs and Shaw (1993) view agenda-setting as a paradigm in itself, which has undergone significant conceptual evolution since its inception during their study of voters during the 1968 US presidential election (McCombs and Shaw, 1972). McCombs and Shaw were interested in the media's power to set limits on public knowledge, not by 'telling them what to think, but what to think about'. Media power, in the authors' view, lay in an ability to tell the public what the important events of the day were by drawing its attention towards certain events and issues (and away from others). Originally, this consisted of research efforts that quantitatively analysed media content to identify those issues receiving the most attention, followed by public opinion polling to ascertain what people saw as being the most important issues of the day (Rogers et al., 1993). The results of the content analyses and polls were then compared to assess similarities between media and public agendas.

Kosicki (1993) sees this initial focus as insufficiently critical, describing a phenomenon of agenda-matching between public and media, rather than describing a process of public manipulation. Subsequently, the paradigm has progressed to a point where it can argue that the power to determine what people think about is prompted by institutional pressures, and indeed often results in the concurrent power to tell people what to think: 'Both the selection of objects for attention and the selection of frames for thinking about these objects are powerful agenda-setting roles' (McCombs and Shaw, 1993: 63).

Edelstein (1993) elaborates on his consideration of what 'thinking about' an issue means. In directing attention towards a certain problematic issue, the media do more than provide information; they also provide interpretative frameworks, suggesting reasons for the problem, suggesting potential solutions in the process. Edelstein identifies five sorts of 'problematics': conditions of need, deprivation, blocking, conflict and uncertainty. Events are presented in the media as representing one of these conditions. However, we may disagree on what an event signifies. Take the example of famine in Africa. Typically such famines are presented as instances of deprivation and conflict; people lack food either because of natural disasters or because of disruptions to supply routes caused by internal political divisions. But famines can be the result of conditions of need created by relations between the industrialized and non-industrialized worlds; that famines are continuing problems speaks to exploitative economic links between the West and Africa. It is clear that the sort of frame one chooses to place such crises within is an ideological decision that points a finger at different villains and solutions: the 'deprivation' and 'conflict' views lay blame at the door of African nations themselves, whereas the 'condition of need' frame accuses the West.

The sorts of issues that the media cue the public to regard as salient can also have a persuasive appeal. Recent history alerts us to the importance frequently attached to the private lives of public figures. Infidelity is a continuing political issue, nowhere more so than during the tenure of office of US President Clinton. There is some question as to the relevance of such matters to a cool-headed evaluation of a politician's service; some argue that the only real issue is the degree to which a person remains faithful to the people. The constant attention paid to personal morality issues in the press can be seen as undermining this position, since its media profile suggests that private matters are highly relevant to the evaluation of a public servant. In shaping the criteria used to make political judgements, we can see how the media's agenda-setting power indeed carries the ability to tell the public what to *think* in telling them what to think *about* (McCombs and Shaw, 1993).

Critical quantification

In some ways, scholars such as Chaffee and McCombs and Shaw suggest moving *away* from audiences towards the analysis of structural factors *preventing* the free circulation of information. Many of these factors have been outlined by Herman and Chomsky (1988), who note numerous connections and common interests between the media, the government and the corporate sector in the US.

But what if we want to work forward, looking at the consequences of such connections for the development of political knowledge and public opinion? This is the question that was pursued by researchers at the University of Massachusetts during the 1990s. The three main players in this research are interesting since, while they use fairly straightforward survey methods that are common in public opinion research, none are pollsters as such: Michael Morgan is a cultivation analyst (of which we will discover more in Chapter 4), while Justin Lewis and Sut Jhally are trained in the British School of cultural studies. Moreover, Lewis has been influential in the development of qualitative audience research. This has placed the researchers in a unique position to follow some of the critical avenues suggested by post-limited effects scholars by augmenting their methods with conceptual insights from other fields.

The University of Massachusetts (Umass) team has approached the connections between media content and public opinion via three case studies: the Gulf War (Lewis et al., 1991), the 1992 US presidential election (Lewis et al., 1992) and the Monica Lewinsky scandal (Lewis et al., 1999). Their general research question is summarized in the latter work, *Libertine or Liberal? The Real Scandal of What People Know about President Clinton*:

> This study forms part of a long-running series of research projects investigating public knowledge of contemporary issues. Our aim is to explore public opinion in more depth by asking people not only what they think, but what they know. Since knowledge . . . provides a basis on which opinions are constructed, we can thereby see what informs public knowledge. The role of the media is instrumental in this context, not so much in directly swaying opinion one way or another, but in providing a very

particular knowledge base. Our concern is to explore the nature of this knowledge base, and to see whether it is informed, uninformed or misinformed. (Lewis et al., 1999: 1)

It is interesting to note that, while divisions between audience researchers are often cast in methodological terms, such as the distinction between the quantitative and the qualitative, the researchers here are using public opinion surveys to critique the work of others who have used the same tools. What is at issue, then, is the way in which the same methods can be used to different ends depending on the conceptual sophistication of the research question.

These projects are related to the problematic outlined by Blumler and Gurevitch (1975): the consequences of articulations between the media and other economic and political institutions. But Lewis and colleagues were also interested in the effects of certain media practices. Their research interest can be best explained within the context of the Gulf War of 1991. One of the paradoxes that has emerged from the study of public opinion is that the more access people have to information, the less interested and informed they seem to be. Was this true of the Gulf War? As Lewis et al. pointed out, the war had presented the US media with the opportunity to brag about the service they provided, not only to the American public, but also to the world. Here truly was a living-room war. Thanks to cable and satellite technology, the CNN network could provide a global audience (at least among those who had access to electricity and satellite television) with 24-hour, real-time coverage. But did this mean that we knew more about the war, and how did the information provided by such sources influence the opinions that people held about what should be done regarding Iraq's invasion of Kuwait? The same principle lay behind the study of the 1992 presidential election and the more recent scandals surrounding Bill Clinton. In both cases the researchers set out to examine, via a quantitative survey asking both attitudinal and factual questions, the relationship between attitudes towards candidates and knowledge about those candidates.

Although the surveys used were methodologically orthodox, conceptually this was not the case. The Umass team departed from survey orthodoxy in adopting an openly partisan position in their research. Whereas earlier researchers, such as Klapper (1960), disguised connections with the media that could explain the 'discovery' of limited effects, Lewis et al. were openly hostile to US news corporations. Indeed, the 1992 study was funded by FAIR (Fairness and Accuracy in Reporting), an organization devoted to the exposure of news media bias. Acknowledging that all research is politically motivated, the team abandoned the search for objective questions. Although in the surveys 'most of [the] questions were open-ended, in order to avoid pushing people into categories of response that they may not, on their own, have thought of' (Lewis et al., 1991: 2), at the same time:

> The factual questions we posed are, like most facts, not politically neutral. [Regarding the Gulf War] some, like the State Department's failure to warn Iraq of the consequences of attacking Kuwait, reflect badly on the [Bush] administration's war policy. Others, like knowledge of Saddam Hussein's use of chemical weapons, could be seen to justify the need for war. (1991: 2)

The rationale for this technique lay in the researchers' understanding of the media's role in such conflicts. In the 1980s, Herman and Chomsky (1988) had pointed to the part that the media had played in the Cold War by publicizing international human rights abuses perpetrated by Soviet bloc nations, while ignoring atrocities carried out by governments who were sympathetic to American interests. Cold War ideology was maintained, Herman and Chomsky argued, less by lying to the public as by deliberately directing their attention towards certain issues, and away from others. Persuasion was thus effected by the selective provision of information.

This can be seen as the inspiration behind Lewis et al.'s work. Despite their academic backgrounds, they addressed fundamental questions in the analysis of public opinion. The rationality of the public mind was assessed by examining the relationship between what people felt and what they knew. In the case of the Gulf War, the question was: to what extent was support for the war connected with a wide range of knowledge concerning both the cases for and against armed intervention. In the two Clinton-related surveys, the aim was to compare what people knew about personal issues surrounding the president with what they knew about his policies.

The surveys were administered via telephone interview to samples deemed to be representative in composition of the general US population. The results of these surveys were presented in a fairly straightforward manner. Often the most startling findings were provided by the simple proportion of respondents giving certain answers to certain questions. For example, the Gulf War study asked:

> In July 1990, just before he invaded, Saddam Hussein indicated that he might use force against Kuwait. How did the US respond?
>
> (a) The US said it would impose sanctions against him.
> (b) The US said it would regard it as a threat to the US.

(c) The US said they would take no action.
(d) The US said that they would support Kuwait with the use of force.

(Lewis et al., 1991: 16)

Respondents were asked to rate each statement as true or false. Only 13.2 per cent of them correctly answered C as 'true'. This compared with the 65 per cent who thought that D was true. On the other hand, 80 per cent of those interviewed were aware that Saddam Hussein had used chemical weapons against his enemies. These results were interpreted as being significant in the sense that they directly related to the then President Bush's claims that the war was fought to preserve long-standing American ideals concerning democracy and human rights. On balance, people were aware of information that supported the view of Saddam Hussein as a modern-day Hitler, but knew little of the US's initial equivocation regarding the invasion, nor of its tolerance of similar occupations in other parts of the world. As Lewis et al. noted, these gaps in public knowledge tended to relate to information that countered moral justifications for the war.

The picture that was emerging was not of an uninformed, uninterested public, but a selectively or misinformed news audience. The pattern was repeated in the Clinton surveys, which found an electorate well schooled in trivia and scandal, but less clued in to policy matters. The 1992 survey asked a series of questions on the policies of both Clinton and Bush, together with more trivia-related questions. Again, using simple response frequencies, the researchers found a public who could, almost *en masse* (82 per cent) name the Bush family's dog, but of whom only 33 per cent knew that Clinton supported cutting capital gains tax, 38 per cent that he supported the death penalty and 37 per cent that he supported the so-called right to work laws opposed by organized labour.

These results suggest an interesting paradox that emerges again in the Lewinsky study. Lewis et al. contend that Bill Clinton is an 'imaginary liberal', that people believe he is far more pro-social welfare, pro-labour and pro-environment than he actually is. While the researchers complain that Clinton differs little from his Republican counterparts, the general public seems to believe that the President holds a far left position. For example, the 1998 survey revealed that only 13 per cent of respondents knew that Clinton had signed a welfare bill originating in the Republican-led Congress. When questioned on his stance on health-care reform, only 26 per cent knew that he favoured maintaining a system that relies on private insurance companies rather than public funding, a system guaranteed to exclude poorer members of society who cannot afford even the most basic insurance premiums.

Most people did know, however, that the president supported abortion rights (74 per cent) and in his 1998 State of the Union address advocated spending a budget surplus on social security instead of tax cuts. In adopting a survey containing questions on policies where Clinton adopted a traditionally liberal stance together with those where he was more conservative, the Umass team again revealed a structured form of public ignorance. This was very different from the sort of ignorance suggested by mainstream political scientists, an ignorance born of laziness or stupidity on the part of the audience. The researchers put it this way: 'Out of the seven questions . . . [in which Clinton's actual position is the more conservative one] . . . the percentages getting the answer right ranged from 13% to 31% . . . This compares with the 69% and 74% of correct responses when the answer involves Clinton taking the more liberal option' (Lewis et al., 1999: 3). They were suggesting that the respondents were in the most part misinformed rather than uninformed. Although many of their answers were wrong, they were conceptually consistent, born of the belief that the president stood further to the left than he actually did.

This notion of the misinformed is a key concept in their research. All three studies showed that political attitudes are formed through the selective provision of information that often misleads the public about the complexity of certain issues. The researchers placed the blame for this situation at the feet of the media rather than the public. Working from the assumption that a little knowledge can be more dangerous that complete ignorance, Lewis et al. complained that in focusing on Saddam Hussein's megalomania, the private lives of politicians, and in presenting the political spectrum as limited to the choice between a conservative Democrat or the Republicans, the media actually discourage public debate. More is less: although we have more news in terms of television hours and newspaper column inches, the content of the news media is relatively homogeneous. This is exacerbated by the fact that contemporary business interests require the news to be entertaining as well as, if not instead of, informative. Hence the emphasis on scandals, or spectacular battlefield images of smart weaponry, in the place of more sober discussion of the issues.

The Umass team explored this point by analysing their data further, examining the role that media use might play in enhancing this process of misinformation. They did this, in the Gulf War and Campaign '92 studies, by using the same technique demonstrated in Table 2.1 (see page 59): the sample was subdivided according to levels of television usage, and television news viewing, respondents being divided into light, medium and heavy users. The sample was further subdivided according to gender, age and education to examine any differences in relationships between media use, attitudes and knowledge in different sectors of the population. These figures revealed that both television watching and television news viewing were significantly related to the tendency to support the war strongly and to give incorrect answers to factual questions concerning foreign policy and welfare spending in the Campaign '92 study. The figures supported the argument that public ignorance was the product of media structures.

Although the authors did not invoke agenda-setting or diffusion studies, their work does address a number of issues raised by these paradigms. The Gulf War study demonstrated the consequences of both information hoarding (the prevention of diffusion mentioned by Chafee, 1975) and the definition of salient topics. The exigencies of war are used to justify a lack of cooperation between military and media, wherein the former justify their silence on the grounds of national interest. This explains why the initially optimistic comments made about the accuracy of allied bombing campaigns were not publicly revised until sometime after the war. It also explains why most people believed the bombing campaigns to be more accurate than they actually were, a belief making military action more morally palatable since it de-emphasizes the danger to civilians. Agenda-setting was also evident in public knowledge of Saddam Hussein's human rights abuses and ignorance of the instances when the US had ignored similar transgressions. The correlation between such knowledge/ignorance and support for the war indeed suggested that the ability to determine what people think about carries with it considerable power to tell them what to think.

The Clinton studies show similar dynamics. The media's preference for entertaining, sensationalist stories that lend themselves to sound-bite coverage militates against the substantive discussion of political issues – hence we could say that there are structural barriers to the diffusion of complex debate. Attitudes towards candidates are thus based on ignorance of their policies.

Conclusion

Public opinion research demonstrates a number of important developments in understanding audiences. Those who set out to study connections between the media and the public mind began to do so on a behaviourist footing, but they soon began to look for less obvious signifiers of media effects. Naked positivism was rejected due to the realization that society could not be neatly divided into independent and dependent variables since the relationship between political institutions, the media and the public was interactive. Moreover, the effects of these interactions often emerged over a long period of time, in the form of deep-seated political orientations. Conceptual evolution could therefore be seen as the driving force behind the development of public opinion research. Methodology does not necessarily lock a researcher into a prescribed scientific philosophy. This is demonstrated by the work of Lewis and colleagues, who show how quantitative opinion polls can be used to ask critical questions which point to the power of political elites and the media to mislead as well as inform.

Exercises

---

1   Collect a group of surveys. These can come from, for example, marketing surveys, opinion surveys or readers' polls in magazines. Examine these surveys and answer the following questions:

(a) What does your survey want to find out?
(b) What types of questions does it use? Open or multiple choice?
(c) How adequately do these questions measure the thoughts of respondents? Do you think any of the questions might put words into people's mouths? Do the questions cover the range of responses that respondents might wish to give?
(d) What sampling strategy does the survey use? Is this strategy good or bad?

2   Collect newspaper reports on the results of significant opinion polls. List the information you need to have to assess the reliability and validity of a poll. Do the news stories contain all of this information? Is there anything missing from these reports that makes it difficult for you to make an informed judgement?

4 Cultivation analysis

Cultivation analysis is a paradigm of audience research that has enjoyed an unusually high public profile. Its founding father, George Gerbner, has acted as adviser to many bodies established by the US government to investigate the problem of television violence (Wober, 1998), and the work he and his colleagues at the University of Pennsylvania carried out has been covered in the mainstream media (Morgan and Shanahan, 1996). But notoriety is not the only reason for devoting a chapter to this body of work. Over the past 30 years, cultivation analysts have demonstrated how the mainstream sociological methods eschewed by cultural studies can be used to move beyond the limitations of the effects tradition. In Chapter 3 we saw how those interested in studying the impact of the media on political knowledge and opinion realized the need to invigorate the conceptual basis of their research in response to a changing media environment which had invalidated much of the work done in the 1940s and 1950s. The same can be said of cultivation analysis in its pursuit of the effects of televised violence.

Despite years of failure to find direct connections between televised and real-world violence, the fear that the medium can turn ordinary people (especially children) into psychopaths remains as what Seiter (1999) calls a powerful 'lay' theory of the media. Each time society is rocked by a gun-related tragedy, the media are dragged back into the dock. Parallels are found between the actions of the killers and movie scenes. Surely such images play a part in fuelling deranged fantasies? And, just as surely, public anger cannot be placated by antiseptic talk of statistical significance and intervening variables.

But can these fears be dismissed as nothing more than a type of latter-day witch hysteria? Barker and Petley (1997) suggest that moral panics surrounding media violence reflect long-standing concerns about the need to regulate popular culture for the sake of social control, and also reveal the way in which 'childhood' functions as a cultural as well as biological and psychological category. In this sense, debates about media violence are really debates about the way we would like to see childhood and our society.

These are useful insights, but they do not explain away public concerns. The danger of seeing these fears as moral panics designed to maintain social divisions via a compliant media culture is that it can lead towards an uncritical celebration of all things popular. For example, is the person who complains of film director Brian de Palma's penchant for voyeuristically depicting the murder of female characters to be simply dismissed as someone who has failed to grasp the subtleties of audience reception? This would seem a strange argument to make, given some of the work by qualitative audience research conducted within cultural studies. In the video *Dreamworlds*, Sut Jhally (1990) describes connections between sexualized depictions of women in music video and the rape scene from the film, *The Accused*. The implication is that degrading representations of women fuel sexist ideologies that in turn underscore the widespread problem of sexual assault. By the same logic, surely we should be concerned about the sexualization of murder seen in films such as *Dressed to Kill* and *Body Double*?

This argument becomes more pressing when viewed from a macrolevel. As we shall see, one of the premisses of cultural studies is that the mass media serve as a key ideological tool, shaping the way in which we understand ourselves and the societies in which we live. The issue of representation, the way in which certain types of people, events and places are depicted, is fundamental to this ideological power. If this is true, then the sorts of widespread depictions of violence persuasively described by Gerbner must have relevance. But if their influence is not behavioural, what else could it be? Cultivation analysis provides some answers to this question, telling us of the ideological influences of television violence, thus rejecting behaviourism without rejecting the violence question itself. Gerbner and his colleagues applied some of the insights of the post-limited effects political communication researchers to the sphere of popular culture. Their work is important since they suggested that fictional entertainment programming could be powerful sources of socialization, a theme having much in common with the ideas of European critical scholars.

Cultivation analysis is also important since it confronts the Kuhnian view of normal science that had informed many qualitative researchers' views of those who use mainstream sociological methods. Kuhn would have it that once a research paradigm is established, those working within it are charged with the task of defending its concepts and methods rather than extending the field into new directions. This is how scholars such as Gauntlett (1998) see cultivation analysis, which is regarded as part of the effects tradition. Closer examination of the work not only of Gerbner and his colleagues but the many other researchers who have pursued the question of cultivation instead shows a significant evolution driven by a number of sharp internal divisions in the areas of theory and method. As such, we are provided with an example of how reflexivity can function within quantitative research.

What is cultivation analysis?

Cultivation analysis has its roots in the debate on media violence. As a brief but intriguing sidelight, violence has been a persistent feature of George Gerbner's life: escaping the Nazi-friendly Hungary of the 1930s, Gerbner fled to America, only to return to Europe as an SOE operative charged with leading Yugoslavian resistance (for more of Gerbner's fascinating biography, see Morgan, 1995). We can deduce from this that Gerbner knows much about both real-world and media violence!

By the 1960s, Gerbner was a professor of communication at the University of Pennsylvania's Annenberg School of Communication. In 1967, amidst fears that television was playing an integral part in the escalation of violence in society, he and his colleagues were commissioned by the United States surgeon general to compile the first of many 'violence profiles'. Using quantitative methods of content analysis, the Annenberg team 'measured' the amount of violence shown on prime-time television. Defining violence as 'the overt expression of physical force, with or without a weapon, against self or other, compelling action against one's will on pain of being hurt or killed, or actually hurting or killing' (Gerbner et al., 1978: 179), the Annenberg team counted the incidence of such actions in samples taken from prime-time television. Their results showed some stark contrasts between television and the real world. From 1969 to 1977, 64 per cent of television characters studied were involved in violence (Gerbner et al., 1978). Taking the 1976 profile as typical, given that 0.41 per cent of the US population had been victims of violent crime in that year, it follows that the televisual world was a far more violent place than that which it supposedly represented. Moreover, it was found that this violence was targeted at specific groups of people. By recording the demographic characteristics of television characters who were both the victims and the perpetrators of this violence, the Annenberg team found that children, women, the old, the working class and non-whites were all significantly more likely to be targets than were white, middle-aged, middle-class men (Gerbner et al., 1977). Here, then, was the evidence that television relied heavily on violence. But, for Gerbner and his colleagues, this was the beginning rather than the end of the puzzle. The patterns noted suggested that television violence was a rich symbolic form that potentially communicated all sorts of lessons about the world that American viewers lived in. This prompted an expanded definition of what counted as violence. Later profiles defined it as:

> a dramatic demonstration of the power of certain individuals . . . and the tendency of others to fall victim to it . . . [the effects may be] lessons of victimization and ways to avoid as well as commit violence; caution and prudence as well as pugnacity; a calculus of one's risks as well as opportunities to be gained from violence . . . a tendency to assume high levels of violence; to acquiesce to the use of violence by others . . . a sense of fear and need for protection. (Gerbner et al., 1978: 184)

The real questions were: why was television so violent, and what impact did this have on the way its viewers made sense of society around them?

This prompted Gerbner and his colleagues to move beyond the content analysis to produce a 'cultural indicators project' that took on three parts: institutional research, examining the broadcasting structures that produced prime-time programming; message system analysis, which outlined the broad symbolic patterns of television, paying special attention to its most repetitive elements; and, finally, cultivation analysis. Here is where we find the audience. This part of the project uses survey data to study correlations between television viewing and the development, or cultivation, of specific beliefs and attitudes about the real world. Cultivation analysis seeks out differences in knowledge and beliefs between light and heavy viewers, seeing if it can find explanations for these differences in television fare (Morgan, 1989; Morgan and Signorelli, 1990; Gerbner et al., 1994). Note that researchers have looked for differences in thoughts rather than behaviours. Gerbner explicitly rejected behaviourism as a justification for his concerns about media violence:

> Conventional wisdom . . . might stress the one in a thousand who imitate violence . . . But it is just as important to look at the large majority of people who become more fearful, insecure, and dependent on authority, and who may grow up demanding protection and even welcoming repression in the name of security. (Gerbner et al., 1978: 196)

Here was the key. The patterns of victimization outlined by message system analysis suggested that television violence carried with it messages about the social structure. Violence was important in that it provided dramatic demonstrations of who were the powerful and who were the powerless. The significance of this is not to produce violence among the audience, but rather 'a sense of fear and the need for protection' (Gerbner et al., 1978: 184).

This fear found its conceptual expression in what the Annenberg team called the 'mean world syndrome' (Gerbner et al., 1980b). Survey analysis revealed that heavy television viewers were more likely than light viewers to overestimate both the amount of violence there was in the real world and their own chances of being the victims of this violence. They also demonstrated greater anomic tendencies, being less trustful of others and less satisfied with their lot in life. While the results of these beliefs may not be directly behavioural, there was evidence nevertheless that such beliefs did have material consequences: they could make people more fearful of leaving their own homes, or make them more favourable towards authoritarian views on law and order.

These findings prompted the Annenberg team to move the emphasis away from violence and towards the relationship between television and the cultivation of general political dispositions. Using data collected by the National Opinion Research Council in the years 1975–9, Gerbner and colleagues (1982) set out to chart the political 'mainstream', researching viewers' opinions towards minority and civil rights, free speech, government spending and taxes. Significant differences were again found between light and heavy viewers. The latter group was found to be more conservative than light viewers in terms of attitude towards anti-racism legislation, homosexuality, abortion and the legalization of drugs. They also tended to be more hostile to communism, and were more in favour of curbing the right to free speech in the defence of American ideals.

Perhaps more significant was the fact that subgroup analysis revealed a process that the researchers referred to as 'mainstreaming'. The samples were divided into demographic and political subgroups (as we saw in Table 2.1, page 59). One might expect that different sectors of society would differ in their opinions according to varying social experiences, along the lines of race, sex, class, education and political ideology. Gerbner et al. found that this was indeed the case, but more so among light viewers than heavy viewers. In almost every case, attitudinal differences observed between light viewers in different subgroups were less pronounced than among heavy viewers in the same groups. For example, among subjects who deemed themselves to be politically liberal, heavy television viewers in fact took on more conservative views than their light-viewing 'comrades'. Interestingly, this worked in the opposite direction for conservatives in the area of welfare spending:

heavy-viewing conservatives were more approving of increasing welfare payments than were light-viewing conservatives. Gerbner et al. interpreted this as indicative of television's power to homogenize the political outlooks of its viewers.

The Annenberg team also researched how television related to perceptions of ageing (Gerbner et al., 1980a). Content analysis had revealed that there were far fewer old people on television than there were in society. In profiles compiled during the late 1970s, it was found that while the over-65s accounted for 11 per cent of the US population at the time, only 2.35 per cent of prime-time television characters fell into this category. Accompanying survey research discovered at the same time that heavy television viewers were more likely than light television viewers to underestimate the numbers of old people in society. They were also more likely to believe that men lived longer than women – which they do on television, but not in real life. This was seen to reflect two structural features of television drama: the fact that, at the time, male characters outnumbered female characters by 3 : 1, and that there were more old men on television than old women. But this tendency to misrecognize basic facts of life was not what troubled the team; more important was the fact that heavy viewers tended to extrapolate these facts into sets of beliefs about the powerlessness and lack of opportunities open to older people, especially older women. Such beliefs hardly have a place in a 'greying' society where the over-65s account for an increasing proportion of the population.

By the early 1980s, Gerbner and his colleagues at the University of Pennsylvania had reached two conclusions. Content analyses of prime-time television told them that patterns of representation found therein significantly distorted social reality. Violence was exaggerated, as were the risks that violence posed towards certain sectors of the community – women, the old, the poor and racial minorities. The medium also displayed a class and age bias: old people and the working classes were virtually invisible. In terms of the effects of these representations, their impact went way beyond behavioural concerns. Television's main influence seemed to be the cultivation of a climate of fear and mistrust. Political consequences followed, with the production of a 'mainstream' of ideological beliefs that leaned towards the right.

These are very different conclusions from those drawn by earlier effects researchers, who either doggedly persisted in the search for direct behavioural effects or else concluded that the mass media had very limited powers. Yet scholars such as Gauntlett (1998) and Wober (1998) see Gerbner's development of cultivation analysis as being a part of the effects tradition. To justify the claim that the Annenberg team's work marked a significant turn in audience research, it is necessary to examine why some people see it as no more than effects research by different means.

Why is cultivation analysis seen as part of the effects tradition?

The short answer to this question is because some view Gerbner's development of the paradigm as betraying positivist and administrative roots. Some of these misgivings are understandable. There are certainly historical parallels between the early 1940s and the late 1960s. In the earlier period, we saw how communication researchers were recruited by the US government to help solve national problems. The US surgeon general's commissioning of the first violence profile was prompted by similar concerns; that is, Gerbner was recruited to help the US government find out if television was a factor in prompting the widespread social unrest of the time. Since that time, Gerbner's concerns about television violence have certainly provided ammunition for those who wish to regulate the US television industry.

On a conceptual level, Gerbner et al.'s work has also been read as a resurrection of the old 'hypodermic needle' notion of media effects. Gauntlett (1998) and Wober (1998) both accuse Gerbner of adopting an elitist view towards audiences who are seen as passive and incapable of resisting media messages. This tendency is represented by the Annenberg team's rejection of selective exposure. From the beginning, Gerbner et al. have contended that television viewing is largely habitual rather than goal directed; people tend to watch by the clock rather than by the programme. Since this habitual viewing tends to fall within the prime-time period, a time when the content of television varies little between channels, this means that viewers are relatively powerless to escape 'mainstreaming' messages. What is more, the early period of cable and the emergence of the VCR appear to have done little to change the picture (Signorelli, 1986). Gauntlett and Wober both claim that numerous studies show much more active audiences, who are diverse both in terms of the programming they view and their responses to what they see.

Another problem with the Annenberg work is that it apparently ignores European critical theory, and explicitly rejects certain premises of qualitative media research. Gerbner's early description of the cultivation project (1970) made no mention of the neo-Marxist scholarship that was highly influential at the time in the development of cultural studies, and cultivation analysts since this time have failed to explore this area. Also, the view of textuality that is integral to a cultural studies approach to media texts has been dismissed as irrelevant. During the 1960s and 1970s, highly influential scholars such as Roland Barthes (1973) and Stuart Hall (1973) urged a re-evaluation of the complexity of popular culture by providing detailed semiotic analyses of mundane media content. Their purpose was to show that the connection between the signifier, in this case the media text, and signified, the meanings that could be attached to that text, were neither straightforward nor guaranteed. Horace Newcomb (1978) picked up on this point in his 'humanistic critique' of cultivation analysis. How, he wondered, could Gerbner et al. use a unitary definition of what counts as violence to measure its prevalence on television when, as we all know, violence can mean different things in different contexts? A slap in the face can be disturbing in a domestic drama, or it can be humorous in a slapstick comedy.

Despite this work, Gerbner et al. have appeared unwilling to consider the differences between media texts and their use of violence. Violence profile no. 8 (Gerbner et al., 1977) rejected the idea that the same violent acts can mean different things in different contexts, since they still contained messages about power. Since then, the Annenberg strand of cultivation analysis has maintained the belief that it is more important to focus on the common messages that pervade television as a whole rather than to look for differences between texts (Morgan and Shanahan, 1996). This could be interpreted as reflecting a 'transmission' view of communication which sees the interpretation of media content as unproblematic, in the sense that the meaning and the reception of violent images are both unambiguous.

The critical rehabilitation of cultivation analysis

It is possible to take a selective view of Gerbner et al.'s work that portrays them as positivists who do little more than provide old wine in new bottles at the behest of institutional sources. But it is also true that George Gerbner has been one of the most vocal academic critics of those same institutional sources over the past 30 years. His view of the nature and role of the American mass media has much in common with political economists such as Herb Schiller (1996) and Ben Bagdikian (1983) who have stressed the ideological power created by the deregulation of the global economy and concomitant rise of transnational media corporations. As such, his work is compatible with other people who have ventured beyond the effects and limited effects paradigms.

One of the problems with cultivation analysis is that, while its findings can be concisely summarized, the route that Gerbner et al. took to these conclusions is complex. We need to understand not only what he and his colleagues have argued, but also why they have made these arguments in the manner they have. The criticisms detailed in the previous section must be confronted and explained. Why, for example, did the Annenberg team dismiss the notion of selective exposure that Wober and Gauntlett see as important if we are to view audiences as active rather than passive? The reason for this is that Gerbner et al. have consistently maintained that mass communication is intimately connected with social power. Wober conflates two very different bodies of research into his notion of selective exposure: the work carried out by people such as Lazarsfeld and Klapper in the 1940s and 1950s, and ethnographic studies of audiences carried out in the past 20 years or so. As we shall see in Chapter 5, these are two very different paradigms functioning from diverging conceptual bases. So, in considering Gerbner et al.'s dismissal of selective exposure, and the related concept of limited effects, we must consider how this related to the earlier research, not the later.

As we have seen, researchers in the 1950s believed that interpersonal communication was just as important as television, if not *more* influential, in shaping people's thoughts and behaviours. It was this that Gerbner objected to. One of the things that marked cultivation analysis as a departure from what had gone before was its sensitivity to the technological, economic, political and social specificities of the television age. Television did not simply represent a medium of communication, but was crucially different from earlier media forms, both in terms of its form and content and also its institutional arrangement. As such, Gerbner claimed that earlier researchers had made the mistake of assuming that concepts applied to other media would be equally valid in the television age.

He directed this criticism against the liberal-pluralist logic of selective exposure and limited effects. The notion of selective exposure only makes sense if we assume that people have diverse messages to select from. This idea derived from the era when the press was the dominant medium. The television era, however, was characterized by greater centralization of ownership, and a narrowing of viewpoint due to restrictions established by commercial concerns that encouraged producers to shy aware from controversial points of view that might alienate viewers and, more importantly, advertisers (Gerbner et al., 1982). This combined with the sheer pervasiveness of the medium to establish an unprecedented opportunity to seize and hold popular consciousness. The ubiquity of television, and the rapid pace at which it became central to America's need for information and entertainment, meant that it eclipsed the importance of interpersonal communication as a source used to orientate oneself to the surrounding world. This was not to say that all television programmes sold exactly the same story all of the time. But it was to say that the institutional arrangements that provided Americans with television, arrangements depending on a symbiosis of interests between the television industry and the government and corporate sectors that regulated and funded that industry, ensured a certain commonality of viewpoint:

> any message is a socially and historically determined expression of concrete physical and social relationships. Messages imply propositions, assumptions and points of view that are understandable only in terms of the social relationships and contexts in which they are produced. Yet they also reconstitute those relationships and contexts. Messages thus sustain the structures and practices that produce them. (Morgan and Shanahan, 1996: 4)

This view stands closer to Carey's (1989) 'ritual' view of communication, influential within cultural studies, whereby the goal of communication is not to change thoughts or behaviours but ensure the longevity of an existing social structure based on a particular set of beliefs and values.

If this is the case, it makes little sense to speak of selective viewing since anything which viewers might select is likely to express dominant social values beneath a veneer of superficial difference. It is this that explains both the prevalence of violence in the media and Gerbner's interest in that violence. In the video *The Killing Screens* (Gerbner, 1995), Gerbner explains the appeal of violence as being its ability clearly and cheaply to demonstrate the political pecking order.

This perspective goes a long way towards explaining the Annenberg team's dismissal of close textual analysis. In fact, this dismissal was more of a commitment to study macro- rather than micro-processes (Morgan and Shanahan, 1996). Cultivation analysis has from its inception been interested in the broad structural features of mass-mediated messages. This is justified on the ground that to deny the limitations placed on the ideological positions offered by television, and the sense that viewers can make of these positions, is at the same time to dismiss the power of culture.

Which brings us to the relationship between Gerbner et al. and the critical theory that was shaping cultural studies at the same time. If, methodologically, cultivation analysis appears to be at one with the mainstream mass-communication tradition, conceptually it is closer to

Marxist and structuralist perspectives. Gerbner's description of television as 'the cultural arm of the industrial order' (1976: 151), combined with his contention that a common symbolic order pervades the medium regardless of genre, producer intent or audience preference, shares much with Louis Althusser's (1972) neo-Marxist structuralism, wherein power relationships are reproduced via ideological state apparatus. Why are such connections ignored? Wober (1998) reminds us that Gerbner's Marxist leanings may have been disguised, since much of his work was conducted in the shadow of the Cold War at a time when leftist sympathies could destroy careers.

Approaching the question from an alternative position, these conceptual similarities also explain why mainstream mass-communication researchers are often equally critical of Gerbner's work. In dismissing transmission views of communication, Gerbner also rejected the idea that quantitative methods could be used from a positivist perspective. The nature of television as a social entity inevitably compromised the integrity of positivist methods. For example, experimental approaches were no longer viable since it was impossible to locate a 'control' group who had never been exposed to television. Nor could the medium be used as an independent variable in the strictest sense, since its form and content shared an interactive relationship with other social forces (Gerbner et al., 1978). Hence the work of Gerbner and his colleagues displayed a good deal of reflexivity towards the methods they used. The differences between cultivation analysis and positivism can be demonstrated by looking at some of the criticisms levelled at the team from other social scientists.

Blood on the tables: cultivation and the Hughes/Hirsch critique

Despite the success and longevity of the Annenberg cultivation project, other quantitative media researchers saw Gerbner's model and findings as fundamentally flawed. These misgivings are best summarized in critiques by Paul Hirsch (1980, 1981) and Michael Hughes (1980). Combining their work, Hirsch and Hughes argued that the case for cultivation was far from solid for five reasons. Three criticisms were levelled at the statistical analysis of survey data. Re-analysis of this data revealed that the perceived correlations between television viewing and attitudes disappeared under simultaneous controls for demographic features such as age, sex, race, class and living environment. What this meant was that these alleged effects were spurious; that is, they were caused by other factors in the viewing environment. Secondly, this problem not withstanding, even those correlations that had been found by Gerbner et al. were extremely weak. Indeed, a meta-analysis of a range of cultivation projects performed by Morgan and Shanahan (1996) found an average cultivation effect of just 0.09. What this means is that television explains around 9 per cent of the variations in belief and ideology observed among the respondents. Finally, Gerbner et al. had failed to establish concrete categories of what counts as light, medium and heavy viewing, thus making a systematic comparison between these three groups impossible.

Conceptually, the Annenberg team was accused of wanting their cake and eating it too. In addition to mainstreaming, Gerbner et al. (1980b) had also developed the idea of 'resonance'. Television's power to produce fear and mistrust was especially potent when its violent messages intersected with reality. Living in a high-crime area, for example, heightened television's power by adding realism to its depictions of violence, a realism which might not be perceived by those without experience of lawlessness. Under such circumstances, television can actually enhance divergences between viewers due to different viewing environments. For Hughes and Hirsch, the combination of mainstreaming and resonance was nothing more than a trick designed to make cultivation findings unfalsifiable. How, they asked, can you argue that television produces both uniformity *and* difference among its audience?

At the same time, the researchers pre-empted Wober (1998) in arguing that cultivation analysis still relied on an outmoded notion of stimulus response, wherein television viewers were powerless to resist the televisual menace. This is due to Gerbner's insistence that television has a distinct and identifiable effect on society. The only real way of getting around this problem, Hughes argued, was to adopt the anthropological approaches that featured in qualitative audience research. The curious thing about the Hughes/Hirsch criticism is the paradigmatic slippages evident therein. While they criticized cultivation analysis for resurrecting direct effects, their dismissal at the same time of cultivation on the grounds of the absence of a universal effect, capable of withstanding multiple controls, seems itself to buy into this way of thinking. This suggests that neither researcher fully understood the conceptual basis of the paradigm, nor the implications of some of its findings. It also indicates that cultivation analysis cannot be neatly housed within positivism.

Let us explore the latter argument by studying how far the Hughes/ Hirsch critique actually fits with the conceptual basis of cultivation analysis. The first point to make is that Gerbner's understanding of the nature of mass communication is not compatible with the stimulus-response model. Gerbner's view of communication has much in common with the encoding/decoding model that will be discussed in Chapter 5. The process of mass communication is characterized by shifting perspectives facilitating polysemous interpretations of messages. An event occurs in the material world; that event is perceived by media workers who then manifest their perceptions into textual form. Their perceptions of the event, however, represent a way of seeing that may be open to reinterpretation. Thus the text does not reflect an incontestable recreation but a signification, an interpretation made from within a specific set of assumptions and production practices (Gerbner, 1976).

Hence, although Gerbner and his associates maintain the belief that generic differences between programmes are relatively unimportant, given the range of common messages pervading the medium as a whole, they did not take this to mean that the consequences of exposure were predictable. Indeed, if this were the case, there would be no need to do survey research. Television's power was seen in terms of agenda-setting rather than direct effects. The medium in America presented an unprecedented opportunity to encode and broadcast the values of the corporate sector. The audience did not 'have to accept [these] messages, but can't help having to deal with them' (Gerbner, 1973: 558).

This has consequences for how mainstreaming is understood. Wober (1998) suggests that this implies the production of uniformity among the audience. But in light of the agenda-setting view of television's power, it is more accurate to say that mainstreaming refers not to the production of uniformity, but the management of difference. Recalling Gerbner et al.'s work on the political views of heavy television viewers, the researchers did not find that the medium obliterated differences between races, classes, sexes and political orientations. Moreover, they found that television apparently cultivated some surprising tendencies: heavy viewers tended to want more, not less, spending on welfare.

This desire for interventionist government policy hinted at a recognition of structural inequalities within American society, an insight running counter to the hegemonic view of the US as the land of opportunity. Yet these same viewers were hostile to civil rights legislation and to increased taxation. Morgan (1989) has explained this phenomenon by reference to television's consumerist logic, which cultivates a desire for more of everything. People want more spending on welfare, as long as they do not have to pay for it. Hence the desire to help the needy is mitigated by hostility to redistributive policies, effectively hamstringing any concerted assault on poverty. This underlines the argument that television has enhanced the control of the corporate sector by pulling the political spectrum to the right. The limits of the debate on how far the government should go in providing a helping hand for the less fortunate is limited by the articulation of socialist principles within an over-arching consumerist framework that makes people hostile not to the poor, but to the concept of personal financial sacrifice. Calls for change are contained rather than silenced.

But this still leaves us with the problem of what Gerbner means by his claim that television has a distinct and identifiable effect. Surely the weakness of the correlation noted by one of his own colleagues (Morgan and Shanahan, 1996) dismisses this conclusion? The Annenberg team's response to this criticism indicates their post-positivist approach to statistical research. Far from ignoring anthropological work on television and society, Gerbner and his colleagues were only too aware of the fact that television's embeddedness within the rhythms of everyday life made it very difficult to locate its effects. Anthropologist Konrad Kottak (1990) suggests that such effects are only visible in the early introduction of a new technology. By the 1960s, America was well past this point. Gerbner acknowledged this by saying that, in absolute terms, there was no such thing as a light viewer (an insight which invalidates the search for concrete categorization of what counts as light, medium and heavy amounts of viewing).

When the Annenberg team speak of television, they are talking about a social institution which is wedded to the governmental and corporate sector. Subsequently, television's independent contribution to the cultivation of ideology can only be small since it expresses what are already dominant values. Hence:

> the observable independent contributions of television can only be relatively small. But just as an average shift of a few degrees can lead to an ice age . . . so too can a relatively small but pervasive influence make a crucial difference. The size of an effect is far less critical than the direction of its steady influence. (Gerbner et al., 1980b: 14)

Under such conditions, the normal rules of positivist social science do not apply. The methods designed by Gerbner and his colleagues were not designed to discover the truth of television's power, but rather to give a glimpse of complex cultural processes that are beyond the grasp of any single methodology.

Further challenges and problems in cultivation analysis

Although many of the criticisms that have been levelled at cultivation analysis are misplaced, as with any research paradigm there are further questions and weaknesses to be addressed within the field. One could argue that, however important the findings of Gerbner and his colleagues are, they are largely descriptive in nature. Although a series of important correlations between television content and the beliefs of audience members have been charted, the fact that the researchers have by their own admission preferred to focus on the macro rather than the micro means that they offer few comments on how exactly cultivation happens (Hawkins and Pingree, 1980). Other researchers have set out to answer this question. Potter (1992) relates cultivation effects to the development of media literacy. Looking at children, he argues that older children are in many ways more open to the cultivating effects of fictional programming, since they are more capable than younger children of making connections between stories and the real world. Shapiro and Lang (1991) and Mares (1996) suggest that cultivation effects can be generated by a tendency to confuse information gained from fictional shows with information gained from the news. The basic idea here is that as time goes by, we remember general patterns of information gained from television but not the precise sources of this information. Under such circumstances, drama can be a more potent ideological force than the news. Shrum (1994) picks up on this point, arguing that distinctive features of television drama make the information it delivers easier to recall for audiences. When asked to make judgements about the world, people use information stored from past experience. Information which is frequently encountered, or which is delivered in vivid form, is the easiest to recall and hence becomes powerful in shaping these judgements. This explains the power of television drama which tends to be more spectacular and hence memorable. Cultivation occurs, then, because popular culture provides a constant stream of information about the world around us that is easier to recall than information from other sources.

The problem with this body of work is that it demonstrates the limitations of quantitative research techniques in dealing with some of the subtleties of reception. This in turn relates back to Gerbner's dismissal of the notion of textuality. Cultivation analysis' use of content analysis as a means of mapping the denotative features of the television environment precludes questions of textual form, limiting the sorts of explanations of the cultivation process that researchers can explore. For example, the issue of whether source confusion can enhance cultivation is prompted by ignoring the various forms of television drama that in turn influence the sorts of relationships viewers can form with the text. It is here that Gauntlett's criticism of the elitism of cultivation analysts rings true. Shapiro and Lang's and Mare's work is premised on the hypothesis that viewers can confuse *NYPD Blue* with the nightly news. Their work also turns on the strict distinction between reality and fiction.

Yet, as Corner (1992) illustrates, the relationship between television and the real world can be very complex due the aesthetic dimensions of realism as an artistic form. The persuasive appeal of a television show is clearly related to its realism; but realism refers not only to the success of a text in faithfully recreating the real world, but also the formal features of that text and the way in which it functions to offer viewers subject positions that can be used to interpret the action we see before us. This debate outlines a relationship between the viewer and television drama that may well explain why cultivation can occur. Numerous researchers have pointed out that the vast majority of television viewers are perfectly aware that the dramas they see are fictional. Why, then, do we become excited or upset by the things that we see? When one of our favourite characters on a show dies, why do we feel sorrow? The reason is that we, as viewers, engage in what is known as a 'voluntary suspension of disbelief'. For the hour or so that we might spend watching a drama, we relate to the people on the screen as real people so that we can develop an emotional connection with the action. This is an exercise in pleasurable imagination. It is also an act of identification, where we create a relationship with a character by imagining what it would be like to be such a character, or to meet such a character (Ang, 1985).

This process will be explored in greater depth in Chapter 5, but for now we can see that these acts of imagination might carry ideological effects with them. If Gerbner is right in arguing that television characters are mostly white, middle-class, middle-aged men, from whose perspective most stories are told, it follows that viewers are enticed over and over again to view the world from this perspective in order to realize the pleasures offered by the medium. So perhaps it is the process of identification offered by television drama that explains cultivation, rather than the audience's tendency to forget where they get their information. The dismissal of the question of textuality prevents researchers from exploring this possibility.

This continues to be a problem since the notion of selective viewing must be constantly re-evaluated in the light of changing media environments. Signorelli's (1986) contention that the VCR and cable and satellite television had yet to make selective viewing a possibility could only be a provisional statement. The continuing proliferation of television stations, the syndication of certain types of programming (especially situation comedies and talk shows) and the development of cable and satellite channels specializing in specific genres call into question

Gerbner et al.'s contention that cumulative viewing is the best way to differentiate television audiences. Perse and colleagues (1994) argue that it is now possible for television viewers to devote the majority of their viewing time to specific genres. Subsequently, they discovered that, while cultivation stalwarts such as mistrust of others and fear of crime can still be found among viewers of programmes originating on broadcast channels, fear of crime was actually negatively associated with heavy viewing of specialized cable channels. Similarly, Davis and Mares (1998) have assessed the cultivating power of the talk-show genre, seeing as it is now possible in both the US and the UK to spend several hours a day watching Jerry Springer and Co. Among other things, they have not surprisingly associated heavy talk-show viewing with a tendency to overestimate the real-life occurrence of certain activities. Hence a changing media environment requires that we pay close attention to generic form.

The need to subvert Gerbner's initial hypothesis in paying attention to the differences between television texts is enhanced by the call for more comparative work on cultivation in different cultures. Does cultivation still occur in countries whose television industries function under different organizational arrangements from those of the United States? Piepe et al. (1990) echoed Wober (1998) in arguing that the British public service ethos produces more diverse content that in turn produces different sorts of cultivation effects, depending on viewing patterns. Heavy soap-opera viewers, for example, were more likely to define themselves as working class than were heavy current-affairs viewers; this was interpreted as reflecting the social realism of British soap which, unlike most television drama, is normally set in blue-collar communities. Piepe et al. (1990) concluded that the diversity of programming produced by a broadcasting system that is funded both through subsidy and advertising means that, unlike America, British television does not produce a homogeneous mainstream. At the same time, technological innovation raises the question of how long this situation is likely to last. In the UK, for example, many satellite and cable channels are dominated by American shows, especially talk shows, situation comedies and action adventure series. Does this reduce the diversity of viewing responses?

Conclusion

Cultivation analysis demonstrates two things: first, quantitative research, specifically content analysis and mass sample surveys, can be used for post-positivist and critical purposes. The power of cultivation analysis lies in its ability to map general and generalizable patterns of televisual representation and audience reactions to these representations. Gerbner and his colleagues have charted persuasive connections between the interests of corporate America, the stories that this corporate sector pays for, and the ideological reactions of viewers to these stories. Overall, they find sets of beliefs among heavy television viewers that are consistent with the maintenance of an unequal power distribution within American society. In doing so, their work is compatible with political economy and European critical theory.

At the same time, the limitations of quantitative methods show that cultivation analysis cannot provide an all-encompassing theory of media power. While the evidence for cultivation is powerful, the explanations of how this process occurs are not. This seems to relate to the dismissal of textuality as an important factor, but perhaps it is more accurate to say that cultivation methods are simply not suited to a consideration of this textuality. Content analysis can map broad denotative characteristics of texts, but can do little more. For this reason, those who have sought to explain the cultivation process via quantitative methods have fallen back upon psychological explanations that, as Barker (1998) notes, provide very limited explanations of audience activity. Ignoring the qualitative aspects of textuality has produced a very limited view of the sorts of relationships that viewers can form with texts. This does not invalidate the paradigm, but it does show that there is more to the relationship between media and audience than cultivation analysis suggests.

Exercises

1   Spend an evening watching broadcast television between the hours of 6 o'clock and 10 o'clock. Count:

   (a) The number of men and the number of women you see (excluding crowd scenes).
   (b) The number of people seen from specific racial and ethnic backgrounds.
   (c) The age groups you see (under 18, 18–25, 26–35, 36–55, 55–60, 60+).

2   Locate each person/character you see into one of the following three categories: (a) professional/managerial (white collar); (b)

manual/blue-collar/working class; (c) unemployed/below the poverty line, criminal. What types of people are most likely to be found in each?

3 Is it possible to discern any underlying values across a variety of television programmes?

4 Consider the problems entailed in this exercise. Did you have any problems coding what you saw? Was it always clear what category characters fitted in to? List specific instances of characters that were difficult to code. Why were they difficult?

5 Perform the same exercise in the classroom, using a clip from a soap opera, sitcom or television drama. Compare notes with colleagues to discern differences in the way in which you code items. What explains these differences? What does this tell us about the use value of content analysis?

5 Cultural Studies and Audience Research

The 1960s and 1970s were a watershed in mass-communications audience research, as older effects approaches were challenged by the agenda-setting and cultivation analysis models. Effects research was also confronted by interpretative modes of social science that jelled into cultural studies. 'Cultural studies' is a contested term. Wright (1998) sees it as eurocentric, having been appropriated by scholars centred at the University of Birmingham's Centre for Contemporary Cultural Studies who were in essence replicating work that had been done in other parts of the world. The account that follows is similarly 'centred' in the UK and the US, and is therefore a particular version of a cultural approach to media audiences.

For strategic purposes, this chapter concentrates on the creation and reception of textual meaning, in addition to outlining methodological issues that will carry over into Chapter 6. The reasons for this are twofold. First, the shift from the analysis of what texts *do* to the audience to what texts *mean* to them is often outlined as the fundamental difference between mass-communication research and cultural studies (Nightingale, 1996). This is important since it shows that the latter paradigm was able to give many of the former's concerns a different conceptual morphology that was to have methodological consequences. But, at the same time, commonality of interest enables us to question the degree of paradigmatic rupture between cultural studies and mass-communications research. Interpretative approaches claimed to provide new forms of knowledge by redefining the goals and means of social research, but the work that led to and followed on from Stuart Hall's (1980) influential encoding/decoding model was driven by questions that were not entirely different from those pursued within mass communication. Equally, the two camps were confronted with similar theoretical and methodological problems. The purpose of pointing to such continuities is to create a productive dialogue between apparently opposing camps. The rationale for such a dialogue begins from the realization that cultural studies is a response to issues that had been raised by mass-communication researchers who were sensitive to the limitations of their own work. This is most apparent in work on the 'public knowledge' question, as framed by the encoding/decoding model.

Interpretative approaches to social science

Distinctions between cultural studies and mass communication must be contextualized within the broader development of interpretative analyses of human thought and behavior. Many opposed the idea that the social studies should ape the natural sciences. The counter-attack began in sociology with Max Weber. Weber did adopt the positivist view that social science could be objective, in so far as it could develop replicable methods of study. But at the same time the sociologist's goal, in his view, was to achieve an understanding of human behaviour that was beyond the scope of the natural sciences (Giddens, 1971; Weber, 1977). For Weber, human action was driven by subjective meanings. Had he been involved in researching media violence, he would not have been interested in reactions to mediated images, but how these reactions could be connected with subjective experiences of these images. This moves social research towards viewing the world from the perspective of the people being studied, reversing as such the dominance of the researcher seen in positivism.

Suggesting that the worlds of nature and human interaction are different in form and function also means questioning whether laws govern thought and action. Winch (1977) sees meaningful human behaviour as being regulated by rules. The distinction here is that, while laws are immutable forces that must be obeyed, rules are produced by context-based human interaction. Every social situation is shaped by pre-existing ideas about what counts as acceptable, but these ideas can be renegotiated according to the actors' view of the specificities of the occasion. Consider going to see a film. Etiquette demands that films be watched in silence in deference to other audience members. Talking loudly, responding to on-screen characters or energetically moving around in your seat during a screening will normally draw some sort of rebuke. However, there are occasions when this is not the case. I remember a particularly riotous late-night showing of Ridley Scott's *Aliens*. Normal viewing rules did not seem to apply, probably due to the fact that the audience was mostly composed of people in their late teens and early twenties who were watching a film that elicited physical responses through the extensive use of gruesome special effects. No one seemed to mind that what little dialogue there was during some scenes was lost amid the screams and wisecracks coming from the audience. If anything, the interaction made for a richer experience. Normal rules of social engagement were re-written in accordance with shifting circumstances. As with the notion of subjective meaning, the analysis of rules has methodological implications in that it encourages us to consider the power of the audience to shape its relationship with the media.

The goals of social science were substantially re-written by the arguments that research is about grasping the meaning of human behaviour, and that this is related to the development of rules through inter-subjective agreement. A rules-based approach dismisses the search for universal laws of communication and persuasion. Jarvie (1977) argues that a cultural phenomenon should be understood in its own right, not as something which represents larger forces. This being the case, experimental media effects research appears an ill-conceived attempt to analyse one context (the everyday impact of media violence) through observation of another (the impact of media violence within a controlled environment). Interpretative approaches to social science thus question external validity, or generalizability as a criterion on which research should be evaluated.

If interpretative social science is not about laws, it most certainly *is* about the values and morals that had been driven out of positivist approaches. Positivism had argued that true knowledge could only grow from inquiries excluding value judgements and subjective experience. Yet qualitative researchers saw this as a mistake, since value judgements and subjective experiences are the substance of human life. Trying to study human behaviour without taking account of the subjective experiences of both researcher and researched is a little like playing football without a ball – it misses the vital ingredient that produces a meaningful result.

Relating this to media studies, Gitlin (1978) and Hall (1980) argued that the effects tradition had substantially misrepresented the social nature and impact of the mass media by ignoring subjective aspects of human experience. For Gitlin and Hall, behaviourism evaded questions about other sorts of effects that could be produced in connection with the meaning of media texts. It also collapsed boundaries between very different sorts of social experiences. Behavioural change could come in the form of reacting to a violent film, buying a different soap powder in response to a brilliant advertising campaign, or changing a voting preference following a political broadcast. Gitlin (1978) claimed that effects researchers saw each of these scenarios as representing variations on the same theme; each functions in pretty much the same way. This ignores how each situation might be viewed in a different way by the audience, and the consequences that differing subjective experiences have on reactions (or the lack of them) to messages. Gitlin and Hall charged that these errors were compounded by effects researchers' failure to reflect upon the power of dominant social institutions to direct research. In fairness, this is a criticism that was recognized by Lasswell. Nevertheless, the fact that effects researchers conceded this point tells us that value-free media studies is an impossibility.

Gitlin and Hall argued that audience research should take an interpretative tack. This new direction was best articulated in the American context by Carey's ritual definition of communication wherein: 'Communication is a symbolic process whereby reality is produced, maintained, repaired and transformed' (Carey, 1989: 23). This quote encapsulates the cultural view that reality, meaning and subjective experience are entwined. Reality is formed through the ritualistic creation and dissemination of meaning. Hence, communication is culturally specific and as such can only be understood as a process from the point of view of the people involved.

A cultural approach to communication would seem to represent a complete rupture from mass-communication research. The implication of Carey, Gitlin and Hall's work was that the entire audience research project needed to be revamped – from theory-building through hypothesis-developing to methodology and method. In combination with general premisses of interpretative social science, they suggested that cultural studies functions according to an entirely different view of investigative objects and procedures, establishing different criteria for what counts as good research.

Re-conceptualizing communication: ideology and institutions

A cultural approach to communication needed a new model of media effects. In Europe, Marxist and neo-Marxist theories of ideology provided the answer. As Raymond Williams (1978) and Terry Eagleton (1990) indicate, ideology is a tremendously complex term whose meaning shifts according to historical, cultural and academic context. Turner (1990), Fiske (1992) and Tudor (1999) provide comprehensive and comprehensible accounts of this. What follows is a shorter consideration of how ideology applies to audience research, and how this led to the development of Stuart Hall's encoding/decoding model.

Let us think again about Nightingale's (1996) argument that while effects research was concerned with behaviours, cultural studies is focused on meaning. This is a slightly misleading suggestion. Behaviourism, in its short-term, laboratory-based incarnation, is certainly rejected. But cultural studies retains an interest in human action. Carey's ritual definition creates a connection between meaning and action – the things that people do in a given situation depends on how they understand that situation. It is more accurate, then, to say that cultural studies is interested in exploring meaningful human action.

Europeans had a more complex view. Carey concedes that the transmission and ritual models are not mutually exclusive. The meanings created and shared within a culture have to have a point of origin – somebody has to make them in the first place. Standing alone, the ritual definition creates the impression that an entire culture is involved in this process. This is not true of mass communication, as Hall states in his essay 'The rediscovery of ideology: the return of the repressed in media studies' (1982). Here, Hall expands upon the doubts that effects researchers such as Lasswell had about their liberal-pluralist assumptions. Much of the mass-communication research of the 1940s and 1950s felt that the media functioned for the common good within an American society that was united in terms of its core values. Yet at the same time, America was replete with social conflicts characterized by the absence of consensus – the civil and gay rights movements, and conflicts over the Vietnam War. Moreover, there was no guarantee that these groups would ever be absorbed within the social mainstream, since their beliefs directly threatened the material interests of those who were already there. Liberal pluralism was replaced by an apocalyptic view of a society comprised of conflicting groups, pursuant of self rather than common interests.

What role did the media play in all of this? Influenced by the work of Karl Marx, Louis Althusser and Antonio Gramsci, Hall argued that the mass media play a crucial role in defining, disseminating, popularizing and protecting the beliefs and values of a social mainstream, dominated by a narrow social elite. This view has its origins in Marx's belief that the ruling class within a society legitimizes its power by creating the ideas that people use to make sense of reality, as such controlling the subjective side of human experience. Gramsci gave these ideas a less deterministic sheen. For him, ideology is the place where competing versions of social reality meet to win over popular consciousness in a never ending struggle to define the world in a particular way (for more on these developments, see Hall, 1983, 1985, 1986a, b).

For Hall, media studies must begin from the question of how the mass media serve to secure 'A universal validity and legitimacy for accounts of the world that are partial and particular' (1982: 65). As a starting-point, this involved the investigation of the institutional context of the media industry – the sort of analysis suggested by Lasswell and Gerbner. Curran (1990) argued that liberal-pluralist media research was based on an invalid model of the organization of mass communication. Liberal pluralism is based on the idea that all social groups have a right to speak within a democracy. This was relatively true in the nineteenth century, since comparatively low start-up costs for newspapers ensured a flourishing radical press. This quickly ceased to be the case as rising costs and, more recently, the continuing deregulation of the media industry created an ever increasing degree of centralization in the production of media messages (Bagdikian, 1983; Schiller 1996). Relating this to the notion of the public sphere, the realities of media ownership and access mean that claims that we live within an 'electronic town hall' ring hollow (Dahlgren, 1991).

Schiller and Bagdikian tend to explain this in orthodox Marxist terms: the fact that capitalist monopolies own media corporations means that they quite deliberately promote the values of these monopolies. But connections between powerful groups and the sorts of messages we find in the mass media can be less direct. In *Policing the Crisis*, Hall et al. (1978) describe how the routinized use of sources from the government, police and judiciary for information and interpretation on issues of law and order gives these groups tremendous power to determine the agenda on which particular issues are discussed. Hence, while in Althusserian terms the mass media are 'relatively autonomous' from other social institutions, routinized practices of media production have an implicit ideological agenda and effect (see Tuchman, 1978 for further examples).

Reconceptualizing communication: ideology, realism and texts

Both cultural studies and effects research are interested in issues of persuasion, and the influence that this has on what people think and do. However, the two camps diverge on what persuasion is and how it is effected. The effects belief in the transparency of communication, where the process simply involves shifting information from sender to receiver, means that the persuasive element of a message is easy to see, as is its success or failure. The notion of ideology however, suggests a more complex process in which texts have both an explicit *and* an implicit agenda. A public health campaign on the importance of using condoms to prevent the spread of sexually transmitted diseases has a clear point of origin and goal. Hall's work on ideology, however, suggested that media power lay in its ability to determine the form as well as the content of public consciousness. Consider the example of the drawing of the old/young woman described in Chapter 1. Ideological power would be affected if someone developed a strategy to fix the perspective from which this diagram was viewed by making it appear that this was the only available position. This involves 'naturalizing' this perspective by denying that it is motivated by the desire to achieve control for certain political ends. In this sense, persuasion is achieved not only through information, but also through controlling how people make sense of information.

Thus the argument ran that the mass media were persuasive in so far as they offered audiences seductive 'knowledge positions' that made sense of a chaotic world. This view was inspired not only by theories of ideology, but also psychoanalysis (see Moores, 1993). This shift explains the more complex view of the relationship between fiction and reality developed by John Corner's work on realism, described in Chapter 1. George Gerbner had argued that the fact–fiction divide was illusory, since television drama conveyed powerful messages about reality. Yet Gerbner's quantitative bias prevented him from exploring the processes that caused this phenomenon.

Semiotics solved the problem (for an account of semiotics, see Fiske, 1982; Lewis, 1991; Seiter, 1992; Moores, 1993). Semiotics teaches us that news and drama are united by the fact that they are first and foremost signifying practices that transform everyday experiences into something else. Routinized news production procedures spin reality by systematically excluding certain voices from its accounts. At the same time, the concept of social realism suggests that drama plays a role too in creating public knowledge by dealing in aspects of reality that are formally excluded from news (Caughie, 1980). The BBC drama *Warriors*, which focused on the experiences of British peace-keeping forces in Bosnia based on interviews with men who had served with the UN, told the story of the civil war from the perspective of ordinary soldiers rather than the politicians who dominated the news coverage. As such, it was better placed to comment on the emotional devastation inflicted on victims of the war. These insights – that news is itself a signifying practice and drama does claim to tell us something real – lead John Corner (1992) to a third definition of realism. Realism is the relationship between a text's formal features and the point of view it offers to the audience. In this sense, all texts are potentially 'persuasive' in terms of their ability to shape views of social reality. The debates on ideology and realism contributed to the development of the encoding/decoding model which operationalized the new hypotheses about connections between communication and power.

Reconceptualizing communication: encoding/decoding

The encoding/decoding model is a vital moment in audience research since it ties together a number of themes within discussions of interpretative social science, ideology, semiotics and, crucially, how these ideas influence the approach we take to media audiences. At the risk of simplifying, all these areas unite to produce a fundamental assumption that represents a distinct break from positivist research: that *our sense of* reality is *often* a matter of intersubjective agreement and is, as such, ambiguous. Please note that the italicized parts of this sentence mean that this is not to argue that reality is entirely what we make of it. This point will become important in later discussions.

The encoding/decoding model defines persuasion as the ability to suppress ambiguity by monopolizing the means that people use to make sense of the world. Its logic is semiotic and, although it was not a term that Hall was to use until much later (1986b), can be described through the idea of 'articulation'. Basic semiotics tells us that the connection, or articulation, between signifier and signified is arbitrary, since it is a matter of cultural convention. Hence the key to political power lies in the ability to make contestable signifier/signified relations seem like common sense. As an example, Hall discusses the war waged by the British prime minister Margaret Thatcher against the welfare state. Thatcher's problem, Hall argued, was semiotic: she had to take a term, 'welfare state', and change the ideas that people associated with it. For some, 'welfare state' referred to a benign commitment to protect vulnerable citizens from the worst ravages of poverty and illness. Put this way, it is hard to see how anyone could support dismantling such a force for good. Thatcherite success in doing just that with relatively little public outcry was facilitated, in Hall's view, by de-coupling positive associations and re-articulating the notion of 'welfare state' with ideas of incompetence, inefficiency and inequality. The welfare state, in short, came to represent the unfair advantage that the work-shy enjoyed at the expense of working people (Hall, 1990).

Political power therefore involves conditioning the subjective side of human experience. This, however, sounds very similar to the 'hypodermic needle' model of media effects. Was this not, after all, the goal of the *Why*

We Fight films studied by Hovland et al. (1949)? Although it has been criticized for resurrecting the notion of direct effects in a different form (Wren-Lewis, 1983; Abercrombie and Longhurst, 1998), the encoding/decoding model does not view mediated communication as a linear process that implants the ideas of the powerful into the heads of the powerless. Influenced by semiotics and the Althusserian notion (1972) of overdetermination, the model argues that the mass media 'encode' reality. What this means is that the real world is used as raw material, and is made to signify in specific ways by technical conventions of media production, which may or may not complement the interests of powerful social groups. These produce texts which have a 'preferred reading', a meaning that is encouraged by the structure of the text and ways of defining reality that are dominant in a given society. Two elements of this model differentiate it from 'hypodermic' thinking. The first is the idea that texts are 'encoded'. A code is a message whose meaning can only be deciphered if we have access to the right interpretative guide. Hall argued that if the audience do not share the producers' 'code', then they are unable (or perhaps unwilling) to decode the message in the intended fashion: hence meanings are preferred rather than enforced.

Consider the 1987 film *Top Gun* as an example. The film tells the story of a young, arrogant, good-looking US Navy pilot's journey towards maturity and hero status. The pilot, played by Tom Cruise, learns to curb his 'maverick' tendencies during a training course that is marred by the death of his crewman. Redeployed on active duty, he overcomes doubts over his ability, temperament and courage by saving the life of a fellow pilot in a spectacular dogfight with Soviet warplanes. What could we say about *Top Gun*'s preferred meaning? Douglas Kellner (1995: 77) is clear on the point:

> Hollywood films . . . are not innocent entertainment, but lethal weapons in the service of dominant socio-economic forces. *Top Gun*'s ideological project is to invest desire in the figure of the heroic fighter pilots and high tech war which it does with attractive star figures, cinematic high tech wizardry and special effects, rock music and the sounds of speed and power, and of course, the sophisticated planes and military gadgets.

This sounds like direct effects. *Top Gun* was a conspiracy cooked up between Hollywood and the Reaganite presidency, designed to stoke the dying Cold War embers. Certainly, as Kellner notes, the US armed forces felt that the film had a positive effect on recruitment. Indeed, the extensive aid it received from the navy, in contrast to the lack of co-operation given to Stanley Kubrick's surreal and critical Vietnam tale *Full Metal Jacket*, indicates a symbiosis of interest. But symbiosis is not equivalence. The conspiratorial tones of Kellner's analysis disguise the fact that while he might be right about the ideological effect of the film, it is probably misleading to say that the film-makers consciously set out to promote militarism. That this happened, if it happened, was the product of an intersection between the desire to create a successful blockbuster film, full of attractive people, impressive locations and spectacular effects, and the navy's realization that they stood to benefit from the ideological fall-out. Add to this implicit assumptions about masculinity (where the successful male is represented as individualistic, competitive, physically and mentally aggressive and sexually irresistible), and you end up indeed with a powerful brew that almost forces the viewer to see the world through red, white and blue tinted glasses. This end result, however, is produced by multiple forces: aesthetic principles, uninterrogated conventions of gender representation, and a political mission. This intersection is what is meant by the notion of overdetermination.

But if the film is as powerful as Kellner suggests, how is it that we are able to identify and explain its persuasive strategies? Showing the film to a group of first-year European students with little experience of media analysis, I was struck by their ability to replicate Kellner's critique despite the fact that none had actually read it. This points to the dislocations that can occur between encoding and decoding. When shown to a group of people who did not share the producer's codes, a different reaction to that implied in the production stage became evident. In general, the students saw *Top Gun* as an example of a film that used conventional themes of masculinity and the 'USA #1' ethos so artlessly that it almost became a parody of itself.

This response can be used to illustrate the importance of encoding/ decoding to cultural studies. Earlier, I argued that cultural studies re-theorized communication with new hypotheses developed to guide empirical research. The early effect of the debates on ideology and realism meant that new research initially came in the form of textual analysis. French semiologist Roland Barthes (1973) described how the most mundane texts – advertisements, songs, news photographs – work to position the reader ideologically. Such attempts, however, led in some quarters to the belief that one could assess the social impact of a text simply by looking at its structure. This idea featured most prominently in the work of the journal *Screen* (Moores, 1993).

Despite the fact that Hall's ideas were largely based upon textual analysis, encoding/decoding implied that the only way to assess the impact of a text was to look at the audience. Aligning himself with the idea that media meaning was best understood from the perspective of people at the receiving end, Hall postulated that audiences could react in one of three ways to a media text: they could accept the *preferred* reading; they could accept parts of the text while rejecting others, constructing what he called a *negotiated* reading; or they could reject what the text was trying to make them think in an *oppositional* reading. Looking at *Top Gun*, we could argue that if indeed there were young men who decided to join the US navy after seeing the film, then they did so on the basis of accepting the preferred meaning. The students that I spoke to, however, were oppositional in their rejection of what the film was trying to say.

Resistance

The encoding/decoding model was an important element in a number of empirical investigations of the audience. But before exploring its methodological applications, it is important to note some conceptual flaws in its original formulation. Consider the responses to *Top Gun* I have described. Although the viewers in question react in different ways to the text, both the navy recruits and the students agreed that the film promotes an orthodox view of militarism. What, however, if audiences disagree not on their evaluation of a text's meaning, but on their comprehension of what this meaning is? Wren-Lewis (1983) argues that, in failing to address this possibility, the encoding/decoding model stops short of a fully semiological position. Consequently, the encoding/decoding model encounters methodological problems similar to those faced by survey researchers *vis-à-vis* the precoding of responses.

'Resistive reading' theories offer a theoretical avenue out of this dilemma. Associated most closely with John Fiske (1987, 1989, 1993), a resistive reading is an interpretation of a text which changes its encoded meaning at the point of reception. Take as an example the argument that *Top Gun* can be read as a gay film. Replete with semi-naked male bodies displayed in multiple shower-room scenes, and centred on intense homosocial bonding, the film has been seen as offering many points of identification for a gay male audience. But this is not an example of an oppositional reading: where the students mentioned earlier rejected the film, a gay reading works within ambiguous textual elements. Fiske sees this as the key differentiation between the oppositional and the resistive. Since the signifier is always potentially ambiguous, it follows that the preferred meaning of a text might be unclear, or might be open to subversion. Where preferred and oppositional readings are different in terms of their valuation of a text, the resistive is different in its interpretation.

Fiske's work has sparked a controversy over the audience's immunity to ideological persuasion. This argument will evolve over the next two chapters, but resistance implies no *necessary* rejection of preferred readings or media power. Hall's understanding of the preferred reading was developed under an Althusserian influence. Despite theories of 'relative autonomy', Althusser (1972) saw the role of the 'ideological state apparatus', of which the media were a part, as being to reproduce a dominant ideology. Preferred readings are thus produced by the relationship between aesthetic practices and political forces. Looking at *Top Gun* in its historical context, we can say that it did not set out to be a gay friendly film. Why can we say this? The navy was hardly likely to co-operate with such a film since it actively discriminates against gay people in its recruitment drives. Add to this the potential loss of audiences that producers who deal with gay themes face, and we can see that there are powerful institutional needs to suppress such a reading. Whatever the theoretical twists and turns that follow, it remains true that a good deal of interpretative audience research retains the belief that media texts are powerful means of persuasion. Vigorous campaigns against the encoding/decoding model have not dissuaded Hall (1994) from the belief that the ability to create and disseminate texts ensures that your version of reality will gain a foothold in public consciousness.

So, with the development of the encoding/decoding and resistive reading models, cultural studies armed itself with a new set of theories about how communication works, and how it relates to issues of social power. The interpretative investigation of media audiences was to be guided by five assumptions, described by Lembo (1994: 34):

1 Society is divided into dominant and subordinate groups that differ in terms of their access to social power.
2 Dominant groups assert their power in cultural as well as political and economic domains.
3 Cultural meanings are linked to the social structure and, consequently, to power relations, and such meanings can only be understood if the history of the social structure and power relations is made explicit.
4 The creation of cultural meanings by those who use the media is relatively autonomous from the institutional production of media objects.
5 This relative autonomy in the creation of meanings in media can serve as a basis for oppositional politics.

Ethnography and the relationship between researcher and researched

Methodologically, relationships between audiences and texts have been studied via methods that are inspired by ethnography. An ethnographic approach to media audiences involved a completely different view of how to approach and analyse media audiences. In order to evaluate this body of work, it is important to set out what the aims of ethnographic research are, and how these differ in kind from the aims and objectives of mass communication research.

The major attraction that ethnography held for audience researchers is that it offered a means to overcome the artificiality of mass-communication research since it is based on naturally occurring data. Its roots lay within the descriptive and interpretative anthropology of Branislaw Malinowski. Malinowski (1922) championed the idea that culture can only be understood for what it is through the painstaking observation and documentation of everyday life. In the manner of Weber, this involved understanding the meaning of cultural phenomena from the participants' point of view. This was applicable to media research since, up until this point, institutional problems rather than the subjective experience of the audience had driven research. This meant that a large part of the media's social function had been ignored (although this dimension is certainly hinted at in Cantril's (1940) *War of the Worlds* study).

A much lighter touch on the part of the researcher is implied. To respect the true nature of social phenomena, ethnographic agendas are set by the people and situations under investigation. This is called 'grounded theory' (Hammersley and Atkinson, 1996), which involves viewing the research process described by Silverman in Chapter 1 in interactive terms. Although research questions are inevitably based to some degree on a priori assumptions, the ethnographer's goal is to create a flexible observational framework that can register and account for unexpected phenomena. Hammersley and Atkinson (1996) suggest that effective ethnographers allow themselves to be 'surprised' by their results. What this means is that, since the goal is to unravel a somehow mysterious culture, he or she must accept that the theories and hypotheses which he or she initially feels to be most useful might not, in fact, offer the best explanations for the cultural patterns observed. This being the case, the researcher should be prepared to reformulate his or her ideas according to the information he or she receives from those under study.

Consequently, the relationship between researcher and researched is very different from that suggested in mass-communication research. Ethnography places researcher and researched on a relatively equal footing, due to political as well as methodological concerns. While ethnography originated with a view to the analysis of obviously 'exotic' cultures, the Chicago School of sociology developed a mode of urban investigation that demonstrated how domestic cultures could be just as puzzling. Deviance – the world of alcoholics, drug users and the homeless – developed as a key concept in revealing the unacknowledged rules of mainstream society (Hammersley, 1989). Many common-sense assumptions made about so-called deviant people were denaturalized as a result.

Analogies can be drawn with the cultural studies approach to audiences. If they were not deviant in the legal sense, viewers, readers and listeners had none the less been demonized by certain strands of effects theory that painted them as potential H-bombs. In 1967, the American sociologist Howard Becker had concluded that ethnography was not an objective science, but was 'on the side' of repressed social elements whose beliefs and values were largely ignored in public debate and policy-making. Hall's (1982) essay, subtitled 'The return of the repressed in media studies' indicates that cultural studies took much the same position *vis-à-vis* the audience. Much of the new audience research was on the side of the viewer, not only in terms of viewing the media from his or her position, but also to represent the larger political views and interests of those who were structurally excluded from the 'electronic public sphere'.

This commitment creates a number of practical problems. The first of these is how to generate research questions that will respect the natural world of the audience. Hammersley and Atkinson (1996) see ethnography as being generically guided by a focus on rule-making. How does culture develop rules that govern interpretation and behaviour? Given this question, one place to begin is to identify regular patterns of human behaviour, then to work backwards to address how these patterns came to be. Whatever scorn Ang (1991) pours on ratings research, statistics do represent a way of identifying regular media habits. Jhally and Lewis's (1993) analysis of *The Cosby Show*, for example, could be justified on the grounds that at the time the show headed prime-time rankings, and was thus a staple of television culture. Broadcasting schedules might also be used as evidence. David Morley's (1980) research into the reception of the British news magazine show *Nationwide* was based on its institutional position as the gateway between the evening news and the prime-time schedule.

Unfortunately, the rules governing social life are often difficult to see, since they are a part of everyday common sense. Audience researchers are especially vulnerable to this problem, since they often study audience cultures of which they are a part. Hammersley and Atkinson (1996) see this as a familiar ethnographic dilemma, which is why 'breaching exercises' become important research tools. A breaching exercise is a moment that disrupts conventions, thus revealing the unspoken rules that guide normal situations. Imagine standing in an elevator. Stopping at the next floor, the doors open and a woman enters. As you take off for the next level, you realize that something is strange: the woman has not turned to face the door. This makes you feel uncomfortable. It also makes you conscious of the rules of normal behaviour in an elevator. On entering, you are supposed to turn your back on fellow passengers. You have never reflected on these rules before, but the woman's aberrant behaviour has suddenly made you aware of them. This is an example of breaching.

Ethnography is reliant on moments of natural breaching since it is based on methods of observation that cause as little disruption as possible to a setting. This idea has been applied in ethnographic media research in a number of ways. Ang (1985) and Katz and Liebes (1990) have studied the reception of *Dallas* in non-American cultures. Since the 1950s, commentators such as Richard Hoggart had warned of the perils of cultural imperialism: the music, movies, magazines and television shows that poured out of the United States, flooding the international media market, served as vehicles for the dissemination of American values, so powerful that they could stifle indigenous cultures (Tudor, 1999). The *Dallas* researchers asked if this were the case, in various ways. They were united in the sense that the fundamental question was whether such a text, which signified a changing symbolic environment, could constitute a 'breach' in custom.

Breaching has also been used as a way to identify projects in public knowledge. Reilly (1999) studied how two outbreaks of concern about BSE or 'mad cow disease' had an impact on what people knew about the problem, and how BSE was connected to new variant CJD, the human form of the illness caused by eating infected beef. In a similar vein, Kitzinger (1999) has studied how AIDS coverage has influenced the shape of public knowledge. Philo and Henderson (1999) have extended these concerns into the area of popular fiction, studying how the dramatic depiction of a suicide caused by an overdose of paracetomol, featured in the BBC drama *Casualty*, impacted upon public awareness of the dangers of the medication. Spectacular events are important since they provide opportunities to ask if the media fulfil their public service commitment.

Theoretical problems can also form the basis for research questions. Generally, these surround the processes through which power is realized or evaded. Since much of the early cultural studies project outlined how the mass media affected ideological power over politically weaker sectors of society, its audience research has tended to look at what actually happens when such people interact with the media. Buckingham's continuing interest in children's relationships with the media (1987, 1993a–c, 1998a, b, 1999) is inspired by his determination to overturn the popular view that children are more susceptible to media influence than adults. In the same vein, relationships between class, gender and ethnicity have been explored. These interests have exerted a powerful methodological influence on the practice of media ethnographies, affecting methods of sampling and data generation.

Naturally occurring data: samples

The importance of naturally occurring data and respect for the specific nature of the cultural world has a significant impact on sampling procedures. Morley (1992) argues that traditional random sampling methods used in experiments and surveys are unable to address subjective social experience since they ignore the social nature of human subjectivity. Such methods treat people as isolated individuals, when in reality we define our identities through affiliations to social groups. With this in mind, sampling in ethnographic audience research normally draws participants as members of collectives. Rather than examining people individually, groups are selected on the basis of shared cultural characteristics. Due to the influence of Marxist theories of power, many of these groups have been chosen according to class position. Morley's (1980) *Nationwide* study looked at how the interpretation of the programme differed among apprentices, trade unionists, students and managers. Although some of the groups also differed in race and gender, class seemed the over-riding factor in determining readings.

Class was originally located as important since it was felt that it implied a political outlook on the basis of common experience. However, the two cannot be equated in any simple fashion. Researchers retaining an interest in class have modified their sampling strategies to gather groups in terms of actual rather than implied experiences and political engagements. Philo's (1990) study of the reception of news about the British miners' strike of 1984–5, which sampled people according to their relationship to the strike, had an implicit class bias. In addition to using general categories based on occupational, residential and special interest groups, Philo also studied striking miners, policemen and women who had been on duty on the picket lines, and women's groups constituted to provide help for the families of the strikers. Similarly, Corner et al. (1990) looked at reactions to documentaries on the nuclear power industry among both general groups (women, children, the unemployed, students, Rotarians), groups with direct political attachments (Labour, Conservative and SLD party members, trade unionists) and groups with direct experience of the industry (nuclear workers). Social experience combined with gender is the rationale behind Schlesinger et al.'s (1992) study of how women view televised violence. The researchers had two aims. The first was to see how women in general interacted with a news programme, a soap opera, a televised drama and a film which all featured violence towards women by men. The researchers were also interested in how these reactions differed between women who had and women who had not been victims of such abuse.

Sampling strategies were also influenced by the emerging realization that audiences were divided along more than class lines. Feminist researchers complained that class provided an incomplete picture of audiences. This body of work will be discussed in greater depth in Chapter 6. But, methodologically speaking, one of the major insights of feminist research was that the relationship between text and audience could not be predicted on the basis of a simple identification between race, class, ethnicity, sexuality and political position (Seiter, 1999).

This is the crux of the differences between sampling theories employed by mass-communication research and cultural studies. It is not true to say that survey research is unaware of collective notions of identity, given the use of subgroup analysis in public opinion and cultivation research. However, sampling within cultural studies approaches demographic variables such as class, gender, age and ethnicity as more flexible points of identification. They denote common fields of experience, perceptions of which can be influenced by other things. Using Schlesinger et al. (1992) as an example, if one might have expected that the women would be united by a common revulsion against physical abuse, what was less expected was the way in which the women differed in their evaluation of its victims. Two of the programmes featured the rape of women in public places – a street at night and a public bar. The other two featured spousal battery. Some of the women who had not been subjected to similar incidents displayed a tendency to blame the victims; the women abused by their spouses, for example, were criticized for pushing their men too far. In this sense, common ways of interpreting social reality that might otherwise unite the women viewers were over-ridden by other facets of their social experience. The way that audiences make sense of the media depends, then, not only on obvious attributes of collective identity, but also on the idiosyncratic factors that influence the contextualized experience of these identities.

Guidelines for sampling within ethnographic audience research are consequently more flexible and situational than those used in mass-communication research. The sort of people gathered depends on the research question at hand, and choice of participants is determined by criteria that are appropriate for a specific study, rather than the field in general. As a related question, one might also ask how many respondents are used in an ideal study. The answer is again situational. For both methodological and pragmatic reasons, qualitative research cannot claim to produce the sorts of generalizable results found in surveys. One reason is that ethnographic work is far more labour intensive. If survey interviews take as little as ten minutes, ethnographic modes of research take at least a few hours; the imperative to get to know the subject means that ethnography cannot deal with the sorts of sample sizes that mass-communication researchers do.

But this does not mean that ethnographic research does not seek to draw inferences about society as a whole, based on the observation of a small subsection. In general, random sampling is replaced with a form of quota sampling, aiming to create a systematic degree of variation within a study. Morley, Schlesinger et al., Corner and Fenton, Philo and his colleagues in the Glasgow Media Group select groups with the greatest degree of ideological variation possible, in order to outline the full range of possible decodings that texts might have. Sample sizes range from just one or two people (Condit, 1989) to over one hundred (Morley, 1980). Livingstone and Lunt (1996) recommend that ethnographers should run interview groups until the information they receive becomes repetitive, suggesting that they have found the limits of interpretative activity. Unfortunately, the resources made available to the researcher often determine the extent to which this advice can be followed. Ethnographic research requires a lot of effort on both the part of the people conducting the reearch and those participating in it. Those who are able to offer their respondents money in return for participation (Schlesinger et al., 1992; Jhally and Lewis, 1993) are thus placed at an advantage over less fortunate researchers who must depend on goodwill alone.

Smaller samples do not necessarily lead to weaker or less useful work. Since ethnographic research almost always works with smaller numbers of people than quantitative projects, the most appropriate method to evaluate sampling strategies is to match them with the scope of the research question at hand. Typically, for example, smaller ethnographic samples have been used as ways of developing knowledge about the relationship between context and reception. Walkerdine (1993) seeks to make a range of statements about audience research in general on the basis of observation of the children in one family viewing one film. Academically, this approach can be justified along Popperian lines: Walkerdine seeks to falsify a number of routine assumptions about television's social role. She begins from the widely held belief that parents should carefully monitor their children's television use due to the danger the medium poses. Walkerdine does not necessarily take issue with this argument, but what she does object to is the idea that irresponsible viewing contributes to problems within dysfunctional families. She makes this argument by studying a family that has been referred to social services. The group, consisting of an often drunken and abusive mother and father, and their three young daughters, are observed watching the musical *Annie*. At face value, the viewing situation fits the stereotypical 'pathological' scenario, where kids are sat in front of the 'electronic babysitter' just to keep them quiet. One might think that since the television prevents the family from interacting, it also blocks any chance of them talking through their problems. Yet, through interviewing the mother and the children, Walkerdine suggests that the film, featuring the adventures of a young orphan who herself faces problems caused by the absence of a stable family, actually provides a vehicle that allows the children to explore their feelings about their own family situation. This is not to argue that television is a panacea. Evidence gathered does, however, problematize the argument that television exacerbates the difficulties of such families by allowing them to ignore real life. Despite the small sample size, Walkerdine's research is generalizable in terms of its demonstration that dominant views of 'illegitimate' television use do not fully explain the relationship between television and its audience.

Naturally occurring data: settings and interviews

The need to study audiences in their natural habitat, and to approach them as members of social collectives rather than individuals, influences where and how samples are studied, once identified. Research inspired by the encoding/decoding and resistive reading models has typically explored the sense that people make of media texts with focus-group interviewing strategies that are more open-ended than those used in survey research. Livingstone and Lunt (1996) comprehensively describe the development and application of focus-group interviews. The authors see a certain continuity between mass-communication research and cultural studies, in that the method was originally applied to media research by none other than Paul Lazarsfeld. Together with Robert Merton and Carl Hovland, Lazarsfeld became convinced that open-ended interviews played a vital part in the exploration of the subjective meanings attached to research variables. The goal of open-ended interviewing is to allow subjects themselves to define the research agenda. Philo (1999) wanted to look at the impact of explicit violence featured in the film *Pulp Fiction*. Had he used a quantitative approach, he might have followed the lead of Schlesinger et al. (1992) in asking the viewers to rate the strength of the violence on a scale of one to five. The problem with this is that this forces the violence issue into the respondents' consciousness, when left to their own devices they might have considered another part of the text as its most striking feature. Open-ended interviews are intended to overcome this problem, recreating a natural viewing experience by allowing the subject to decide for him or herself what the most salient aspect of his or her media experience is.

Contemporary ethnographic audience research differs from Lazarsfeld, Hovland and Merton in using open-ended interviews as primary rather than secondary analytic modes. Mass-communication research tended to use focus groups to check the reliability of surveys; assuring, for example, that the meaning of survey questions was clear, or predicting any potential problems in ambiguity of response. Since cultural studies is interested in textual interpretation and variability in response, this technique represents the closest approximation possible to the actual sort of relationship the audience forms with texts.

What, then, differentiates an open-ended interview from a casual conversation? It would be erroneous to conclude 'not much', since a priori research interests influence the formulation of questions. Schlesinger et al. (1992) suggest a 'funnelling' process, where the interviewer begins to ask general questions, moving on to more specific ones that reflect the original goals of the research. Following a screening one might begin by asking what viewers thought of the text in general, before moving on to specific aspects of it. This allows the researchers both to pursue the initial question and also to see how relevant that question is to actual audience experience.

Should interviews be conducted individually or on a group basis? There are two reasons for choosing the second option. The first is practical: interviewing people individually requires more time and effort. The second is theoretical. Carey's (1989) culture definition of communication suggests that meaning creation is a collective process. One of the arguments against group interviews is the idea that some people are more confident about expressing their opinions than others, and can therefore dominate these interviews and change the way that less talkative interviewees interpret texts. Philo (1990), however, argues that this is exactly what happens in real life – meaning is negotiated rather than immanent, and is influenced by our perceptions of other people's opinions. Think, for example, about the hype surrounding *The Blair Witch Project*. By the time the film was released in the UK, audiences had been so bombarded by positive reviews that it was almost inexcusable to see it as anything less than brilliant. Interviewing people together is important since it accesses real processes involved in the negotiation of meaning.

But on what basis are these groups to be constituted, and where should they be interviewed? Morley's (1980) approach to these questions in the *Nationwide* project has been criticized for not taking adequate steps to replicate a natural viewing environment. Groups were assembled according to demographic characteristics and were interviewed in a formal university setting. The research context, watching a programme in an unfamiliar environment with people you do not know, replicated the artificiality that was a problem in surveys and experiments (Lunt and Livingstone, 1996).

Some researchers have tried to overcome these problems by using 'interpretative communities', groups of people who naturally gather to watch films or television programmes (Machin and Carrithers, 1996). Katz and Liebes (1990) used this approach in their *Dallas* study, locating individuals who were willing both to take part and also to invite friends and families into their home for screenings and interviews. Such situations represent the closest thing that audience research can get to natural viewing situations. However, it is important to note that privacy and safety issues mean that this ideal might not always be attainable.

The main problem with this sort of ethnographic research is that it is very difficult to get people to commit the time and effort needed to study the domestic reception of media messages. Some of these obstacles can be overcome if respondents are paid, as in the case of Katz and Liebes (1990), Schlesinger et al. (1992) and Jhally and Lewis (1993). But what is to be done by the less well resourced? Hope is provided by the realization that interpretative communities do not only exist in the home or in the workplace. Ien Ang (1985) studied *Dallas* fans by placing an advertisement in a Dutch women's magazine, asking viewers of the show to write to her to explain why they were fans. Although this methodology has the weakness of excluding responses from those who are uncomfortable expressing themselves in written form, it has become increasingly relevant with the rise of interpretative communities whose interactions take place on Internet message boards. Bielbe and Harrington (1994) and Ruddock (1998a) have used message boards to pose questions to fans of certain television shows. The advantage of this approach is that it is cheap and potentially very fruitful. The disadvantage is that the researcher loses the power to introduce systematic variation in the sample, since he or she cannot control the sorts of people who respond.

The chief weakness of focus group interviews is that they furnish researchers with accounts of interpretations and behaviours that might differ from interviewees' non-observed media experiences. However much ethnographers prize naturally occurring data, interviewing means that the researcher's presence inevitably registers on what people will say. Consider again the students who were critical of *Top Gun*. Surprised as I was by these cool and distanced responses, at the same time they were elicited in an environment where the students were called upon to function as intellectuals, not fans. As a result, I have no way of knowing if the students would have felt the same way had we been informally chatting whilst they were voluntarily watching the film in their own homes. Ethnography requires people to reflect on their perceptions of themselves, the interviewer and the interview situation as well as the subject at hand. Those in the *Top Gun* study would have tailored their answers in accordance with their perception of what they were supposed to think as media students as much as their feelings towards the film. Barker and Brooks (1999) point to a similar tendency whereby participants in audience research projects screen what they say according to their view of 'intellectuals'. Ethnography requires participants to make personal feelings public. As a result, not surprisingly, there is a considerable tendency towards self-censorship. I would suggest that in the *Top Gun* case study, it was actually easier to make the critical reading than to admit to liking the film, since the latter response would reveal a world of desires that most of us would prefer to remain hidden. All of us would love to live in a world where we were sexually irresistible, but few of us would admit to such fantasies.

There are two ways around this problem. The first is to produce some sort of triangulation in research, whereby responses to interview questions are checked against other data. David Morley's *Family Television* (1989) pursues this strategy in comparing what people say about their media habits with direct observation of these habits in action. This technique belies claims made by many of the men in the study that they are only interested in factual programming.

The drawback of triangulation is again related to resources: is it possible for the researcher to interview and observe, and are participants willing to donate the time required? These problems have led others to develop strategies that allow us to get around self-censorship within conscious responses. Greg Philo's (1990) method of getting people to write stories based on a series of media images has been particularly fruitful. In the miners' strike research, participants were asked to write a news story based on a number of photographs showing miners, the police and a gun. Despite the fact that the groups had varying interpretations of the strike, reflecting their diverse experiences, startling similarities between them emerged. All of the stories produced by the groups emphasized the violence of the picket lines, despite the fact that many had felt that the news overdramatized physical conflict. All of the groups also placed the gun in the hands of the miners. Hence whatever their explicit statements about who was at fault in the strike, or how biased media coverage had been, the groups were relatively homogeneous in their recollections of the media coverage, often being able to recall actual reports almost verbatim.

The same technique and tendency was found in Philo and Henderson's (1999) research into the way in which young viewers watch *Pulp Fiction*. A group of 10- and 11-year-olds were given pictures of the scene in which two hitmen, played by Samuel L. Jackson and John Travolta, torment, torture and murder a group of young men. The researchers were amazed and more than a little horrified by the children's ability to recite not only the general narrative but also the precise dialogue of the scene.

David Gauntlett takes a more hi-tech approach in *Video Critical* (1996). Gauntlett worked with children in developing their own scripts and producing their own video documentaries on environmental issues. His goal was to assess the match between media representations of environmentalism and the childrens' perceptions of the most salient environmental issues. Gauntlett justified this on the grounds that, since the media are so powerful in determining political consciousness, a self-made video on environmental issues is as much a response to the media as is an answer to a focus-group question.

Analysing data

Focus-group interviews produce data in the form of verbatim transcripts. But how is the researcher to use this information? As Jhally and

Lewis (1993) point out, interviews furnish thousands of pages of information that does not speak for itself; it is the researcher's task to interpret the meaning of these data, and present their most salient features in coherent form. This presents a theoretical dilemma, speaking to distinctions between critical materialism and positivism. Ethnography is not entirely divorced from positivism: the painstaking detailing of every aspect of a culture can be connected with the desire to recreate that culture objectively for the reader (Hammersley, 1992). In focus-group research, interviews are transcribed word for word since the transcript is supposed to be a faithful record of what took place.

Can this claim be justified? Morley (1992) views transcripts as texts about texts; a transcript is a representation of an interview that is crucially different in form from the original. This is because communication in interviews can be both verbal and non-verbal. How is body language to be recorded? Even words can be difficult to transcribe; what about emphasis and tone of voice? Additionally, one could argue that focus group interviews suffer problems of artificiality since they do not account for the daily context in which they take place. Suppose a participant is especially belligerent during an interview. Is this because he or she is belligerent by nature or has he or she had a bad day? If the latter is true, does this mean that the interview would have been different if conducted a day earlier or later? Often we do not know. Critical materialism must take these issues into account. People's words constitute evidence about real political positions that ultimately have a social effect, but they do not speak for themselves; their significance has to be interpreted, and a part of this interpretation involves considering how the research process itself influences the information gathered.

The second problem in transcript analysis is how to establish criteria for identifying and interpreting significant comments. Interviews always generate more information than can be used, so the researcher's task is to report those sections of interviews that shed most light on the research question at hand. The danger of this task is that it threatens to undermine the commitment to allow audiences to set the agenda. Radway (1996) argues that the selective reporting of comments allows the researcher to use the audience as a sort of ventriloquist's dummy, reporting those comments that lend greatest support to the point the researcher wishes to make.

Given that it is impossible to reproduce transcripts in their entirety, as this would make projects unreadable, the best way around this problem is to be as explicit as possible about identifying criteria for sorting the more significant comments from those that are less relevant. Within research on the reception of meaning, this can involve assessing the degree of fit between the languages of text and audience. This is relatively straightforward in Greg Philo's work, which centres on the ability of audiences to regurgitate the language of news and film. Often the task is less straightforward. The *Nationwide* study is more explicit about how similarities between official and public languages are indicative of ideological effects. Beginning from a close analysis of the text, Morley (1980) used transcripts to look for places where audiences seem to inhabit frames of reference established by the text, and places where they departed from the view of reality offered by *Nationwide*.

I used this approach in a study of the reception of news of the US invasion of Haiti in 1994 (Ruddock, 1998b, c). Showing participants an edition of ABC news' *Nightline* programme, which featured on the scene reporting of the conflict together with a debate between opposing members of Congress on the pros and cons of the invasion, I asked them about their perceptions of both the conflict and also the programme's adequacy in explaining the situation to them. *Nightline*'s persuasive power was assessed by comparing critical comments with those where the audience accepted its interpretations of events. But I also learned that it can be as important to consider what remains unsaid. At the time of the invasion, the debate on whether or not America should intervene surrounded the issue of how quickly the situation could be resolved, and how deserving Haiti was of such help. Arguments for and against the invasion were ideologically united by the belief that American foreign policy is driven by human rights concerns. Yet some believe that US/ Haitian relations have been consistently driven by economic self-interest (Farmer, 1994). Regardless of which of these arguments holds most water, what can be said is that the latter was absent from both *Nightline* and my respondents' comments. I took this as evidence of *Nightline*'s power to determine the limits of the viewers' debate on Haiti, even if they were very critical of many aspects of its coverage.

One way of making transcripts more manageable is to construct questions that impose an interpretative agenda. Katz and Liebes (1990) were able to compare the way in which different ethnic groups interpreted *Dallas* by asking all of them to retell the story of the episodes viewed – in this way, the transcripts were all comparable in terms of the way in which participants reconstructed the narrative. Some researchers employ methods used in mass-communication research as a way of establishing patterns in transcripts. Schlesinger et al. (1992), for example, used Likert scales. The women in their study, in addition to being interviewed, were also asked to assess the programmes they saw on a scale of one to five in terms of how disturbing and violent they were. This information was used as evidence of general orientations to the programmes as a means of contextualizing what the women said about them. Yet researchers must also try to account for responses falling outside their initial frames of reference and interest. Barker and Brooks (1999) suggest that the best way to do this is to scour transcripts for recurrent phrases and themes that might indicate common perceptions that occur naturally.

Analysing transcripts inevitably lacks the precision of methods such as survey research. Computer packages are available that perform functions such as identifying recurrent words and phrases. Such aids may be of little use, however, since ethnography is interested in significance as much as recurrence. Also, the same word or phrase might mean different things in different contexts, something which a computer may not be able to account for. The only real way forward is to be as explicit as possible about criteria for evaluating transcripts, and as honest as possible in reporting data which reflect the position of respondents rather than the researcher.

Encoding/decoding research: findings and conclusions

David Morley (1993) sees the history of audience research as oscillating between despair over the media's power to dominate hapless and helpless audiences and an euphoric celebration of the very same audiences' power to evade textual oppression. While some of the work to be discussed in Chapter 6 can be accused of utopianism, the projects considered here occupy a midpoint on Morley's pendulum. Despite Curran's (1990) complaint that ethnographic audience studies have achieved nothing more than the resurrection of uses and gratifications theory, research inspired by the encoding/decoding model stays close to the Marxist idea that human agency – the power to shape one's own personality and destiny – is subject to structural constraints. Transplanted into audience research, while the crude determinism of the direct effects model is rejected, at the same time audiences are not free to make what they will of media content.

Encoding/decoding and resistive reading research is generally credited with empowering the audience. Certainly this is an important feature of this work, produced by its determination to confront mass communications and its use of ethnographic methods that are 'on the side' of the people being studied. Cultural studies was very concerned about media power, but two features of this concern differentiated it from the direct effects tradition. First, the nature of both media texts and media influence was far more complicated than had previously been thought. Secondly, viewing audiences as vast agglomerations of dopes fostered anti-democratic elitism among academics. So, in a very strange way, deep concern about the media's political power, where this power influenced much more than what soap powder people bought or who they voted for, had to work its way through a view of the relationship between audiences and media wherein the former played an active role.

This was the significance of studies such as Ien Ang's *Watching Dallas* (1985), Dorothy Hobson's study of the British soap *Crossroads* (1982), David Morley's *The Nationwide Audience* (1980), Katz and Liebes's *The Export of Meaning* (1990) and Janice Radway's *Reading the Romance* (1983). These works share the common theme of confronting the relationship between the sorts of texts deemed by direct effects to have the most insidious influences on the sorts of audiences most vulnerable to manipulation. On the ethnographic evidence gathered, it appeared that women were not encouraged to accept patriarchy passively (Ang and Radway), international audiences did not uncritically slice into 'American pie' (Ang, Katz and Liebes), and the working classes were not sucked into a mainstream of upper middle-class values (Morley). In general, audiences were often highly critical of media texts, and were not afraid of complaining when their expectations were violated (Hobson).

All of these findings were based upon the general discovery of media literacy. Media content was not simply there for all to see, but could only be appreciated through an understanding of textual form. Radway's (1983) study of women who were fans of romance novels, for example, showed that their ability to differentiate bad from good stories was based on an intricate knowledge of the format of these novels. This literacy is shaped by the background of the reader as much as it is by the story's textual form. Katz and Liebes's *Dallas* study (1990) showed how different cultural backgrounds produced different ways of relating to and retelling stories: where US audiences tended to view narrative as being driven by individual action, Soviet *émigrés* saw *Dallas* through various themes on life in America, a fact explained by their training in criticizing capitalism.

The 'validation of popular culture' (Schudson, 1987) brought with it a re-evaluation of fictional fantasy. Earlier paradigms had associated fantasy with escapism. Whether this escapism was seen as a juvenile refusal to deal with everyday life, or a mature decision to take a break from reality to rest and recuperate, fictional fantasies were seen as entirely divorced from the real. Ethnographic studies of textual reception went beyond the fact/fiction divide by showing relations between fantasy and social context. In her *Dallas* study, Ang extends the notion of realism by developing the idea of emotional realism. This refers to the way in which audiences can identify with fictional characters with whom they would appear to have nothing in common. While Dutch women shared little materially with fictional American oil millionaires, they did know what it was like to experience the sorts of interpersonal conflicts that are the stuff of soap operas, and it was these moments that opened the possibility of identification between viewers and characters. Identification, defined as a recognition of a fictional character as representative of ourselves as we are or as we would like to be, or as representative of a type of person who we encounter in our own lives (Ang, 1985), is a crucial aspect of describing fiction's real-world impact. Radway's romance readers' voracious consumption cannot be dismissed as mere escapism, since it becomes clear that the women's criteria for judging what makes a good male protagonist is based on actual definitions of what makes a good partner. Since the real men in their lives often fail to live up to this criteria, it becomes clear that talking about fictional characters is a means of talking about actual experience. Buckingham (1993a), Philo and Henderson (1999) and Walkerdine (1993) reach similar conclusions in their studies of child audiences, in which fictional characters are used as a means of policing ideas about gender and appropriate modes of behaviour. Press and Cole (1994) and Celeste Condit (1989) extend identification into macro-political issues, showing how dramatic depictions of the abortion issue allow audiences to negotiate their position on the debate.

It is at this point that Curran's (1990) criticism that encoding/decoding does little more than reinforce the liberal-pluralist assumptions of uses and gratifications theory holds most weight. The mass media simply cannot ride roughshod over the audience, since reception is a creative process where viewers bring their own experiences to bear. Moreover, theories of identification suggest that the media play a therapeutic role, exorcizing the demons of bad relationships. The problem with this conclusion is that the dismissal of direct effects was intended to be the base camp rather than the summit of critical audience research. So while Morris (1996) might complain of endless toasts to audience autonomy, it remains the case that a significant strand of research has followed a less utopian path.

As early as 1987, Anne Gray had warned that audiences who exert no influence over the production of media texts can never be autonomous; their 'activity' involves making the best of a bad deal. At the furthest end of the resistive scale, we could argue that the homeless men who Fiske (1993) watched re-writing *Die Hard* are still powerless in the sense that they live in a world where their stories will rarely be told.

This speaks to the general point that audiences would not need to create imaginative links with ostensibly different people and places if media dramas dealt more often with ordinary settings.

Based on this view, a tradition has remained at least within British media studies that retains an interest in structural limitations placed on audience behaviour, leading to important forms of media power. The Glasgow Media Group presents the most coherent part of this trend. Greg Philo and his colleagues have pointed to the media's colonization of popular consciousness, determining not only the frameworks of public debate but also the language used within it. Corner et al. (1990) show how varying public reactions to documentaries on the nuclear power industry are united in an uncritical acceptance of the contestable journalistic commitment to objectivity. Schlesinger et al.'s (1992) work on women viewing violence shows again how varying reactions are united beneath common trends, most notably the fear that media dramas generate about venturing into public places without male accompaniment.

Jhally and Lewis (1993) provide one of the most disturbing interpretations in their analysis of white audiences of *The Cosby Show*. The authors outline how institutional pressures forced Bill Cosby to understate the extent of contemporary racism in America. Prejudice was only discussed in the show as an historical peculiarity, something which had affected Cliff Huxtable's parents, but which never touched himself or his children. For many of the white viewers studied, this encouraged the belief that racism was a thing of the past, simultaneously eradicating the need for affirmative action, or any measures designed to aid impoverished racial minorities. *The Cosby Show* reassured white audiences that everything was all right, encouraging attitudes that amounted to what Jhally and Lewis called an 'enlightened racism'.

So what can we say about encoding/decoding/resistive reading work in terms of its relationship to earlier research paradigms? Despite some obvious similarities, it would be wrong to conclude that this work parallels earlier ideas about opinion leaders and limited effects. Negotiated, oppositional and resistive readings are different from selective perception in the sense that viewing is constitutive rather than reflective of ideological positioning. For the girls and their mother in Walkerdine's (1993) study, *Annie* did not simply allow them to express thoughts on the ideal family that already existed in their heads, but it provided them with a means and a setting which allowed them to express these thoughts in cogent form. Media reception is not just about reinforcement, but facilitation where audiences express things that might otherwise remain silent. Having said this, it is not true to think that people can make what they will of media texts. Condit (1989) describes how when faced with an episode of *Cagney and Lacey* that is clearly pro-choice in the abortion debate, a pro-life activist can do nothing other than reject it; he or she cannot bend the text to fit his or her own views.

At the same time, there is significant conceptual resonance between encoding/decoding/resistive reading research and some of the post-positivist mass-communications paradigms. Schlesinger et al.'s work replicates Gerbner's 'scary world' hypothesis, showing how televised dramas provoke fears about the outside world. Agenda-setting research is also complemented by the Glasgow Media Group's and Corner and Fenton's work on the role news plays in determining the ideological frames used by audiences to discuss key debates. Methodologically speaking, ethnographic researchers have also faced problems shared by quantitative researchers. So, while it radically complicated the view of what communication is, and produced a kaleidoscopic view of the sorts of effects it could have, this strand of cultural studies audience research is not irrevocably set adrift from mass-communication research.

Exercises

1   This exercise is developed from the work of Greg Philo (1990). Conduct a group analysis of a piece of televised news. Select a news item focusing on a controversial issue (a strike, a riot, a court hearing, a political scandal, a war). Watch the item with the sound turned off, and write a script to accompany the visuals. This script should describe the situation you see, identifying protagonists, 'villains' and 'victims'. Compare and contrast your stories with other members of the group. What are the similarities and differences you see? What assumptions have you made in writing these scripts? Where do these assumptions come from? Personal experience? The media? Now watch the clip with the sound on. How close are your scripts to the actual soundtrack? What explains the fit, or lack of fit, between the two accounts?

2   Select any media text which you find interesting from an ideological point of view. Discuss why you find the text interesting, what is it trying to say, and how does it function to position the audience? Next, think about a series of open-ended questions that you could use to assess the impact of this

text on another viewer. Show the text to a classmate or friend, and put your questions to him or her. How closely do your readings match? Does your viewer reflect the effects which you expected? Does he or she come up with any responses which you didn't expect? What might explain these differences?

3 Generate a research topic based on a 'breaching' episode that reveals implicit rules of engagement between institutions, media and audiences.

6 Audiences, Media and Consumption

Cultural studies has recently witnessed a growing interest in consumption, defined as the meaningful appropriation of goods and services. This interest is partly a reaction to the limitations of encoding/decoding/resistive reading research. Abercrombie and Longhurst's (1998) critique of the model, which they rename the 'incorporation/resistance paradigm' (IRP), accuses Hall, Morley and Co. of falling into the same trap that had ensnared effects researchers. Both 'incorporation/resistance' and effects models made the mistake of taking on unresearchable questions. The problem of hegemony could no more be addressed with focus groups than effects could be measured in experiments; in both cases, grand claims about society were made on the basis of unreliable snapshots. Abercrombie and Longhurst (1998) claim that the IRP has ignored this problem, becoming the sort of self-contained, self-deluding paradigm that Kuhn (1962) sees as impeding progress. The IRP's hegemonic influence within media studies prevented, in their view, the exploration of important questions falling beyond its jurisdiction; where Raymond Williams had advocated an analysis of culture as a 'whole way of life', the IRP offered a radically truncated view of what counts as cultural activity.

Studies of consumption, as they relate to texts, technologies and connections between media and other commodities, address these issues by incorporating audience research into everyday life. But this creates another set of problems for media researchers: how can you make a whole way of life researchable, and how is media and audience research to be distinguished from other disciplines that investigate human activity?

These questions can be answered by understanding methodological and conceptual challenges offered by debates on the adequacy of culture studies' appropriation of ethnography and the emergence of postmodern theory. While these developments have been read as illustrating the impossibility of knowing audiences (Allor, 1988), the reading I will offer takes a more positive position. Michel Foucault's thinking on discourse, the postmodern concept that inherits the crown worn by ideology in modernist paradigms, has suggested important new directions for audience research and has also made a valuable contribution to the question of how one can research broad questions of power. This potential has been realized in feminist research and in studies of fan culture and the domestic appropriation of media technologies.

Challenges to the IRP: modernist/methodological

Some of the challenges to IRP work come as a reaction to its perceived Marxist tendencies and methodological limitations. In Abercrombie and Longhurst's (1998) view, the influence of Marx, Althusser and Gramsci limited views of what counts in media reception. The complexities of viewing, reading and listening were reduced to the role that these processes play in reinforcing or opposing dominant ideologies. Yet even the paradigm's practitioners felt that there was more to reception: in the 'critical postscript' to the *Nationwide* project, Morley (1992) acknowledges the crudity of sorting audience responses into the preferred, negotiated and oppositional categories. The problems that Morley identifies in his work are indicative of weaknesses with the IRP in general. He pre-empts Abercrombie and Longhurst in seeing that, in some ways, encoding/decoding was guilty of resurrecting a transmission model of effects, albeit in a more theoretically elegant guise. Asking whether the audience accepts or rejects a text's version of reality is fine when dealing with overtly political programming such as news or current affairs, but these criteria might be less relevant in other contexts. Additionally, decoding is a multi-faceted phenomenon, including perceptions of relevance, attentiveness and comprehension that all happen before audiences form ideological responses. Morley was struck in his *Nationwide* study by the fact that while some of the groups engaged with and took a position on the show's implicit class politics, others found its themes simply irrelevant. This sort of 'opposition' was very different from that shown by groups who felt that the programme foisted middle-class values on its viewers. Where the latter groups objected to what they understood as the show's message, the former did not care. Morley's argument has a methodological component. The mistake he had made in the *Nationwide* project was similar to the sorts of error Bourdieu found with survey research. The encoding/decoding model had produced questions that forced Morley's ideological problematic upon the audience, regardless of how relevant it was to their own subjective experience of the show. This pushed him closer to methods that were better suited to the development of grounded theory.

For Buckingham (1999), Morley's 'critical postscript' signifies the death knell of encoding/decoding research. While this conclusion radically undervalues the contribution of the IRP, it is true that cultural studies had written theoretical cheques that encoding/decoding's methodologies could not cash. Richard Johnson (1987) argued that an effective critique of ideology needed to show connections between media meanings and everyday social practices. Focus-group methods that rely on self-reporting, or are unable to comment on how responses to questions relate to thoughts and actions beyond the interview, are unable to address Johnson's link.

Abercrombie and Longhurst's (1998) comments about the inability of ethnographic methods, as practised in the IRP, to address hegemony also speak to issues of generalizability. While small-scale studies could initially be justified as efforts to falsify notions of direct effects, by the late 1980s this task had been achieved. Reception was evidently a complex procedure, to the extent that, as Abercrombie and Longhurst point out, all audiences are 'active' to a degree. The task that lay before cultural studies was no longer, therefore, to detail this activity, but to reflect upon what it meant for the way that people led their lives.

Challenges to the IRP: postmodernist/conceptual

Methodological problems encountered by the IRP were exacerbated in the late 1980s and early 1990s by the growing influence of postmodernism. Concerns over the ability of ethnographic and other methods to deliver on key research questions were inflamed by a social theory questioning the very nature of truth and our ability to know it. Debates over method are premised on a materialist orientation bearing positivist traces. Grossberg (1996a) argues that political audience researchers must believe in the existence of a reality that is more than the product of the way we understand our social world; there is an objective element to subjective social experience. Hence, while reality will always exceed the limits of the means we use to describe it, some methods offer better explanations than others.

The most radical fringes of postmodernism deny even this possibility: reality is reduced to a series of interchangeable language-games, none of which offers access to an external truth. This offers nothing of use to audience research. However, postmodernism is a contradictory body of theory. Some see similarities between postmodernism and modernism (Smart, 1993). Modernism is aligned with positivism in the sense that it believed that the natural and social worlds could be tamed via the application of rational thought. Yet, as we saw in Descartes' thinking, true knowledge could only be distinguished from prejudice by viewing reality with suspicion. It is this same radical doubt that is at the core of postmodernism. The question is – where does this doubt stop? For Descartes, it terminated at an unquestionable belief in his own rational powers and the existence of God (Flew, 1971). For radical post-modernism, the doubt does not stop. Barry Smart (1993) quotes Fredric Jameson in concluding that postmodernism differs from modernity in its insistence on 'depthlessness' or the rejection of meaning. However this idea works its way through social theory, it does not apply to audience research. The problematization of meaning and narrative have provided important insights, but these are still married to a cumulative project whose goal is to develop a better understanding of audiences; a project which is doomed to failure by radical postmodernist standards.

Why then do important figures in audience research such as Angela McRobbie (1994), Joke Hermes (1995) and Ien Ang (1996) cite post-modernism as an influence? Perhaps an answer can be provided by thinking about the work of French philosopher Michel Foucault. Foucault is often associated with postmodernist thinking, and with the problematization of many of the ideas on which the IRP was based. Yet, at the same time, Hall (1986b) sees similarities between Foucault's work and some of the neo-Marxist theories of ideology which he ostensibly rejects. As radical as Foucault's ideas might seem, his thoughts on the nature and analysis of power can be read not as a postmodern complaint of the futility of research, but rather as a call for greater conceptual clarity and sophistication, and more thorough methodologies.

Far from dismissing reality as a language-game, Foucault was com-mitted to a materialist study of power. Power, in his view, was principally produced by the categorization and organization of the body. 'Truth and Power' (Foucault, 1984) provides a concise summary of Foucault's thoughts on the problems of ideological analysis, and his own view of the nature of cultural power, as realized though the concept of discourse. Foucault concludes, somewhat unfairly, that ideological analyses are premised on the juxtaposition between true and false. Related to media studies, audiences inhabiting preferred readings are in the grip of ideologies that misrepresent reality. Researchers, then, are special people having access to the truth. Ideological analysis had, of course, long since abandoned this argument. Hall's (1990) review of Thatcherism, for example, acknowledged that Conservative ideology had become real in the sense that it served as a powerful guide for social policy. Gramscian definitions of ideology are consistent with Foucault's idea of discourse, in the sense that both describe ways of both defining and acting towards social situations. Where ideology and discourse part company, however, is in the cognitive bias of the former. Ideological analyses see power as running from mind to body. Where subjective meaning can be conditioned, so compliant behaviour will follow. Foucault's discourse reversed this polarity. In *The History of Sexuality, Part I* (1976), Foucault argues that power has been based on the analysis and organization of the body since the seventeenth century. He explores this idea in *Discipline and Punish* (1979). As an example, he describes how the French army of the eighteenth century transformed peasant recruits into soldiers first and foremost by engineering their physiques, based on the belief that a soldierly bearing would foster a military mentality. His work on panopticanism, as a means for changing convicts into law-abiding citizens, also stressed the physical elements of producing compliance. The panopticon was a design for a prison in the shape of a wheel; at the hub was an observation tower from which radiated 'spokes' tipped by lit cells. Each cell contained one convict. The beauty of the design was that, since the cells were lit and the tower was not, prisoners were never aware of whether or not they were being watched; they would thus be forced to internalize prison discipline and correct behaviours, becoming their own jailers.

The panopticon can be seen as a model for the way in which power works in society in general. The panopticon individualizes the prisoner, opens him or her to constant examination and in doing so encourages the convict to internalize the values of the centre. Foucault's work surrounded the ways that branches of knowledge, particularly medicine and psychology, produced ideas that could be used to individualize people and classify them. These classifications created modes of self-surveillance that were far more effective in maintaining social order than punitive measures. If the outcome of these discourses appears similar to the products of ideology, the process of compliance production is quite different. If ideology is taken as false consciousness, then power is achieved through refusing to interrogate reality. Discursive power, however, is based on the investigation and classification of every aspect of existence. Foucault provides an example in his analysis of sexuality, which confronts the idea that the twentieth century witnessed a relaxation of repressive attitudes to sex typifying the Victorian era. To begin, the nineteenth century was not, in his view, a repressive era, but rather saw a rapid increase in discourses on sex and sexuality. Since population had become a central issue for the state, sexuality had to be actively policed. This policing came in the form of evolving analyses of sexual behaviour that were the basis of attempts to classify the normal and the abnormal, something that could only be done if people could be compelled to confess their deepest darkest desires, whether in the confessional box or on the psychiatrist's couch. All of these cases – the development of discourses around military training, health, sexuality and crime – were aimed at social control centred on the body and 'its disciplining, the optimization of its capabilities, the extortion of its forces, the parallel increase of its usefulness and its docility, its integration of efficient economic controls' (Foucault, 1976: 139). These discourses of the body were all the more powerful since, unlike false consciousness versions of reality, they could not be dismissed as illusory. Discourses were true and real in so far as they had tangible effects on the movements of bodies and the consequent organization of social structures. As a result the cultural critic's goal is not to perceive truth, but rather to pursue a more modest description of the way in which differing 'regimes of truth' shape society.

What legacy do these ideas bequeath audience research? Conceptually, the focus on the body raises a number of questions about the physical experience of media consumption ignored by the IRP. Foucault argued that discourses are powerful since their physicality delivers non-conscious results, aided by the production of physical pleasures. This was an idea that was largely missing from encoding/decoding research. Barker (1999b) complains that the paradigm has led audience research into a cul-de-sac by an over-emphasis on the notion of meaning. In research completed with Kate Brooks on the audiences for the film *Judge Dredd* (1999), he argues that narrative structure (and hence textual and ideological closure) is often irrelevant for action/adventure audiences. A huge part of the pleasure of going to see such films lies in what Grossberg (1992) calls the 'affective element' of reception centred on physical and emotional experiences. It would be possible to see Keanu Reeves's *Matrix* as an allegory for the new virtual age, based on Marx's theory of base and superstructure, but it is easier to experience it as a series of enjoyable special effects accompanied by a great soundtrack. Barker and Brooks (1999) argue that in films such as this the main job of the narrative is to stay out of the way; with the right aesthetic ingredients, all the storyline has to be is plausible. In focusing on the ideological elements of textual closure, the IRP is guilty of providing a very limited view of the audience's experience, since it ignored emotional and physical pleasures.

This has been read as a rejection of power as an object for audience research. However, it is also possible to read Foucault as suggesting that the analysis of cultural power must become more detailed, since it pervades every area of life. His argument also contains methodological lessons. The demands of ideological analysis are simply too great; how can anyone gather the resources to cut through 'a whole way of life'. Isn't it better to choose a containable case study, such as the development of psychiatry in the nineteenth century, so that you can say something meaningful based on concrete case studies? Far from rejecting research, Foucault called for a more rigorous empirical approach to power that was grounded in concrete social situations rather than theoretical abstractions.

For audience researchers, this involved going further into ethnographic research methods. Consider again Morley's *Nationwide* (1980) study, Katz and Liebes's (1990) study of *Dallas* and the work of the Glasgow Media Group. In focusing on overt political content, these studies address participants as citizens. Desires, thoughts and feelings belonging to what is normally thought of as the private realm are less conspicuous. Foucault's vision of discourse, however, suggests that this is where power begins. The emergence of discursive theories of power thus encouraged methodologies based upon greater immersion into the worlds of audiences that took on board notions of pleasure and affect in addition to meaning. Yet, despite Barker's misgivings, this research emerged in part from studies of textual meaning, particularly as they related to the worlds of fans and women readers and viewers.

Fan cultures

The analysis of fan culture is a significant moment since it signified a change of course in audience research. While still tied to questions of textual meaning, fan studies showed how the significance of this meaning spilled into other areas of life, and as such had to be coupled with non-textual pleasures.

Fans emerged as objects of study since they are conceptually representative of a number of popular and academic fears concerning media power. Jensen (1992) sees debates about fans as standing on the cusp of the mass-culture debate, which in turn speaks to differences between modernism and postmodernism. For modernism, knowledge is attained through the distanced, unemotional appreciation of beauty generally associated with the high arts. Passion and an uncontrolled emotional attachment are associated with an uncritical intellectual weakness. Since fans of popular culture often allow their favourite shows or performers to take over their lives, they are thus representative of the worst aspects of mass culture: its ability to produce political complacency by allowing people to withdraw into a fantasy world of imaginary friends. Fans, according to this critique, replace the social with the parasocial, wherein their social network consists of mediated personalities with whom they can have no real contact. It could be argued that this is a natural part of a world where mediated celebrities cannot be avoided. Take the British example of the marriage of England football star David Beckham and Spice Girl Victoria Adams. Marrying the worlds of sport and music, and characterized by a spectacular combination of goods looks, questionable fashion decisions, ostentatious spending and at times monumental displays of stupidity on stage, on the field of play and in interviews, the couple are a celebrity car wreck that cannot be ignored, not least because they monopolize media time and space that could be devoted to other things. While most of us manage to break free of such trivia from time to time to consider more weighty matters, fans spend all of their time pursuing such social relationships. What is worse, the people whom they pursue are often not even real. Fans are, in short, ultimate victims of realism as textual practice; people who are entirely convinced by media artifice.

Modernism thus pathologizes media pleasures (Jensen, 1992). From this perspective, fans might be looked upon as special cases providing warnings concerning the fate of those who become too enmeshed in popular culture. But from a postmodernist perspective, fan cultures provide a means to confront modernist prejudices. Heeding the advice that unresearchable, macro questions about cultural power should be avoided in favour of more containable descriptions of discourse, fan cultures also represent relatively self-contained and hence more researchable phenomena.

While Ien Ang's *Dallas* study (1985) featured the responses of people who were clearly fans in one sense, fan studies since this point have explored communities of people who take more active approaches to their media consumption. This is based on the idea articulated by Fiske (1992) that, in order to be pleasurable, texts must be 'producerly', that is serve as a basis for some form of creativity on the part of the audience. This creativity might come in the form of musing over possible interpretations of a text, but for Fiske it often takes on a more radical guise in creating new ways of life.

Fan culture is easily researchable since it is often based on the creation of communities. Henry Jenkins's work on science fiction and Star Trek fans has been particularly instructive in this regard (1992a, b). His choice of topic is surely not innocent, since science fiction fans in general, and *Star Trek* fans in particular, are the most pathologized of all pathological media dopes. Yet, in considering how such texts become real for their fans, Jenkins discovers a network of practices extending beyond parasociality. Fan cultures are sustained by a number of practices including the recording and circulation of video-tapes, the collection of souvenirs and the often voracious consumption of supporting material on the making of shows and films. Fan activity is therefore an intertextual affair featuring consumption of both textual materials and media technologies (Jenkins, 1992b). As well as consuming primary texts, fans also produce their own materials in the form of Internet discussion groups, newsletters and, in the case of *Star Trek*, their own literature and songs. These sorts of artefacts are vital for researchers with limited resources, since they represent ways of researching audiences and meanings without having to interview people. This has the additional attraction of offering naturally occurring data.

Where interviewing is desirable, fan activity also provides access to ready constituted groups. Both Jenkins (1992a, b) and Barker (1993) have used fan conventions to interview and observe or at least recruit participants for future research. As with newsletters and the like, conventions offer naturally occurring evidence of the pleasures offered by fandom. At a *Star Trek* convention, Jenkins observed what is known as a 'filking' session, where fans gather to sing songs they themselves have written about the show and their own experiences as sci-fi *aficionados*. This 'filking' episode encapsulates the differences between modernist/condemnatory and postmodernist/celebratory approaches to fan culture. From outside 'Trekkiedom', it is difficult not to smirk at the thought of adults singing songs they have written about their feelings for Kirk and Co. to like-minded individuals. The scene is reminiscent of the *Saturday Night Live* sketch, where William Shatner outrages *Star Trek* conventioneers with a keynote address advising them to 'get a life'. Both the joke and the modernist orientation are based on logic connecting fantasy with escapism and a refusal to deal with everyday life. Yet Jenkins argues that 'filking' demonstrates an acute awareness of and attempts to deal with genuine social problems. The participants are alienated in various ways, as members of sexual, ethnic and gender groups that suffer from degrees of social exclusion. But their actions confront this reality; the 'filking' session gives access to a community feeling that is denied in other areas of life. A similar dynamic is seen in the production of 'slash' novels. These are works written by 'Trekkies' that takes the show's commitment to explore new worlds into areas unimagined by Gene Roddenberry. The novels ponder what it would be like had Spock pursued a love relationship with Nurse Chapel or Captain Kirk. As a distinction between modernist and postmodernist views, the latter category is most interesting. Given that gay men were all but invisible in prime time drama until the 1980s, it is unlikely that a show from the 1960s would have openly courted sexual ambiguity. Speculation over Kirk and Spock's sexuality is doubly infantile given that they are not real people.

Abercrombie and Longhust (1998), however, argue that it is this modernist argument that is shallow and naïve. For them, fan activity is a discourse, a way of thinking and behaving that has more to do with the organization of the self than it does the aesthetic appreciation that is central to modernist reception. Similarly, the fan-based production and distribution of texts inspired but not confined by *Star Trek* are true and real in the sense that they provide fans with rare opportunities to express desires or participate in some form of pleasurable social inter-action.

Studies of fans have helped to overcome some of the limitations seen in encoding/decoding research. Discourse rather than ideology is more appropriate to this field since fandom is as much a matter of social action as it is textual reception. Although meaning is still a central concept, the meanings investigated here involve those invested by fans themselves in the range of activities surrounding texts that are more appropriated than received. Meaning in this sense concerns engagement with way of life, not struggling with an ideological problematic that is not of your own making. The movement towards discourse has methodological implications. Foucault sees discourse as rejecting questions of true and false in favour of asking what the material results of discursive practices are. This drives audience researchers further towards methods that respect the audience's subjective experience, since the task is to understand rather than evaluate what people do.

The question is how far are fans analogous to general audiences. Those who have written about fans differ as to how far this is their goal, but Fiske (1992) bases much of his thinking on the resistive oppor-tunities offered by mass culture on the idea that fans differ from every-day audiences in degree rather than kind. Abercrombie and Longhurst (1998) argue that this overestimates the extent of normal audience activity; while all audiences are active in terms of their ability to play around with and form various responses to texts, few go the spectacular lengths observed by Jenkins (1992b). As a result, this sort of research only travels so far into the world of everyday audiences.

Feminist audience research

While feminism inspired the analysis of gender as an important part of IRP studies, it has also been at the forefront of appropriating postmodernism into materialist analyses of audiences, and developing methodologies which allow commentary on the diffuse aspects of discourse. Since the 1980s, feminist researchers have been aware that textual meaning can only be explained within the total context of reception. The first demonstration of this idea came in Janice Radway's *Reading the Romance* (1983). Although based on the role that romance novels play in the perpetuation or subversion of patriarchy, Radway discovered that, for the women she interviewed, the act of reading and the context in which it was realized was as important as the stories they would find in the novels. Irrespective of quality, picking up a novel and putting it in front of their face was a way for these women to signify to husbands, partners and children that they were unavailable for domestic service. The physical act of reading was as significant as the interpretation of the narrative.

Joke Hermes (1995) reaches a similar conclusion in *Reading Women's Magazines*. Although her work is based on focus-group interviews rather than participant observation, Hermes manages to address context by asking questions about where, when and why women read magazines. Her conclusions about the role such magazines play in women's lives show how discourse combines postmodernism with a concern for inequalities of power. Hermes's work integrates Radway's insistence on defending female audiences that are often the butt of modernist complaints about mass culture with concerns about the over-emphasis of the power of resistive audiences (Seaman, 1992; Morris, 1996). Hermes sets out to 'respect' rather than 'defend' her female respondents. She recognizes that, while women's magazines cannot be dismissed as mere ideological attempts to confine women, at the same time they are implicated within patriarchal discourses. Above and beyond the fantasies and solutions these magazines might offer for real-life predicaments, women's magazines are popular because of their superficiality; as objects that can be picked up and put down, they insert themselves perfectly into lifestyles where moments of leisure are constantly interrupted. This is especially useful for those who work in the home, who are never truly off duty. Since these people are principally women, whatever the opportunities for escapist and resistive fantasies they offer, women's magazines are nevertheless inserted into gender discourses. Their relevance can only be understood by appreciating how magazines are appropriated as commodities before they are read as texts.

Modleski (1996) and Seiter (1999) explore this idea in their work on women and television. As with Radway and Hermes, the question in these works centres less on the meaning of texts and more on the significance of genre preferences and modes of viewing. Modleski and Seiter both argue that domestic media reception must be understood as a bridge between the worlds of duty and leisure for women who work in the home. Modleski argues that women prefer quiz shows and soap operas because they offer an escape from the social exclusion homeworkers suffer. Viewing in this sense becomes a social occasion where women can interact with regular casts of characters whom they can recognize, if not necessarily identify with. Viewing, like reading romance novels, provides a break from the domestic economy. Seiter (1999) elaborates this in her work with Christian fundamentalist women in America. Despite the fact that their faith denounces television as morally corrupt, the women whom Seiter interviewed form an ambiguous relationship with the medium: while they accept their church's teachings, at the same time television serves an invaluable babysitting role that helps them as wives and mothers.

Electronic media and the texts they deliver thus serve an ambiguous role. Ideological 'resistance' can be seen in Modleski's (1996) work, where women recognize their exclusion from the public sphere. But at the same time, as with magazines, listening to the radio and watching television are discursive acts that insert women into a patriarchal domestic economy, making it easier for them to perform their roles by providing regulated breaks. Feminism was responsible, then, for demonstrating how the concept of discourse could be researched. The practicalities of power could only be understood by studying the private sphere where it was ultimately reproduced. As a result, feminism has also been at the forefront of debates on the practicalities and ethics of studying private worlds.

It is virtually impossible to separate conceptual and methodological issues in this area. Seiter et al. (1996) are troubled by ambiguities in the ethnographic relationship between researcher and researched. While critical audience studies have tried to be on the side of the researched, ethnography's roots in nineteenth-century colonial practices suggest a more exploitative relationship. Nineteenth-century ethnographers are accused of complicity in a Foucauldian project to exoticize the colonized: the practices of indigenous peoples were painstakingly described not to appreciate them on their own terms, but to demonstrate how far they stood from civilized European sensibilities, hence validating colonial rule. Seiter et al.'s (1996) concern is that media ethnography could serve a similar function, producing an audience of infantile 'others' in need of policing.

This could only be overcome by developing a wider range of methods to create greater immersion in the worlds of audiences. This often requires using techniques that collapse boundaries established by objective social science. Seiter (1999) and Gillespie (1995) have used relationships formed outside the research context to engender trust and develop a thick appreciation of the research setting. Gillespie used her role as a teacher in Southall to access local Hindi families, on the basis that having taught in the area for a year, she had a good sense of what the culture was like. Similarly, Seiter used contacts made in a parents' support group for her work on women television viewers. Seiter was a member of the group for two years before she approached them about participating in the project.

This is a controversial approach to sampling and research. Seiter justifies it by pointing out that most ethnographic researchers spend too little time with their subjects to develop any clear sense of what their lives are like. The ethical problem is, however, that research data come in both formal and informal guises – Seiter uses casual conversations as well as more recognizable methods such as diaries and interviews. There is some question then, as to when the respondents are 'on' and when they are 'off'. Having said this, it could be argued that this sort of extensive personal contact is necessary to build the kind of trust needed in studies of the private realm.

But even if Seiter's methods and ethics can be accepted, this raises another problem. What happens if the quality of your research depends more on your social network than your research skills? What if a researcher has no natural connection with the people he or she wishes to study? Radway (1983) and Gray (1992) overcame this with 'snowball' sampling methods which identified pre-existing audience communities. Radway attracted respondents for her romance study by contacting the owner of a bookstore that specialized in these novels, who put her in contact with regular customers. Gray did the same thing with a video club. The advantage of these techniques is that they provide access to the same sorts of naturally occurring communities found by Jenkins, but in a more everyday context.

Television and the family

Feminism has also been instrumental in replacing the concept of identity with the process of identification in audience research. Grossberg (1996b) argues that identity is erroneously seen as referring to the existence of a stable self which in turn reflects an objective position within material culture. It was precisely this model of identity that underwrote the limited effects and selective perception models. Identification, however, refers to the way in which people take on contingent masks in relation to the specificities of shifting cultural forces. This idea grows from the postmodernist insight that identity cannot be stable since the human subject is the point of intersection between often contradictory collective associations. Black feminist writers have explored this by speaking of the way in which the experience of being a woman is inflected by issues of class and ethnicity (Wallace, 1990). This being the case, identity is not an internal quality, something to be carried around like a passport, an objective statement of who you are no matter who is asking. Instead, it is a form of interaction between people. This is not to say that identity is free of material constraint, but it is to say that the significance and the meanings we attach to gender, class, sexual and racial identities are somewhat fluid.

Identity is less about the self than it is about the relation between the self and other people. It is therefore tied to communication (Grossberg, 1996b). This produced new methodological directions for audience research. Seiter (1999) argues that female audiences are best interviewed and studied apart from partners and children. For women with husbands, interviewing them with their men present might influence what the women say. Men also have a tendency to dominate conversations in group situations. There is nothing wrong with this position but, as Barker (1999b) argues, the analysis of gender involves men as well as women. If identities are context specific, and depend on the presence of the other, it follows that gendered media reception must study relations between men, women and children.

As a result, the family has emerged as an important site of media research. In addition to accessing postmodernist processes of identification, the family is also the locus of discursive forms of power permeating both the public and the private spheres. As the major unit of production and consumption in the industrial and consumer revolutions, the family has been the place where social change has been most acutely felt and fought over:

> [The home] . . . is gendered and highly differentiated according to geography, class position and culture. It can be a place of conflict and despair as well as peace and security. It can be a haven or a prison. And our interiors are not just physical spaces. They are social, economic and political spaces. And they are technological spaces. And in all these dimensions our domesticity is unsettled and vulnerable, extending . . . into a world of change, of movement. (Silverstone, 1994: 25)

For the interests of media studies, the family also promised a means of resolving the artificiality of focus-group interviews by providing examples of reception in its natural environment. David Morley took the first step in this direction in his *Family Television* (1989). Centring on interviews with 29 families in London, Morley shifted the emphasis from ideological textual meaning to the issue of how gender determined genre preferences and ways of using household media. Morley concluded that habits of media were just as, if not more, interesting than ideological responses to specific texts. Questions of how families decide what to watch, how decisions are made on the use of the VCR, who possesses the remote control, and *how* different family members watch television are significant in their demonstration of how discourses of gendered power run through the home. In homes where the male partner was the primary wage-earner, Morley witnessed unsurprising patterns: the male made the majority of viewing and recording decisions. Women were more likely than men to watch in a distracted manner while performing other household tasks. Although texts were mentioned in terms of genre, with men expressing a preference for factual programmes rather than more 'feminized' fictional fare, the main conclusion was that the act of watching was the primary mechanism through which the medium entered domestic gender politics. But media usage was presented as being constitutive rather than reflective of pre-existing patterns of gendered power. This was supported by the fact that a degree of role reversal was seen in houses where women were the primary earners. In this sense, media use was one of the areas in which gender power was achieved, not simply expressed.

The new emphasis on technologies rather than texts moved audience research closer to studies of consumption. Family-based consumption of media technologies, as the above quotation from Silverstone (1994) indicates, was one of the major places where individuals collided with macro-economic and political trends. Bausinger (1984) argues that it is wrong to see the development of media technologies as a story of how new inventions force themselves upon a helpless society. To be sure, technological and economic factors have great power to determine what media we use and how we use it. The fact that nearly all computer users rely on Microsoft Windows is largely a result of Bill Gates's monopoly power. But the concrete applications of media technologies are also influenced by the idiosyncrasies of the family.

Silverstone et al. (1994) pursue Bausinger's thinking in outlining their thesis of the 'moral economy'. Before we can concern ourselves with the ideological implications of the texts that media technologies deliver into the home, we must appreciate that the decision to bring the technology itself into the domestic sphere is soaked in economic, moral and political factors. The decision is in part determined by external economic factors: in Britain, Sky and OnDigital's decision to promote their services by providing free decoding technologies makes digital television accessible to a wide audience. But the decision to bring a technology into the home is also influenced by moral and aesthetic values. Even as the cost of PCs continues to tumble, still some parents might resist the urge due to concerns over Internet safety. The same worry creates problems over where to place a PC in the house. Parents who wish to supervise their children's use of the PC might wish to place the machine in a common area of the house, but this in turn creates problems of overcrowding and clashes between people engaged in different activities.

Communication technologies are implicated in power struggles on two fronts: between the household and the outside world, and within the household in differences between family members. General economic and political trends do create forces which households are ultimately powerless to resist. The fact that, in Britain, analog television transmissions are due to end in 2006 means that viewers will have to succumb to the digital revolution. Yet Silverstone et al. (1994) contend that households exercise some agency in determining the nature of the impact of domestic technologies. This is because these machines pass through four stages in their journey from sale room to the home, each of which offers the family an opportunity to struggle over and impose a moral agenda. First, 'appropriation' refers to the various factors lying behind the decision to buy a technology. Secondly, 'objectification' is the way in which the object is positioned in the home. Next, 'incorporation' refers to the actual use to which the technology is put, which may diverge from its intended or potential uses. Finally, 'conversion' is the process through which a technology can be used as a communicative device to convey to others an image of status. The point of this classification system is to show how technologies play a role in shaping internal family relations and also mediating between the private and the public.

Tim O'Sullivan (1991) applied these ideas to his study of television's introduction into British homes in the 1950s and 1960s. O'Sullivan capitalizes on the fact that we live in an age where we still have access to the people who were the first to experience the medium. Similar to techniques used by the Glasgow Media Group, O'Sullivan tapped the significance of television by asking people simply to tell the story of how it was that they or their families came to the decision to buy the first set, and how it was positioned in the home. His interviews provided evidence of connections between the public and the private, as clear cultural patterns emerged from the stories of private purchasing decisions. Buying a television in the 1950s and early 1960s was connected to general discourses of gender, class and consumption. At this time, television was seen as a luxury, so that buying one signified a surrender to the booming consumer culture. When the decision was made, it tended to be made by men by virtue of their status as breadwinner and technical expert.

Issues of social class were also important. As with future technologies, a television was something of a status symbol. Ironically, given modern-day concerns, television was seen as an educational tool in its early days. Class concerns were also evident in deciding where to place the set. British homes of the time often featured a living room and a parlour. Where the living room was a place for relaxation, the parlour was a more formal room where families might entertain guests. Conflicts sometimes emerged when the television was placed in the parlour as it disrupted other sorts of social interaction. The television was also blamed for evaporating the distinction between living room and parlour, as the casualization of viewing practices brought a concomitant relaxation of parlour rules. This trend was accelerated by the introduction of commercial television from 1956 onwards which tended to feature less formal programming than that offered by the BBC. Television was instrumental in altering the temporal as well as the spatial dimensions of family life. As with radio before it (Moores, 1988), television schedules were instrumental in demarcating domestic time – signifying tea-time, bedtime for children and so on.

James Lull (1990) and Anne Gray (1992) pursue these issues within contemporary settings and technologies. Lull's work is in many ways complementary to Morley's *Family Television* (1989). But, methodologically, the fact that Lull is influenced by North American mass-communication research and also more traditional ethnographic methods produces different approaches. Lull's project is bigger in scale. One of his studies uses 97 families made up of 400 people drawn on a quota sampling basis. When selected, researchers spent three days with the family. Two days were spent simply watching the family watch television and pursuing other home-based leisure activities; the third day was spent interviewing. This gave him an advantage over Morley in that Lull was able to triangulate words with actions. Surveys using multiple choice questions were also used to map out patterns of preference and action. Lull concluded that television was primarily significant as a means of mediating rules of family conduct. He identified two sorts of rule. Habitual rules were firmly established patterns of use that were not open to negotiation between family members. An example would be a restrictive regulation, such as sending children to bed at the nine o'clock watershed. Parametric rules were those more open to negotiation, such as decisions on what to watch and when. Both sorts of rule were tied in to established lines of power within the family, but the existence of the parametric element suggests that they were also the place where this power was tested and challenged.

Anne Gray (1992) explores the issue of gendered power as it relates to the introduction of the VCR into British homes. Gray's work stands as a clear illustration of connections between apparently mundane actions and the creation and subversion of power. She begins by considering the role of the VCR in illustrating women's technological ineptitude. In many societies, mythology has it that women are somehow less technically capable than men. Gray approaches this argument as a discursive reality rather than a piece of false consciousness: the women she studied indeed knew less about the VCR than the men in their lives, and tended to leave its programming to their partners. But this is not, Gray argues, evidence of a natural technical ineptitude but rather a culturally constructed social reality; it is materially true, but since this truth is produced by distinct social forces, not innate and immutable natural laws, it can be changed.

Gray explores this idea through a technique whereby families in her sample were asked to colour code domestic technologies. The patterns she found were unsurprising: where men were the experts with VCRs, televisions, stereos and telephones, the pattern of gendered expertise was reversed when it came to things such as ovens, irons and microwaves. The latter is significant in that techniques for programming VCRs and microwaves are very similar. Hence the relative inability of women to use the VCR is read by Gray as signifying male domination of the leisure sphere; they know more about the VCR because the machine is there primarily for their use, tied as it is to domestic relaxation which is less open to women who work in the home. She also sees a strategic logic to the 'ignorance' she observes. Women might not wish to become media savvy since this would do nothing more than extend the range of their domestic duties.

Media technologies also help negotiate relations with the external world. Charlotte Brunsdon (1996) and Sean Moores (1996) both describe how the growth of satellite television in the UK has been connected with images of class. Aesthetic dimensions of satellite television in Britain inevitably bring the family into contact with macro-political issues. Unlike unobtrusive cable technology, satellite television requires users to place a receiving dish on their homes. This brings the home-owner into conflict with other people's aesthetic sensibilities, and even questions of national heritage. For many people, the visibility of these dishes is offensive; they signify a vulgarization of British culture associated with the proliferation of working-class tastes. The problem has been poignantly felt in 'heritage' areas where homes are semi-public property due to historical features (Brunsdon, 1996).

Moores explored these issues in his study of 18 families living in North Wales. As the issue of taste was articulated through class, Moores selected families from different areas of the city, from working-class through middle-class to upper-class areas. His task was relatively simple in one sense, since potential respondents could be identified by walking through parts of the city associated with varying levels of affluence looking for houses with dishes. He argued that his interviews showed how the decision to purchase satellite systems acted as a source of both solidarity and conflict in collective relationships. Satellite television was associated with social bonding between men, given the high profile of sport, action-adventure films and pornography it delivered. It also appealed to masculine tastes for gadgetry. However, satellite dishes also prompted inter and intra-home conflict. In one area of Edwardian houses, a 19-year-old man was in conflict with his father about the appearance of the dish, which the latter felt was out of keeping with the locale. This raises an issue also mentioned by Livingstone (1998) in her comments on children and new media technologies. Both Moores's and Livingstone's work point to the role that media gadgets play in mediating inter-generational conflict. Very often, televisions, stereos, computers, telephones and video-games are used by children to mark their own space that is relatively autonomous of parental control. Moores also illustrates how satellite dishes can be used to mark people off from their neighbours, either by demonstrating disdain for the aesthetic tastes of others or as a mark of conspicuous consumption.

Moores's work lends empirical weight to Morley's (1994, 1996) argument that domestic media use is integral to relationships formed between families and external social and political structures. A key part of the twentieth-century revolution in electronic media is the way in which it facilitated new forms of what Benedict Anderson calls 'imagined communities' (1995). Nations are imagined communities in that our sense of nation depends on our ability to form emotional connections with others who we never meet or see. The BBC's televised coverage of Elizabeth II's coronation in 1953 demonstrated the medium's capacity to allow simultaneous participation in national ceremonies. If this event outlined television's nationalistic potential in a country where the technology had yet to take off, its actual power became clear in the coverage of the death and funeral of Princess Diana in 1997. Given the success of radio and television in permeating almost every corner of life, it became impossible not to become part of the national mourning; on the day of her death the country's most listened to radio station, Radio One, abandoned its usual programming to provide a day of ambient music. BBC and ITV both covered the funeral in its entirety, and both terrestrial and UK-based satellite stations observed a two-minute silence. However one felt about the issues surrounding Princess Diana, it was impossible not to become part of the event in some way. Its media coverage provided a powerful means of articulating or disavowing a sense of national identity. While part of the process was textual it was also technological in the sense that it depended on the ability to achieve saturation coverage.

Such occasions show how private acts of consumption are implicated in global forces (Morley, 1996). Mary Gillespie (1995) describes this in her study of Hindi families living in Southall, London. These families are confronted by diasporic problems. How are they to maintain faith and traditions in an increasingly multicultural but predominantly Christian country? Some of these tensions have been alleviated by cable, satellite and video technologies which allow for the reception and circulation of programmes such as *The Mahabharata*, the dramatization of a Hindu holy book. These texts and technologies play an important role in reversing cultural imperialism, allowing the maintenance of traditional communities despite the challenges of time and space.

Consumption, objects and meanings

The intersection of technology, interaction and identity reconnected media analysis with the original goal of cultural studies. Concerns over the material nature of ideological or discursive power demand attention to meaningful social activity (Johnson, 1987). This activity has increasingly been placed beneath the banner of consumption. The media are connected with consumption in two ways. First, the technologies are themselves objects to be consumed, as such addressing discourses of purchasing. Secondly, the media give symbolic clues to audiences on how to position themselves in consumer culture. Consumption is important, then, since the media play a central part in motivating consumer culture, and also acts of consumption provide examples of how mediated meanings become actualized.

Consumption represents a coming home of sorts for cultural studies, since it addresses the world of leisure that has always stood at the heart of tensions between politics and culture. Tony Bennett (1986) illustrates this in his analysis of how Blackpool, a coastal town in the North of England, came to be the premier working-class holiday destination in the nineteenth and early twentieth centuries. From a Marxist perspective, leisure became an acute political problem due to the fruits of the industrial revolution. Industrialization produced a new working class which possessed greater discretionary income and leisure time than its agrarian predecessor. Yet leisure could not be autonomous since its functional attribute was the reproduction of labour power. For public order and economic reasons, the state and those owning the means of production had a vested interest in ensuring leisure time was used correctly. At the same time, nineteenth century leisure pursuits popular with the working classes bore traces of earlier folk festivals, characterized by excess and a disregard for authority. Blackpool developed as a resort due to a combination of economic reasons and a clash between working-class and upper middle-class definitions of appropriate leisure pursuits. Hence, holiday-makers were confronted with contradictory discourses: on the one hand, Blackpool offered common access to spa culture, based on upper middle-class beliefs about the health benefits of taking in the sea air; on the other hand, it also offered the possibility of indulging in the vices of drinking and gambling. The development of the town thus reflected contradictory impulses that tried to defend genteel leisure pursuits while at the same time cashing in on the working-class market (Bennett, 1986).

Media studies are related to the cultural analysis of leisure since media consumption is itself a major recreational activity, and is also central to the policing of 'downtime'. But if cultural studies is about the politics of leisure, and if media meanings are to be related to material practice, then it follows that audience research is about more than the relationship between viewers, texts and technologies. This can be appreciated by thinking further about identification as a process. The examination of media technologies shows that the use of these technologies is about creating and projecting a sense of self. Consumption studies show how this is potentially true of any object. Leiss and colleagues' (1990) history of advertising shows an industry which increasingly focuses on the 'communicative function' of goods. They argue that, since by the early twentieth century the consumer market was flooded with functionally similar goods, persuasive appeals centred on the role that consumables could play in the construction and projection of identity; goods were purchased not only for their function, but what they said about the user.

Debates on the politics of consumption theoretically mirror the development of thinking on audiences. Warde (1994) illustrates this in his essay on Zygmunt Baumann's understanding of consumption. Baumann oscillates between pessimism and optimism in his views of consumer society. In dystopian mood, he argues that consumption divides society into two groups: the seduced and the repressed. The 'seduced' are those with enough money to participate in a consumer society that indeed works for them; their needs are met so well that they never have to call on other people or the state to satisfy wants. The 'repressed' are those excluded from this affluence who must subsequently be policed. Consumption is in this sense a conservative force that drives the majority of people into privatized worlds negating collective modes of identity and action. The 'seduced' are obsessed by a project of self-construction via consumption that amounts to a Foucauldian exercise in self-surveillance.

If this bears heavy traces of mass-society theory, at the same time consumption also has more liberatory elements. For Abercrombie (1994), consumption provides a means for ordinary people to assert a form of authority that is otherwise denied to them. He sees society as being divided according to four sorts of authority. The first three are the property of the elite: authority of expertise, authority of deference and authority of taboo. Each of these authoritative forms is characterized by the external imposition of power. Authority of meaning, however, allows for popular power. As with media texts, the meanings that people attach to objects and the ways in which these meanings are used to create a sense of identity are not exclusively determined by macro-political forces.

The idea of an appropriated authority based on the power to impose meaning on an object has been the basis for the investigation of youth or subcultures. Dick Hebdige's *Subculture: the Meaning of Style* (1979) and *Hiding in the Light* (1988) neatly summarize 'the politics of style'. Hebdige argues that since the nineteenth century at least, young working-class people have used fashion to project specific identities into the public sphere. This accelerated in a post-war period that plunged Britain into a series of identity crises. Educational reform, rising working-class wages, immigration and the growth of feminism as a political force created a society in which pre-war gender, class and racial identities had to be renegotiated. This gave birth to a number of sub-cultures, which could all be read as responses to the new environment. Some, such as the mods of the 1960s (represented in the film *Quadrophenia*), embraced class mobility, androgyny and multiculturalism; others, such as the skinheads, responded with an image that was aggressively working class, masculine and white. In all cases, each sub-culture phrased its views of the New Britain in the language of style.

Style was evidently related to consumption, but not in any obvious sense. While the fact that these identities were heavily dependent on the consumption of clothes, records, films and services was connected to elite concerns about seduction and, in the UK, Americanization, these fears neglected youth's power to combine these goods in new ways to produce new meanings. Hebdige (1988) considers the case study of the Italian motor scooter, as made by Vespa and Lambretta. Scooters were originally designed with the urban female shopper in mind. That they came to be associated with mod subculture, and the violence that sometimes accompanied scooter rallies, speaks to the power of the consumer to subvert an object's preferred meaning. These sorts of phenomena demonstrated how consumption could be used to construct and project identities that subverted ways of being which were foisted upon the young by parent cultures. Members of youth subcultures constructed themselves as spectacles, objects that ostentatiously resisted social norms.

The relationship between subculturises and consumers is similar to that between fans and general audiences. Hebdige's work was fascinating, imaginative and theoretically enriching, but it was also guilty of exoticizing ubiquitous youth practices. Just as fan cultures gave researchers ideas that could be used to investigate less 'specialized' audiences, so subcultural studies have primarily been useful as case studies of more general cultural practices.

For Willis (1998), the emergence of consumption and its connection with creative symbolic human activity signals the demise of subcultural studies. This explains the movement away from subculture towards the idea of lifestyle. Fans and members of subcultures were the vanguard for what Abercrombie and Longhurst (1998) call the 'spectacle/performance paradigm'. This model, suggested as a replacement for the 'incorporation/resistance paradigm' based on encoding/decoding, provides a bridge between reception and meaningful activity. Identity construction is about projecting a sense of self by a performance that draws the attention of others. It is easy to see how this applies to subculture: clothes, hair, tattooing and body piercing simultaneously draw the attention of 'ordinary' people, while at the same time marking a difference between these people and the bearer of the look. But consumption studies suggest that everyone is involved in this sort of activity to a degree.

Frank Mort (1996) explores this in his study of masculinity and style. He explains the success of men's magazines in the UK as a function of their central role in connecting consumer goods with masculine identity. Complementing Willis (1998), Mort sees style as a generally used means of orientating oneself to a world of shifting identification, rather than the preserve of a subcultural elite. Regarding men, magazines give clues as to how style can be used to reconcile a feminized obsession with the self and appearance with more traditional forms of masculinity. While his analysis centres on upmarket titles such as *Arena* and *The Face*, his argument becomes clearer when looking at UK magazines such as *Maxim*, *FHM* and *Men's Health*. These titles combine fashion, grooming and health tips with soft pornography and articles on sport, cars, money and boy toy gadgetry. This gives evidence of a multi-centred form of masculinity that is built around but also renegotiates a traditional core.

To what extent does this signify 'seduction'? Willis (1998) argues that 'seduction' is misleading since it undervalues the complexity of consumer choice. While the choice available to television viewers might be limited by media structures, the world of goods in general offers far more possibilities. Corporate capitalism offers such a wide range of goods and services that it has started to eat itself: the development and affordability of computer and digital technology, for example, has provided the consumer with ways of evading the clutches of record companies by downloading music from the Internet. Factors such as these encourage Miller (1995a) to view the seduction hypothesis as being based on four myths. These are that consumption relates to the homogenization of culture, the absence of authenticity, the emphasis on anomic individuality and a consequent reduction in sociality. Miller agrees with Willis in arguing that these ideas are based on a Marxist notion of alienation that need not apply to consumption. For Willis, alienation refers to the manner in which the working classes are robbed of self-worth by using their labour power to produce profit for others. This idea cannot be transferred to consumption, since the work involved in building a sense of self through the appropriation of goods and services does more than simply produce profits for the providers of these commodities. Miller takes the baton, arguing that consumer activity does not necessarily produce individualized cultures fostering political apathy. The proliferation of goods provides multiple opportunities for identification, and as such reduces the need for one group of people to assert their authority over another. Modern marketing has to an extent abandoned rigidly defined gender, race and class identities that have been used to facilitate and justify oppression. The multi-faceted opportunities for identification offered by consumption, together with the growth of interest in ethnographic and postmodern market research methods designed to tap the qualitative feel of the new consumer culture (Arnould and Wallendorf, 1994; Belk, 1995; Brown, 1995), mean that markets are no longer addressed as male, female, black, white, Asian, middle class, working class, straight or gay but rather as 'avant-gardians, pontificators, self-admirers, self-exploiters, chameleons, token triers, sleepwalkers and passive endurers' (Nixon, 1992: 157).

Consumption can also form the basis for strategic collective identities that become powerful sources of political identity and action. The activities of consumer activist Ralph Nader in the US have demonstrated how the experiences of consumption can motivate people to political action, in the form of product boycotts, far more effectively than traditional party politics (Miller, 1995a). Consumption has played an important part in organizing resistance to unethical business practices, such as Barclays Bank's investment in the South African apartheid regime in the 1980s.

Consumption can also project acts of political resistance into public spaces. Increasingly, services which were once the preserve of the state are being redefined as commodities to be sold in the market. University degree courses are forced to market themselves by addressing students as customers, which in turn creates the problems of compromised academic standards as a result of concerns over satisfaction (Keat, 1994). Bewilderingly, police forces have been encouraged to build modern corporate profiles by regarding both villains and victims as consumers who must feel they have been treated fairly (Heward, 1994). These trends are relevant in that they again address the erosion of the distinction between the public and private, as the state surrenders its authority for the provision of culture to market forces.

The political ramifications of this are seen in places such as the heritage industry. Where once museums and heritage sites were designed for didactic purposes, today they compete for audiences by providing a range of pleasurable physical and emotional experiences that augment their informational functions. As with the BBC, contemporary museums must entertain as well as inform. But this does not dilute the role of these centres in promoting politically contestable views of the past and the present meaning of heritage. Hetherington (1992) uses this idea to explain recent controversies around the use and abuse of Stonehenge. This circle of stones has witnessed a series of clashes between the police and 'new age travellers'. The travellers have been prevented since the 1980s from observing the summer solstice at the site since it was decided that their presence was damaging an important part of national heritage. The travellers responded that a part of this heritage was the right to use public land and resources, a right that was being denied to them. Violent clashes with the police have resulted, based on competing versions of Britain's past and future. As with the appropriation of goods, the consumption of services is tied to a sense of self and other.

Consumption, everyday life and media

Consumption as a concept offers a resolution to many of the problems besetting the IRP, but it also raises the danger of setting oneself an unresearchable problem. Consumption has been theorized to the point where it embraces all social activity. One must ask how valid this expansion is. Regardless of this question, audience researchers must also ask how media studies can retain a distinct identity within an area embracing economics, sociology, psychology and political science. As important as it is to create connections between the media and everyday life, at the same time audience research needs to retain the media as a touchstone.

This can be done in a number of ways. Media technologies and services can themselves be regarded as commodities that are subject to the same sorts of discourse as other goods. For example, disagreements over whether or not public services should be left to the free-market wolves are relevant to the issue of public-service broadcasting. In the UK, football's gradual migration from broadcast channels to cable, satellite and even pay-per-view services has been accompanied by arguments over whether the public has a right to watch the game and if, as such, it can be treated exclusively as a commodity. And, of course, media texts are implicated in debates over public culture as the major forums in which the agenda is defined and discussed.

The second strategy is to pursue projects where there is a clear line of intertextual connection between media texts, technologies and other areas of life. Miller's (1995b) study of the reception of the US soap opera *The Young and the Restless* is one example that connects the show's appeal with general economic concerns; its excessive displays of wealth were welcomed in a culture encouraged to live for the moment by boom and bust fiscal cycles. Livingstone (1998) makes a similar argument in her review of new directions for research into children and the media. On a certain level, this has become an inevitably intertextual area demonstrating deep connections between consumption and media texts. Where can you draw a line between media and everyday life when looking at audiences who turn characters from cartoons and video games into resources for playground activities? And how can you distinguish between texts and goods where sometimes cartoons are primarily used as advertisements for toys? This can apply to audiences in general. What is the 'text' for *Star Wars* – the film, the accompanying literature, the video games or the toys? At the same time, the media and media meaning retain a centrality as a major guide to how audiences can orientate themselves to the world of goods.

Exercises

---

1 Write an account of 'media appropriation'. How is it that you or your family reached a decision to purchase a technology? Who made the decision? How has that technology been positioned in the home? Do these personal decisions reflect external forces in any ways?

2 How could you use personal contacts to generate a 'snowball' sample? How could this be justified academically?

3 Keep a record of your media use for a day. What media do you consume? How long, in a 24-hour period, are you exposed to the media? What are the different social functions of the media in your everyday life? Do you ever use media as a means to regulate social relationships (does it influence the way you interact with others in your home)? Do you always pay the same amount of attention to the media?

4 Consider an issue of a contemporary men's magazine. How many of the articles focus on consumption (what clothes to wear, what gadgets, food and cosmetic products to purchase)? How do these articles integrate these products into an overall image of lifestyle, i.e. how are their uses connected with wider issues of well-being and self-identity?

5 Look at the advertisements in the same magazine. Are they easily distinguishable from articles? What distinguishes them? What are the similarities and differences between the form and content of the information delivered in articles versus advertisements?

6 Consider any magazine dealing in any way with health and fitness. In what way does this magazine represent a 'means of correct training'? To what extent would you say its advice is based on culturally specific versions of health?

Conclusion: Multiple Realities, Multiple Methods

This book began with a Kuhnian vision. The history of audience research can be read as a tale of rival paradigms. Sharp epistemological and ontological differences have provoked a science war that is nowhere near its end. Scholars cannot agree on what counts as media influence, whether this influence exists in the first place, or where and how we can begin to look for it.

Can we rescue anything useful from this academic brawl? The answer is yes and no. Important paradigmatic distinctions remain, but at the same time it is also true that apparently competing approaches to audiences have cumulatively enriched the quality of the debate on media power. For all of the dead-ends and arguments, it is true to say that we have a better grasp of how complicated relations between media and audiences are, thanks to successes and failures in both mass-communication research and cultural studies. Moreover, these apparently competing paradigms have encountered similar theoretical and methodological obstacles. These similarities place a question mark against the borders that are normally drawn in audience research.

Instead of subdividing audience studies into binary oppositions, where mass communication faces off against cultural studies, or quantitative and qualitative methods compare truth claims, perhaps it is more profitable to begin with a different query: what is critical research, and how are different paradigms positioned on this question? Ontologically, critical research believes that social reality is a fluid and complex material phenomenon; something that is real, but is difficult to see, describe and measure (Ang, 1996). Something that can be said with certainty, however, is that society is not a harmonious organism. Instead, the social world is characterized by a power struggle between different groups. The media enter this struggle as a tool used by these groups to popularize their view of reality (Rosengren, 1996). Epistemologically, the dream of objective social science evaporates. Caught in a war of 'haves' and 'have-nots', the media tend to side with the powerful. The only choice left to the civic-minded media researcher is to try to redress the balance by joining with disempowered elements in the audience.

These views imply a rejection of much of the work that was discussed in Chapters 2–4. Effects research, especially in its behaviourist, experimental form, was hamstrung by a reliance on methods that were incapable of dealing with the morphology of social reality. This was demonstrated by methods that violated rather than respected real audiences by studying media effects in artificial settings, removing reception from the contexts that made it meaningful. To make matters worse, effects researchers also reneged on their civic duties, allowing themselves to be led by governments, business interests and conservative crusades against mediated sex and violence. That the consequent reseach questions often flew in the face of both common sense and their own findings did nothing to lure effects researchers away from the behaviourist path.

Faced with this history, the only thing that critical scholars could do was to make a clean break, effecting a paradigmatic rupture by completely rewriting the conceptual and methodological foundation of audience studies. But how accurate was the picture of the effects tradition detailed above? American mass-communication research in the 1940s and 1950s was driven to a significant extent by the positivist search for causal laws, encouraged by the structure of institutional funding. Nevertheless, key figures such as Lazarsfeld, Berelson and Lasswell were aware that they had been hijacked by administrative interests, and that qualitative concepts and methods had a valuable part to play in enriching the understanding of how communication functioned. Of course, they did not do very much about this situation, but their inaction is partly explained by the exigencies of hot and cold wars, and the spectre of McCarthyism that blocked excursions into European theory.

But this was not true of all mass-communication scholars. Cultivation analysis provides an interesting moment as an example of how quantitative researchers changed their view on the nature of empirical research, prompted by the acknowledgement that social reality had to be interpreted as well as measured. George Gerbner's (1976) model of communication resonates with Stuart Hall's (1980) encoding/decoding paradigm in acknowledging the role that perception and interpretation play in forming human understandings of social reality. This has influenced the way in which cultivation analysts view data generated by survey research. Where positivists believe that such data speak for themselves, Morgan and Shanahan (1996) argue that survey responses offer clues to possible effects that need to be interpreted. Cultivation analysis has been dismissed on the grounds that it is based on weak correlations between television viewing and the development of social attitudes. Morgan and Shanahan retort that this dismissal is itself based on a positivist orientation that cultivation analysts have abandoned; if cultivation effects are small, it is remarkable that they should be found at all given the embeddedness of television within industrialized cultures, and the interactive nature of social variables. This response acknowledges potential ambiguities in quantitative research, building an epistemological foundation acknowledging the role of interpretation in social research. In terms of the accuracy of the sort of history that Gauntlett (1998) offers of mass-communication research, it follows that while the cap he has fashioned sits neatly on behaviourism's head, it does not fit all of the research that is habitually described as part of the effects tradition.

A second question that creates a less-ruptured view of audience research history is: to what extent has cultural studies been plagued by the same troubles inflicted upon mass-communication scholars? This was raised by Curran (1991), Seaman (1992) and Morris (1996), who complained that, in stressing the agency of viewers, readers and listeners, cultural studies has done nothing more than reinvent uses and gratifications research. Morley (1993) and Cobley (1994) refuted this charge on the basis that cultural studies is premised on a collective view of subjectivity and remains interested in power.

Yet the critique has emerged again with greater force from the Glasgow Media Group. Greg Philo and David Miller (1998) draw clear parallels between the failures of effects research and similar problems they see in the current state of the art in so-called critical studies. Effects researchers had failed to account for the full range of media power due to methodologies that only allowed them to look for certain *sorts* of influences in certain places. Philo and Miller argue that cultural studies has been guilty of the same mistake. Their argument is a response to the more radical fringes of audience theorizing found in Bennett (1996), Barker (1998, 1999b) and Barker and Brooks (1999). Since reality is complex and fluid, Bennett sees audience research as being primarily useful as a means of pointing to the impossibility of textual closure: we can never be sure about media effects since texts are never univocal. His views explain why Abercrombie and Longhurst (1998) conclude that the question of power has been marginalized in audience research.

Running with the ball, Barker (1998) inverts the relation between consumption and passivity seen in both mass-communication and encoding/decoding work. Taking an implicit swipe at cultivation analysis, Barker argues that heavy media consumption can be highly 'active' and critical. In his work with cinema audiences and sci-fi comic fans, Barker has found that the more involved viewers and readers are with a film or a comic, the more effort they put into preparing for the reception experience (planning an evening's viewing that will include not just watching a film, but reading reviews and discussing it with friends before and after viewing). They are also more likely than casual viewers to voice their displeasure if their a priori expectations are unfulfilled. For Barker, the heavy viewer is the committed viewer, and in this sense is more 'critical' than the person for whom the media matter little.

In effect, Barker concurs with Bennett in critiquing the notion of 'influencability' that lies at the heart of both quantitative and qualitative ideas about media power. Both effects and encoding/decoding research function according to a crude dichotomy between active and passive that gets nowhere near real media experiences. Notions of preferred, negotiated and oppositional readings, for example, are hugely unhelpful since they tend to lump very different responses to media texts into the same category. Sut Jhally (1994) mentions this problem in discussing reactions to sexualized images of women on MTV. Under the auspices of the encoding/decoding model, his objections to rock videos, outlined in *Dreamworlds*, would be classified as an oppositional reading of these texts, placed as such alongside conservative concerns. The nature of his objections are, however, very different; where the moral majority are offended by sexualized depictions *tout court*, Jhally objects to a media world in which only women are objectified and sexualized. His answer to the problem is not to have less sex on television, but more, transforming objectification into a transgendered experience. So the problem with the notion of oppositional readings is that it conflates completely different political positions. Building from this argument, Barker questions the notion of 'effects' on the grounds that the active/passive distinction does no justice to kaleidoscopic reactions to the media. The implication is that it is still too early to ask what power the media have, since there is so much about reception that we do not understand.

Philo and Miller see this argument as premature, reactionary and elitist. Concurring with Livingstone (1999), the Glasgow-based scholars warn that we abandon the notion of textual determination at our peril. To illustrate, the absence of certain sorts of people and ideas in media discourse matters if the audience has no first-hand experience that can act as a counterweight. Take Lewis et al.'s (1991) Gulf War study as a case in point. In a response to a conference paper I presented (Ruddock, 1999), Barker (1999b) complained that the problem with Lewis et al.'s work was that it assumed that we can differentiate between 'good' and 'bad' information, that the audience somehow wants more of the good, and if they were to get it they would magically become more enlightened. In other words, this is another example of quantitative elitism directed at the straw target of the passive audience.

But the argument is quite different. Lewis et al. did not define political knowledge as the ability to regurgitate facts; nor were they arguing for a simple correspondence between factual knowledge and ideological positioning. What they were saying was that in a material world where things really do happen raw factual information is important. Regarding the Gulf War study, knowing that the US had indicated to Iraq that no action would be taken in the event of an invasion of Kuwait, or that the US was tolerating and even supporting similar occupations in other parts of the globe, would not automatically lead to anti-war feeling. However, the presence of such information did make it harder to justify support for the war on moral grounds. What Lewis et al. were saying was that in a society where most people turn to television as their primary source of news information and analysis, the narrow range of information and commentary offered by that medium limited what people knew about the war, and this has a relationship to what they could say about it. I made the same argument in my research on news about the invasion of Haiti. Although responses to this news were far from passive, at the same time they were, as my audience was aware, poorly informed. This had a *pacifying* effect, in the sense that it limited people's confidence in voicing opinions and questioning official versions of what was going on.

In the same response, Barker (1999b) takes issue with the argument made by Morley (1992) and repeated by Philo and Miller, that the encoding/decoding model still works with news programming, since in this realm we can still speak of distinctions between reality and representation. This argument turns, in Barker's view, on a distinction between fact and fiction that ignores the role that television news plays as a form of entertainment. Yet the practices he mentions regarding news viewing might also have pacifying effects. Are we really to read the fact that someone tunes in to news about East Timor, or Chechnya, or Kosovo because he or she finds the newsreader attractive, or because they find images of real-life war exciting, as a dismissal of textual determination? Philo and Miller would argue that in this context, content *is* more important than form, regardless of audience preferences. If television news is one's only connection to the political world, then watching it for the presenter or the visual action rather than for the stories signifies a withdrawal. It also buys into the logic of media institutions that value ratings far above public service. This is, in many respects, a passive response, one that is conditioned by cultural forces beyond the viewer's control.

The problem with the argument made by Barker and Bennett is that it risks relativizing questions about quality and judgement to the point where efforts to address and transform inequality in mediated communication are abandoned (Corner, 1994; Philo and Miller, 1998; Livingstone, 1999). Philo and Miller defend the Gramscian position. As the regulation of media culture is gradually handed over to free-market forces that radically de-emphasize the public-service ethos, media scholars have a duty to re-emphasize connections between communication and citizenship (Livingstone, 1999). Instead, the concentration on pleasure is at one with the free-market spirit, centring on questions of what people like and want as consumers rather than what they need as citizens. Philo and Miller see history repeating itself. Just as uses and gratifications research, which stressed the power of media over audiences, developed at the same time as television became absolutely central to social and political life, so too as media corporations spread their global tendrils: 'Academics have become industry groupies . . . mistaking [the consumption of popular culture] for resistance. Others have examined the 'social relations of media consumption' which could come down to asking if people listen to the radio whilst doing the ironing' (Philo and Miller, 1998: 14).

The dismissal of the passive viewer and the notion of 'influencability' is premature, as it was in the early 1960s. But it also has a methodological component. As Morley (1992) acknowledges, early focus-group research was as artificial as experiments in the sense that it abstracted reception from its natural context. But Kubey (1996) sees more systematic problems in sampling techniques. The dismissal of passive audiences is not surprising, given the use of sampling strategies that systematically attract those who have the most to say about the media. In fairness, Barker and Brooks (1999) are very open about the problems of trying to get people to commit to ethnographic research when they have little invested in reception. Nevertheless, many of the studies that use 'snowball' sampling techniques are indeed based on the identification of audience groups who are highly involved in media practices. The range of audiences that are likely to become involved in research projects is narrowed by the fact that ethnography is a labour-intensive process, meaning that often getting in contact with willing participants depends on personal contacts and luck (Gillespie, 1995; Buckingham, 1999; Seiter, 1999).

If these problems are inevitable, what is more troubling is the implicit bias produced by the idea that the scholar should be on the side of his or her subjects. This has influenced the sorts of audiences that appear in academic accounts, based on the belief that research is best conducted among those with whom the researcher shares a worldview. As Barker (1999b) himself has argued, this excludes certain sorts of genres and audiences, especially those associated with male cultures. Even when conflicts between researcher and researched do arise, there is a temptation to translate the latter's concerns into terms that make sense to the former. Seiter's (1999) argument that Christian fundamentalism appeals to the women she studied for economic reasons, since it offers a means of social advancement that would otherwise be denied, shows a refusal to confront religious and moral differences that are incommensurable with her feminism.

Another problem with the idea that research should be on the side of the audience is the power given to viewers, readers and listeners to determine the direction a project should take. Although this is in keeping with the development of 'grounded theory', it is at odds with other important ideas in ethnographic methodology. Although insider accounts are an important part of cultural analysis, it is also sometimes true that the rules and patterns characterizing a specific setting are best observed from an outsider's perspective. This is relevant to Philo and Miller's objections, since critical media research should be about more than what audiences like and what they think. While viewing the media from the audience's position was an important tool in overturning simplistic notions of media power, it is worth asking how relevant this orientation is to the current state of the art. There is more to audience research than what people have to say about their experiences.

One lesson to be drawn from all of this is that critical audience research is not as distinct from mainstream mass-communication research as some would like to think. Not only has cultural studies been faced with practical and theoretical issues that echo the past, but also the time has come to ask how far the paradigm should distance itself from orthodox sociological concerns. Methodologically, Press (1996) argues that cultural studies has been guilty of wanting to have its cake and eat it too, aspiring towards empirical status while at the same time using the critique of empiricism to avoid tricky technical questions. Indeed, Fine (1993) argues that ethnographers are as guilty as other social researchers of concealing methodological flaws.

If Press (1996) is a little over-zealous in questioning the reflexivity of audience ethnographies, at the same time it could be argued that the critique of method has itself blunted cultural studies' political edge. In the face of multiple practical problems, it has become easier to write about what we *can't* say about audiences than what we can. Sonia

Livingstone (1999) writes that the problem with the dismissal of the notion of media power and general effects is that (a) generalizability is the unacknowledged subtext of all forms of audience research; and (b) the refusal to deal with this surrenders important definitions of media power to other forces. In the end, a materialist analysis of culture requires sorting the probable from the possible. Livingstone rejects Bennett's argument; critical audience research is *not* about the impossibility of textual closure. Culture only works if meaning can be closed down in crucial moments. Just as we are not free to make what we will of social reality, so too audiences are only relatively autonomous, and a key task of audience research is to discover the processes that limit this freedom.

So how are we to view audience research as a whole? It would be facile to see it as some sort of Enlightenment project moving towards the utopia of perfect knowledge. Different models have indeed been marked by a varying methodological and conceptual baggage, influencing their view of how communication works and how it can be studied. But what if we ask a different question: what can we say about media and audiences that we could not say in the early part of the twentieth century? Livingstone argues that, if nothing else, academic wrangling over what audiences are, how they relate to the media and how they should be studied has pushed them to the very centre of debates on politics and culture.

But more than this, regardless of paradigmatic orientation, contemporary scholarship agrees that relations between media and audiences are so complex that they require multiple methods. Jensen (1996) sees social research as involving the investigation of occurrence and recurrence, process and product. Cultural power is something that has to be both described and explained. Description and quantification have a part to play in critical research since, in the end, power is a material force that can in part be measured; cultural cohesion can only happen if a majority think and act in certain ways (Lewis, 1997). Quantitative research is therefore important as a means of mapping the denotative aspects of power. Qualitative methods are useful as ways of analysing how these formations of consensus are created, maintained and diverted. In the end, audience research should be assessed according to the degree of fit between method and the question at hand. Knee deep in a lake of effects, audience researchers must acknowledge the strengths and weaknesses of a variety of approaches to their subject.

References

Abercrombie, N. (1994) Authority and consumer society. In R. Keat, N. Whitely and N. Abercrombie (eds), *The Authority of the Consumer*. London: Routledge.

Abercrombie, N. and Longhurst, B. (1998) *Audiences*. London: Sage.

Allor, M. (1988) Relocating the site of the audience. *Critical Studies in Mass Communication*, 5: 139–51.

Althusser, L. (1972) Ideology and ideological state apparatuses. In L. Althusser (ed.), *Lenin, Philosophy and Other Essays*. London: New Left Books. pp. 119–73.

Amin, S. (1989) *Eurocentrism*. New York: Monthly Review Press.

Anderson, B. (1995) *Imagined Communities*. London: Verso.

Anderson, J. (1996) The pragmatics of audience in research and theory. In J. Hay, L. Grossberg and E. Wartella (eds), *The Audience and its Landscape*. Boulder, CO: Westview Press. pp. 75–93.

Ang, I. (1985) *Watching Dallas*. London: Routledge.

Ang, I. (1991) *Desperately Seeking the Audience*. London: Routledge.

Ang, I. (1996) *Living Room Wars*. London: Routledge.

Angus, I. (1994) Democracy and the constitution of media audiences. In J. Cruz and J. Lewis (eds), *Viewing, Reading, Listening: Audiences and Cultural Reception*. Boulder, CO: Westview Press. pp. 233–52.

Arnould, E.J. and Wallendorf, M. (1994) Market oriented ethnography. *Journal of Marketing Research*, 31: 484–504.

Aronowitz, S. (1995) The debate over science studies. *Cultural Studies Times*.

Babbie, E. (1992) *The Practice of Social Research*, 6th edn. Belmont, CA: Wadsworth.

Bagdikian, B. (1983) *The Media Monopoly*. Boston, MA: Beacon.

Bandura, A. (1978) Social learning theory of aggression. *Journal of Communication*, 28 (3): 12–29.

Barker, M. (1993) Seeing how far you can see: on being a fan of 2000 AD. In D. Buckingham (ed.), *Reading Audiences: Young People and the Media*. Manchester: Manchester University Press. pp. 159–83.

Barker, M. (1998) Critiques 'Я' us. In R. Dickinson, R. Harindranath and O. Linne (eds), *Approaches to Audiences*. London: Arnold. pp. 184–91.

Barker, M. (1999a) Response to 'Methodological boundaries and public knowledge: can we measure culture? Private communication.

Barker, M. (1999b) The coming crisis in audience studies. Paper presented at the

Conference on Researching Culture. University of North London, 11 September.

Barker, M. and Brooks, K. (1999) *Knowing Audiences: Judge Dredd, his Fans, Friends and Foes*. Luton: University of Luton Press.

Barker, M. and Petley, J. (1997) *Ill Effects*. London: Routledge.

Barthes, R. (1973) *Mythologies*. London: Paladin.

Bausinger, H. (1984) Media, technology and daily life. *Media, Culture and Society*, 6: 343–51.

Becker, H. (1967) Whose side are we on? *Social Problems*, 14: 239–48.

Becker, H. (1986) *Doing Things Together*. Evanston, IL: Northwestern University Press.

Belk, R.W. (1995) Studies in the new consumer behavior. In D. Miller (ed.), *Acknowledging Consumption*. London: Routledge. pp. 58–95.

Bennett, T. (1986) Hegemony, ideology, pleasure, Blackpool. In T. Bennett et al. (eds), *Popular Culture and Social Relations*. Milton Keynes: Open University Press.

Bennett, T. (1996) Figuring audiences and readers. In J. Hay, L. Grossberg and E. Wartella (eds), *The Audience and its Landscape*. Boulder, CO: Westview Press. pp. 145–60.

Berelson, B. (1949) What missing the newspaper means. In P. Lazarsfeld and F. Stanton (eds), *Communications Research 1948–9*. New York: Harper. pp. 111–29.

Berelson, B. (1948/1953) Communications and public opinion. In B. Berelson and M. Janowitz (eds), *Reader in Public Opinion and Communication*. Glencoe, IL: Free Press. pp. 448–62.

Berelson, B. (1952/1975) Democratic theory and public opinion. In R. Carlson (ed.), *Communications and Public Opinion: a Public Opinion Quarterly Reader*. New York: Praeger. pp. 587–614.

Bernstein, R. (1988) *Beyond Objectivism and Relativism*. Philadelphia, PA: University of Pennsylvania Press.

Bielbe, D. and Harrington, C. (1994) Reach out and touch someone: viewers, agency and audiences in the televisual experience. In J. Cruz and J. Lewis (eds), *Viewing, Reading, Listening: Audiences and Cultural Reception*. Boulder, CO: Westview Press. pp. 81–100.

Blumer, H. (1948) Public opinion and public opinion polling. *American Sociological Review*, 13: 542–54.

Blumler, J.G. and Gurevitch, M. (1975) Towards a comparative framework for political communication research. In S. Chafee (ed.), *Political Communication: Issues and Strategies for Research*. London: Sage. pp. 165–94.

Blumler, J.G., Katz, E. and Gurevitch, M. (1974) Utilisation of mass communication by the individual. In J. Blumler and E. Katz (eds), *The Uses of Mass Communication: Current Perspectives on Gratifications Research*. New York: Sage. pp. 19–34.

Boston, R. and Donohew, L. (1992) The case for empiricism: clarifying fundamental issues in communication theory. *Communication Monographs*, 59: 109–29.

Bourdieu, P. (1990) *In Other Words: Essays Toward a Reflexive Sociology*. Cambridge: Polity Press.

Brady, N., Henry, E. and Orren, G. (1992) Polling spectacles: sources of error in public opinion surveys. In T. Mann and G. Orren (eds), *Media Polls in American Politics*. Washington, DC: Brookings Institute. pp. 55–94.

Brown, S. (1995) *Postmodern Marketing*. London: Routledge.

Brunsdon, C. (1996) Satellite dishes and the landscapes of taste. In J. Hay, L. Grossberg and E. Wartella (eds), *The Audience and its Landscape*. Boulder, CO: Westview Press. pp. 343–57.

Buckingham, D. (1987) *Public Secrets*. London: Verso.

Buckingham, D. (1993a) Boy's talk: television and the policing of masculinity. In D. Buckingham (ed.), *Reading Audiences: Young People and the Media*. Manchester: Manchester University Press. pp. 89–115.

Buckingham, D. (1993b) Re-reading audiences. In D. Buckingham (ed.), *Reading Audiences: Young People and the Media*. Manchester: Manchester University Press. pp. 202–18.

Buckingham, D. (1993c) Young people and the media. In D. Buckingham (ed.), *Reading Audiences: Young People and the Media*. Manchester: Manchester University Press. pp. 1–23.

Buckingham, D. (1998a) Children and television: a critical overview of the research. In R. Dickinson, R. Harindranath and O. Linne (eds), *Approaches to Audiences*. London: Arnold. pp. 131–45.

Buckingham, D. (1998b) Review essay: children of an electronic age? *European Journal of Communication*, 13: 557–65.

Buckingham, D. (1999) Researching children's media culture. Paper presented at the Conference on Researching Culture. University of North London, 12 September.

Cantor, J. (1994) Fright reactions to the mass media. In J. Bryant and D. Zillman (eds), *Media Effects: Advances in Theory and Research*. Hillsdale, NJ: Lawrence Erlbaum. pp. 213–45.

Cantor, J., Wilson, B. and Hoffner, C. (1986) Emotional responses to a televised nuclear holocaust film. *Communication Research*, 13: 257–77.

Cantril, H. (1940) *The Invasion from Mars: a Study in the Psychology of Panic*. Princeton, NJ: Princeton University Press.

Carey, J. (1989) *Communication as Culture*. Boston: Unwin Hyman.

Caughie, J. (1980) Progressive television and documentary drama. *Screen*, 21: 9–35.

Chafee, S. (1975) The diffusion of political information. In S. Chafee (ed.), *Political Communication: Issues and Strategies for Research*. London: Sage. pp. 85–128.

Chapman, G. (1996) The Sokal affair. *Annals of Academia* (http://www.feed-mag.com/96.06chapman).

Charters, W.W. (1933/1953) Motion pictures and youth. In B. Berelson and M. Janowitz (eds), *Reader in Public Opinion and Communication*. Glencoe, IL: Free Press. pp. 397–406.

Cmiel, K. (1996) On cynicism, evil and the discovery of communication in the 1940s. *Journal of Communication*, 46 (3): 88–107.

Cobley, P. (1994) Throwing out the baby: populism and active audience theory. *Media, Culture and Society*, 16: 677–87.

Comstock, G., Chafee, S., Katzman, N., McCombs, M. and Roberts, D. (1974) *Television and Human Behavior*. New York: Columbia University Press.

Condit, C. (1989) The rhetorical limits of polysemy. *Critical Studies in Mass Communication*, 6: 103–22.

Converse, P. (1975) The nature of belief systems in mass publics. In S. Welch and J. Comer (eds), *Public Opinion*. Palo Alto, CA: Mayfield Press. pp. 92–106.

Corner, J. (1992) Presumption as theory: realism in television studies. *Screen*, 33: 97–102.

Corner, J. (1994) Debating culture: quality and inequality. *Media, Culture and Society*, 16: 141–8.

Corner, J. (1996) Media studies and the knowledge problem. *Screen*, 36: 147–86.

Corner, J., Richardson, K. and Fenton, N. (1990) *Nuclear Reactions*. London: John Libbey.

Curran, J. (1990) The new revisionism in mass communication research: a reappraisal. *European Journal of Communication*, 5: 135–64.

Curran, J. (1991) Rethinking the media as a public shere. In P. Dahlgren and C. Sparks (eds), *Communication and Citizenship*. London: Routledge. pp. 27–57.

Dahlgren, P. (1991) Introduction. In P. Dahlgren and C. Sparks (eds), *Communication and Citizenship*. London: Routledge. pp. 1–24.

Davis, S. and Mares, M. (1998) Effects of talk show viewing on adolescents. *Journal of Communication*, 48: 69–86.

Defleur, M.L. and Lowery, S. (1988) *Milestones in Mass Communication Research*. New York: Longman.

Denzin, N. and Lincoln, Y. (1994) Introduction: entering the field of qualitative research. In N. Denzin and Y. Lincoln (eds), *Handbook of Qualitative Research*. London: Sage. pp. 1–18.

Diener, E. and Woody, L. (1981) Television violence, conflict, realism and action: a study in viewer liking. *Communication Research*, 8 (3): 281–306.

Donnerstein, E. (1980) Aggressive erotica and violence against women. *Journal of Personality and Social Psychology*, 39: 269–77.

Donnerstein, E. and Hallam, J. (1978) Facilitating effects of erotica on aggression against women. *Journal of Personality and Social Psychology*, 36: 1270–7.

Donnerstein, E., Donnerstein, M. and Evans, R. (1975) Erotic stimuli and aggression: facilitation or inhibition. *Journal of Personality and Social Psychology*, 32: 237–44.

Doob, A. and MacDonald, G. (1979) Television viewing and fear of victimization: is the relationship causal? *Journal of Personality and Social Psychology*, 37: 170–9.

During, S. (1990) *The Cultural Studies Reader*. London: Routledge.

Eagleton, T. (1990) *Ideology: an Introduction*. London: Verso.

Edelstein, A.S. (1993) Thinking about the criterion variable in agenda-setting research. *Journal of Communication*, 43: 85–99.

Eldridge, J. (ed.) (1993) *Getting the Message: News, Truth and Power*. London: Routledge.

Farmer, P. (1994) The uses of Haiti. Speech given at the University of Massachusetts, Amherst, September.

Fay, B. (1996) *Contemporary Philosophy of Social Science*. London: Blackwell.

Festinger, L. (1963) The theory of cognitive dissonance. In W. Schramm (ed.), *The Science of Human Communication*. New York: Basic Books. pp. 17–27.

Fine, G. (1993) Ten lies of ethnography. *Journal of Contemporary Ethnography*, 22: 267–94.

Fiske, J. (1982) *Introduction to Communication Studies*. London: Methuen.

Fiske, J. (1987) *Television Culture*. London: Routledge.

Fiske, J. (1989) *Understanding the Popular*. Boston: Unwin Hyman.

Fiske, J. (1992) The cultural economy of fandom. In L. Lewis (ed), *The Adoring Audience: Fan Culture and Popular Media*. London: Routledge. pp. 30–49.

Fiske, J. (1993) *Power Plays, Power Works*. London: Verso.

Flanagan, O. (1995) Behaviourism. In T. Honderich (ed.), *The Oxford Companion to Philosophy*. Oxford: Oxford University Press. pp. 81–2.

Flew, A. (1971) *An Introduction to Western Philosophy*. London: Thames and Hudson.

Foucault, M. (1976) *The History of Sexuality*. London: Penguin.

Foucault, M. (1979) *Discipline and Punish: the Birth of the Prison*. New York: Vintage.

Foucault, M. (1984) Truth and power. In P. Rabinow (ed.), *The Foucault Reader*. New York: Pantheon. pp. 51–75.

Gary, B. (1996) Communication research, The Rockefeller Foundation, and mobilization for the war of words, 1938–1944. *Journal of Communication*, 46 (3): 124–47.

Gauntlett, D. (1996) *Video Critical*. Luton: John Libbey.

Gauntlett, D. (1998) Ten things wrong with the effects tradition. In R. Dickinson, R. Harindranath and O. Linne (eds), *Approaches to Audiences*. London: Arnold. pp. 120–30.

Geer, J.G. (1991) Critical realignments and the public opinion poll. *Journal of Politics*, 53: 434–53.

Geertz, C. (1973) *The Interpretation of Culture*. New York: Basic Books.

Gerbner, G. (1970) Cultural indicators: the case of violence in television drama. *Annals of the American Academy of Political Social Science*, 388: 69–81.

Gerbner, G. (1973) Cultural indicators: the third voice. In G. Gerbner, L. Gross and W. Melody (eds), *Communication and Social Policy*. New York: Wiley. pp. 555–73.

Gerbner, G. (1976) Studies in mass communication. Unpublished monograph.

Gerbner, G. (1995) *The Killing Screens*. Northampton, MA: Media Education Foundation.

Gerbner, G., Gross, L., Eleey, M., Jackson-Beeck, M., Jeffries-Fox, S. and Signorelli, N. (1977) TV violence profile #8. *Journal of Communication*, 27: 171–80.

Gerbner, G., Gross, L., Eleey, M., Jackson-Beeck, M., Jeffries-Fox, S. and Signorelli, N. (1978) Cultural indicators: violence profile #9. *Journal of Communication*, 28: 176–207.

Gerbner, G., Gross, L., Morgan, M., Jackson-Beeck, M. and Signorelli, N. (1979) The demonstration of power: violence profile #10. *Journal of Communication*, 29: 177–96.

Gerbner, G., Gross, L., Morgan, M. and Signorelli, N. (1980a) Aging with television: images on television drama and conception of social reality. *Journal of Communication*, 30: 37–47.

Gerbner, G., Gross, L., Morgan, M. and Signorelli, N. (1980b) The mainstreaming of America: violence profile #11. *Journal of Communication*, 30: 10–29.

Gerbner, G., Gross, L., Morgan, M. and Signorelli, N. (1981) A curious journey into the scary world of Paul Hirsch. *Communication Research*, 8: 39–72.

Gerbner, G., Gross, L., Morgan, M. and Signorelli, N. (1982) Charting the mainstream: television's contributions to political orientations. *Journal of Communication*, 32: 100–27.

Gerbner, G., Gross, L., Morgan, M. and Signorelli, N. (1994) Growing up with television: the cultivation perspective. In J. Bryant and D. Zillman (eds), *Media Effects: Advances in Theory and Research*. Hillsdale, NJ: Lawrence Erlbaum. pp. 17–43.

Giddens, A. (1971) *Capitalism and Modern Social Theory*. Cambridge: Cambridge University Press.

Gillespie, M. (1995) Sacred serials, devotional viewing and domestic worship. In R. Allen (ed.), *To Be Continued*. London: Routledge. pp. 254–80.

Gitlin, T. (1978) Sociology: the dominant paradigm. *Theory and Society*, 6: 205–53.

Gray, A. (1987) Reading the audience. *Screen*, 28: 24–35.

Gray, A. (1992) *Video Playtime*. London: Routledge.

Grossberg, L. (1992) Is there a fan in the house? In L. Lewis (ed.), *The Adoring Audience: Fan Culture and Popular Media*. London: Routledge. pp. 50–65.

Grossberg, L. (1996a) The circulation of cultural studies. In J. Storey (ed.), *What is Cultural Studies? A Reader*. London: Edward Arnold.

Grossberg, L. (1996b) Identity and cultural studies: is that all there is? In S. Hall and P. du Gay (eds), *Questions of Cultural Identity*. London: Sage. pp. 87–107.

Grossberg, L., Nelson, C. and Treichler, P. (1992) *Cultural Studies*. New York: Routledge.

Guba, E. and Lincoln, Y.S. (1994) Competing paradigms in qualitative research. In N. Denzin and Y. Lincoln (eds), *Handbook of Qualitative Research*. London: Sage. pp. 105–17.

Gunter, B. (1985) *Dimensions of Violence*. Aldershot, Hants: Gower.

Gunter, B. (1994) The question of media violence. In J. Bryant and D. Zillman (eds), *Media Effects: Advances in Theory and Research*. Hillsdale, NJ: Lawrence Erlbaum. pp. 163–211.

Hall, S. (1973) The determination of news photographs. *Working Papers in Cultural Studies*, 3: 53–87.

Hall, S. (1980) Encoding/decoding. In S. Hall et al. (eds), *Culture, Media Language*. London: Hutchinson. pp. 128–38.

Hall, S. (1982) The rediscovery of ideology: the return of the repressed in media studies. In M. Gurevitch et al. (eds), *Culture, Society and the Media*. London: Methuen. pp. 56–90.

Hall, S. (1983) The problem of ideology: Marxism without guarantees. In B. Mathews (ed.), *Marx 100 Years On*. London: Lawrence Wishart. pp. 57–86.

Hall, S. (1985) Signification, representation, ideology: Althusser and the post-structuralist debates. *Critical Studies in Mass Communication*, 2: 91–114.

Hall, S. (1986a) Gramsci's relevance for the study of race and ethnicity. *Journal of Communication Inquiry*, 10: 5–27.

Hall, S. (1986b) On postmodernism and articulation. *Journal of Communication Inquiry*, 10: 45–60.

Hall, S. (1990) *The Hard Road to Renewal*. London: Verso.

Hall, S. (1992) The birth and death of the modern subject. In S. Hall, T. McGrew and D. Held (eds), *Modernity and its Futures*. Cambridge: Polity Press. pp. 273–326.

Hall, S. (1994) Reflections on the encoding/decoding model. In J. Cruz and J. Lewis (eds), *Viewing, Reading, Listening: Audiences and Cultural Reception*. Boulder, CO: Westview Press. pp. 253–74.

Hall, S., Crichter, C., Jefferson, T., Clarke, J. and Roberts, B. (1978). *Policing the Crisis*. New York: Holmes and Meier.

Hammersley, M. (1989) *The Dilemma of Qualitative Method: Herbert Blumer and the Chicago Tradition*. London: Routledge.

Hammersley, M. (1992) *What's Wrong with Ethnography*. London: Routledge.

Hammersley, M. (ed.) (1993) *Social Research: Philosophy, Politics and Practice*. London: Sage.

Hammersley, M. and Atkinson, P. (1996) *Ethnography: Principles in Practice*. London: Routledge.

Hansen, A., Cottle, S., Negrine, R. and Newbold, C. (1998) *Mass Communication Research Methods*. London: Sage.

Harris, R.J. (1994) The impact of sexually explicit media. In J. Bryant and D. Zillman (eds), *Media Effects: Advances in Theory and Research*. Hillsdale, NJ: Lawrence Erlbaum. pp. 247–72.

Hawkins, R. and Pingree, S. (1980) Some processes in the cultivation effect. *Communication Research*, 7: 193–226.

Hay, J. (1996) Afterword: the place of the audience. In J. Hay, L. Grossberg and E. Wartella (eds), *The Audience and its Landscape*. Boulder, CO: Westview Press. pp. 359–73.

Hebdige, D. (1979) *Subculture: the Meaning of Style*. London: Methuen.

Hebdige, D. (1988) *Hiding in the Light*. London: Comedia.

Herbst, S. (1993) The meaning of public opinion. *Media, Culture and Society*, 15: 437–54.

Herman, E. and Chomsky, N. (1988) *Manufacturing Consent: the Political Economy of the Mass Media*. New York: Pantheon.

Hermes, J. (1995) *Reading Women's Magazines*. Cambridge: Polity Press.

Hertzog, H. (1943/1953) What do we really know about daytime serial listeners? In B. Berelson and M. Janowitz (eds), *Reader in Public Opinion and Communication*. Glencoe, IL: Free Press. pp. 352–65.

Hetherington, K. (1992) Stonehenge and its festival. In R. Shields (ed.), *Lifestyle Shopping: the Subject of Consumption*. London: Routledge. pp. 83–98.

Heward, T. (1994) Retailing the police. In R. Keat, N. Whitely and N. Abercrombie (eds), *The Authority of the Consumer*. London: Routledge. pp. 240–52.

Hirsch, P.M. (1980) The scary world of the non-viewer and other anomalies. *Communication Research*, 7: 403–56.

Hirsch, P.M. (1981) On not learning from one's own mistakes. *Communication Research*, 8: 3–37.

Hobson, D. (1982) *Crossroads: the Drama of a Soap Opera*. London: Methuen.

Hovland, C. (1948/1953) Social communication. In B. Berelson and M. Janowitz (eds), *Reader in Public Opinion and Communication*. Glencoe, IL: Free Press. pp. 181–92.

Hovland, C., Lumsdaine, I. and Sheffield, F. (1949) *Experiments in Mass Communication*. Princeton, NJ: Princeton University Press.

Hughes, M. (1980) The fruits of cultivation analysis. *Public Opinion Quarterly*, 44: 287–302.

Iyengar, S. and Kinder, D. (1987) *News that Matters*. Chicago: University of Chicago Press.

Janis, I.L. (1963) Personality as a factor in susceptibility to persuasion. In W. Schramm (ed.), *The Science of Human Communication*. New York: Basic Books. pp. 54–64.

Jarvie, I. (1977) Understanding and explanation in sociology and social anthropology. In F. Dallmayr and T. McCarthy (eds), *Understanding and Social Inquiry*. Notre Dame, IL: University of Notre Dame Press. pp. 189–206.

Jenkins, H. (1992a) *Textual Poaching*. London: Routledge.

Jenkins, H. (1992b) Strangers no more we sing. In L. Lewis (ed.), *The Adoring Audience: Fan Culture and Popular Media*. London: Routledge. pp. 208–36.

Jenks, C. (1993) *Culture*. London: Routledge.

Jensen, J. (1992) Fandom as pathology: the consequences of characterization. In L. Lewis (ed.), *The Adoring Audience: Fan Culture and Popular Media*. London: Routledge. pp. 2–29.

Jensen, K.B. (1991) Humanistic scholarship as qualitative science. In K.B. Jensen and N. Jankowski (eds), *A Handbook of Qualitative Methodologies for Mass Communication Research*. London: Routledge. pp. 17–43.

Jensen, K.B. (1996) After convergence: constituents of a social semiotics of mass media reception. In J. Hay, L. Grossberg and E. Wartella (eds), *The Audience and its Landscape*. Boulder, CO: Westview Press. pp. 63–73.

Jhally, S. (1990) *Dreamworlds*. Amherst, MA: Media Education Foundation.

Jhally, S. (1994) Intersections of discourse: MTV, sexual politics and *Dreamworlds*. In J. Cruz and J. Lewis (eds), *Viewing, Reading, Listening: Audiences and Cultural Reception*. Boulder, CO: Westview Press. pp. 151–68.

Jhally, S. and Lewis, J. (1993) *Enlightened Racism*. London: Routledge.

Johnson, R. (1987) What is cultural studies about anyway? *Social Text*, 16: 38–80.

Kagay, M. (1992) Variability without fault: why even well-designed polls can disagree. In T. Mann and G. Orren (eds), *Media Polls in American Politics*. Washington, DC: Brookings Institute. pp. 95–124.

Katz, E. (1963) The diffusion of new ideas and practices. In W. Schramm (ed.), *The Science of Human Communication*. New York: Basic Books. pp. 77–93.

Katz, E. and Liebes, T. (1990) *The Export of Meaning*. New York: Oxford University Press.

Keat, R. (1994) Scepticism, authority and the market. In R. Keat, N. Whitely and N. Abercrombie (eds), *The Authority of the Consumer*. London: Routledge. pp. 23–43.

Kellner, D. (1995) *Media Cultures*. London: Routledge.

Kitzinger, J.A. (1999) A sociology of media power: key issues in audience reception research. In G. Philo (ed.), *Message Received*. Harlow: Longman. pp. 1–20.

Klapper, J.T. (1960) *The Effects of Mass Communication*. New York: Free Press.

Kolakowski, L. (1993) An overall view of positivism. In M. Hammersley (ed.), *Social Research: Philosophy, Politics and Practice*. London: Sage. pp. 1–8.

Kosicki, G. (1993) Problems and opportunities in agenda-setting research. *Journal of Communication*, 43: 100–27.

Kottak, C. (1990) *Primetime Society: an Anthropological Analysis of Television and Culture*. Belmont, CA: Wadsworth.

Krippendorf, K. (1995) Undoing power. *Critical Studies in Mass Communication*, 12 (2): 101–32.

Kubey, R. (1996) On not finding media effects: conceptual problems in the notion of an active audience. In J. Hay, L. Grossberg and E. Wartella (eds), *The Audience and its Landscape*. Boulder, CO: Westview Press. pp. 187–205.

Kuhn, T. (1962) *The Structure of Scientific Revolutions*. Chicago: University of Chicago Press.

Kuhn, T. (1974) Logic of discovery or psychology of research? In P. Schilp (ed.), *The Philosophy of Karl Popper*. La Salle, IL: Library of Living Philosophers. pp. 798–819.

Lane, R. and Sears D. (1975) The problem of intensity. In S. Welch and J. Corner (eds), *Public Opinion*. Palo Alto, CA: Mayfield Press. pp. 28–48.

Lasswell, H.D. (1927) *Propaganda Techniques in the World War*. New York: Knopf.

Lasswell, H.D. (1927/1953) The theory of political propaganda. In B. Berelson and M. Janowitz (eds), *Reader in Public Opinion and Communication*. Glencoe, IL: Free Press. pp. 176–80.

Lasswell, H.D. (1941/1953) Democracy through public opinion. In B. Berelson and M. Janowitz (eds), *Reader in Public Opinion and Communication*. Glencoe, IL: Free Press. pp. 469–82.

Lasswell. H.D. (1944/1953) Why be quantitative? In B. Berelson and M. Janowitz (eds), *Reader in Public Opinion and Communication*. Glencoe, IL: Free Press. pp. 265–78.

Lasswell, H.D. (1972/1975) Communication research and public policy. In R. Carlson (ed.), *Communication and Public Opinion: a Public Opinion Quarterly Reader*. New York: Praeger. pp. 605–14.

Lazar, D. (1998) Selected issues in the philosophy of social science. In C. Seale (ed.), *Researching Society and Culture*. London: Sage. pp. 7–22.

Lazarsfeld, P.F. (1950) The obligations of the 1950 pollster to the 1984 historian. *Public Opinion Quarterly*, 14: 617–38.

Lazarsfeld, P.F. (1952/1975) Public opinion and the classical tradition. In R. Carlson (ed.), *Communications and Public Opinion. A Public Opinion Quarterly Reader*. New York: Praeger. pp. 615–29.

Lazarsfeld, P.F., Berelson, B. and Gaudet, H. (1949) *The People's Choice*. New York: Duell, Sloan and Pearce.

Lazarsfeld, P.F. and Dinerman, H. (1949) Research for action. In P. Lazarsfeld and F. Stanton (eds), *Communications Research 1948–9*. New York: Harper. pp. 71–110.

Leiss, W., Kline, S. and Jhally, S. (1990) *Social Communication in Advertising*. Scarborough, Ontario: Nelson Canada.

Lembo, R. (1994) Is there culture after cultural studies? In J. Cruz and J. Lewis (eds), *Viewing, Reading, Listening: Audiences and Cultural Reception*. Boulder, CO: Westview Press. pp. 33–54.

Lent, J. (1995) Interview with George Gerbner. In J. Lent (ed.), *A Different Road Taken*. Boulder, CO: Westview Press. pp. 85–98.

Levitt, T. (1995) The world's highest IQ. *Cultural Studies Times.*

Lewis, J. (1991) *The Ideological Octopus.* London: Routledge.

Lewis, J. (1997) What counts in cultural studies. *Media, Culture and Society,* 19: 83–97.

Lewis, J., Morgan, M. and Jhally, S. (1991) *The Gulf War and Public Opinion.* Amherst, MA: Center for Communication Research.

Lewis, J., Morgan, M. and Jhally S. (1999) *Libertine or Liberal? The Real Scandal of What People Know about President Clinton.* Amherst, MA: Center for Communication Research.

Lewis, J., Morgan, M. and Ruddock, A. (1992) *Images/Issues/Impacts: the Media and Campaign '92.* Amherst, MA: Center for Communication Research.

Lippman, W. (1922) *Public Opinion.* New York: MacMillan.

Livingstone, S. (1998) Mediated childhoods. *European Journal of Communication,* 13: 435–56.

Livingstone, S. (1999) Audience research at the crossroads. *European Journal of Cultural Studies,* 1: 193–217.

Livingstone, S. and Lunt, P. (1996) Rethinking the focus group in media and communications research. *Journal of Communication,* 46: 79–98.

Lull, J. (1990) *Inside Family Viewing.* London: Routledge.

McCombs, M.E. and Shaw, D.L. (1972) The agenda-setting function of the mass media. *Public Opinion Quarterly,* 36: 176–87.

McCombs, M.E. and Shaw, D.L. (1993) The evolution of agenda-setting research: twenty-five years in the market place of ideas. *Journal of Communication,* 43: 58–67.

McLeod, J.M., Kosicki, G.M. and McLeod, D.M. (1994) The expanding boundaries of political communication effects. In J. Bryant and D. Zillman (eds), *Media Effects: Advances in Theory and Research.* Hillsdale, NJ: Lawrence Erlbaum. pp. 123–62.

McQuail, D. (1987) *Mass Communication Theory.* London: Sage.

McQuail, D. (1998) With the benefits of hindsight: reflections on the uses and gratification paradigm. In R. Dickinson, R. Harindranath and O. Linne (eds), *Approaches to Audiences.* London: Arnold. pp. 151–65.

McRobbie, A. (1994) *Postmodernism and Popular Culture.* London: Routledge.

MacDonald, D. (1959) A theory of mass culture. In B. Rosenberg and D. Manning-White (eds), *Mass Culture: The Popular Arts in America.* New York: Macmillan. pp. 59–73.

Maccoby, E.E. and Holt, R.R. (1946/1953) How surveys are made. In B. Berelson and M. Janowitz (eds), *Reader in Public Opinion and Communication.* Glencoe, IL: Free Press. pp. 499–510.

Maccoby, N. (1963) The new scientific rhetoric. In W. Schramm (ed.), *The Science of Human Communication.* New York: Basic Books. pp. 41–53.

Machin, D. and Carrithers, M. (1996) From interpretative communities to communities of improvisation. *Media, Culture and Society,* 18: 343–52.

Malinowski, B. (1922) *Argonauts of the Western Pacific.* London: Routledge and Kegan Paul.

Mann, T. and Orren, G. (1992) To poll or not to poll . . . and other questions. In T. Mann and G. Orren (eds), *Media Polls in American Politics.* Washington, DC: Brookings Institute. pp. 1–18.

Mares, M. (1996) The role of source confusions in television's cultivation of social reality judgements. *Human Communication Research*, 23: 278–97.

Merton, R.K. (1947/1953) Mass persuasion: the moral dilemma. In B. Berelson and M. Janowitz (eds), *Reader in Public Opinion and Communication*. Glencoe, IL: Free Press. pp. 465–68.

Milgram, S. and Shotland, R.L. (1973) *Television and Antisocial Behavior*. New York: Academic Press.

Miller, D. (1995a) Consumption as the vanguard of history. In D. Miller (ed.), *Acknowledging Consumption*. London: Routledge. pp. 1–57.

Miller, D. (1995b) The consumption of soap opera. In R. Allen (ed.), *To Be Continued*. London: Routledge. pp. 213–33.

Modleski, T. (1996) The rhythms of reception: daytime television and women's work. In H. Baehr and A. Gray (eds), *Turning it On*. London: Arnold. pp. 104–11.

Moores, S. (1988) 'The box on the dresser'. Memories of early radio and everyday life. *Media, Culture and Society*, 10: 23–40.

Moores, S. (1993) *Interpreting Audiences*. London: Sage.

Moores, S. (1996) *Satellite Television and Everyday Life*. Luton: John Libbey Media.

Morgan, M. (1989) Television and democracy. In I. Angus and S. Jhally (eds), *Cultural Politics in Contemporary America*. London: Routledge. pp. 240–53.

Morgan, M. (1995) The critical contribution of George Gerbner. In J. Lent (ed.), *A Different Road Taken*. Boulder, CO: Westview Press. pp. 99–117.

Morgan, M. and Shanahan, J. (1996) Two decades of cultivation research: an appraisal and meta-analysis. *Communication Yearbook*, 20: 1–45.

Morgan, M. and Signorelli, N. (eds) (1990) *Cultivation Analysis: New Directions in Media Effects Research*. New York: Sage.

Morley, D. (1980) *The Nationwide Audience*. London: British Film Institute.

Morley, D. (1989) *Family Television*. London: British Film Institute.

Morley, D. (1992) The *Nationwide* audience: a critical postscript. In D. Morley, *Television, Audiences and Cultural Studies*. London: Routledge. pp. 119–30.

Morley, D. (1993) Pendulums and pitfalls. *Journal of Communication*, 14: 13–19.

Morley, D. (1994) Between the public and the private: the domestic uses of information and communications technology. In J. Cruz and J. Lewis (eds), *Viewing, Reading, Listening: Audiences and Cultural Reception*. Boulder, CO: Westview Press. pp. 101–23.

Morley, D. (1996) The geography of television: ethnography, communications and community. In J. Hay, L. Grossberg and E. Wartella (eds), *The Audience and its Landscape*. Boulder, CO: Westview Press. pp. 317–42.

Morris, M. (1990) Things to do with shopping centres. In S. During (ed.), *The Cultural Studies Reader*. London: Routledge. pp. 295–319.

Morris, M. (1996) Banality in cultural studies. In J. Storey (ed.), *What is Cultural Studies? A Reader*. London: Arnold.

Mort, F. (1996) *Cultures of Consumption*. London: Routledge.

Mowlana, H., Gerbner, G. and Schiller, H. (1992) *Triumph of the Image: The Media's War in the Persian Gulf*. Boulder, CO: Westview Press.

Newcomb, H. (1978) Assessing the violence profile studies of Gerbner and

Gross: a humanistic critique and suggestion. *Communication Research*, 5: 264–82.

Nightingale, V. (1989) What's ethnographic about ethnographic media research? *Australian Journal of Communication*, 16: 50–63.

Nightingale, V. (1996) *Studying Audiences: the Shock of the Real*. London: Routledge.

Nixon, S. (1992) Have you got the look? In R. Shields (ed.), *Lifestyle Shopping: the Subject of Consumption*. London: Routledge. pp. 149–69.

O'Keefe, G. (1975) Political campaigns and mass communication research. In S. Chafee (ed.), *Political Communication: Issues and Strategies for Research*. London: Sage. pp. 129–64.

O'Keefe, G. and Reid-Nash, K. (1987) Crime news and real world blues. *Communication Research*, 14: 147–63.

O'Sullivan, T. (1991) Television memories and cultures of viewing, 1950–1965. In J. Corner (ed.) *Popular Television in Britain: Studies in Cultural History*. London: British Film Institute. pp. 159–81.

Palmer, P. (1936/1953) The concept of public opinion in political theory. In B. Berelson and M. Janowitz (eds), *Reader in Public Opinion and Communication*. Glencoe, IL: Free Press. pp. 3–13.

Park, R.E. (1939/1953) Reflections on communication and culture. In B. Berelson and M. Janowitz (eds), *Reader in Public Opinion and Communication*. Glencoe, IL: Free Press. pp. 165–75.

Perse, E., Ferguson, D. and McLeod, D. (1994) Cultivation in the newer media environment. *Communication Research*, 21: 79–104.

Peters, J.D. (1996a) Tangled legacies. *Journal of Communication*, 46 (3): 85–7.

Peters, J.D. (1996b) The uncanniness of mass communication in interwar social thought. *Journal of Communication*, 46 (3): 108–23.

Philo, G. (1990) *Seeing and Believing: the Influence of Television*. London: Routledge.

Philo, G. (1999) Children and film/video/television violence. In G. Philo (ed.), *Message Received*. Harlow: Longman. pp. 35–53.

Philo, G. and Henderson, L. (1999) Audience responses to suicide in a television drama. In G. Philo (ed.), *Message Received*. Harlow: Longman. pp. 82–90.

Philo, G. and Miller, D. (1998) *Cultural Compliance: Dead Ends of Media/ Cultural Studies and Social Science*. Glasgow: Glasgow University Media Group.

Piepe, A., Charlton, P. and Morley, J. (1990) Politics and television in England: hegemony or pluralism? *Journal of Communication*, 40: 24–35.

Plato (1989) The Republic. In R. Davis and L. Finke (eds), *Literary Criticism and Theory*. White Plains, NY: Longman. pp. 44–59.

Popper, K. (1974) Replies to my critics. In P. Schilp (ed.), *The Philosophy of Karl Popper*. La Salle, IL: Library of Living Philosophers. pp. 961–1174.

Potter, J. (1992) How do adolescents' perceptions of television reality change over time? *Journalism Quarterly*, 69: 392–405.

Powlick, P.J. (1991) The attitudinal basis for responsiveness to public opinion among American foreign policy officials. *Journal of Conflict Resolution*, 35: 611–41.

Press, A. (1991) *Women Watching Television*. Philadelphia: University of Philadelphia Press.

Press, A. (1996) Toward a qualitative methodology of audience study: using ethnography to study popular culture. In J. Hay, L. Grossberg and E. Wartella (eds), *The Audience and its Landscape*. Boulder, CO: Westview Press. pp. 113–30.

Press, A. and Cole, E. (1994) Women like us: working class women respond to television representations of abortion? In J. Cruz and J. Lewis (eds), *Viewing, Reading, Listening: Audiences and Cultural Reception*. Boulder, CO: Westview Press. pp. 55–80.

Radway, J. (1983) *Reading the Romance*. Chapel Hill, NC: University of North Carolina Press.

Radway, J. (1986) Identifying ideological seams: mass culture, analytical method and political practice. *Communications*, 9: 93–125.

Radway, J. (1996) The hegemony of specificity and the impasse in audience research: cultural studies and the problem of ethnography. In J. Hay, L. Grossberg and E. Wartella (eds), *The Audience and its Landscape*. Boulder, CO: Westview Press. pp. 235–46.

Reeves, B. and Thorson, E. (1986) Watching television: experiments on the viewing process. *Communication Research*, 13 (3): 343–61.

Reilly, J. (1999) Just another food scare? Public understanding of the BSE crisis. In G. Philo (ed.), *Message Received*. Harlow: Longman. pp. 128–46.

Rogers, E., Dearing, J. and Bregman, D. (1993) The anatomy of agenda-setting research. *Journal of Communication*, 43: 68–84.

Rosengren, K. (1996) Combinations, comparisons and confrontations: toward a comprehensive theory of audience research. In J. Hay, L. Grossberg and E. Wartella (eds), *The Audience and its Landscape*. Boulder, CO: Westview Press. pp. 23–52.

Ross, A. (1995) Culture wars spill over. *Cultural Studies Times*.

Rothschild, M. (1975) On the use of multiple methods and multiple situations in political communications research. In S. Chafee (ed.), *Political Communication: Issues and Strategies for Research*. London: Sage. pp. 237–62.

Rubin, A., Perse, E. and Taylor, D. (1988) A methodological examination of cultivation. *Communication Research*, 15: 107–34.

Ruddock, A.D. (1996) Seems like old times: US foreign policy, media audiences and the limits of resistance. *Journal of International Communication*, 3: 94–113.

Ruddock, A.D. (1998a) Active netizens: television, realism and the *ER* website. In N. Moody and J. Hallam (eds), *Medical Fictions*. Liverpool: Eaton Press.

Ruddock, A.D. (1998b) Doing it by numbers. *Critical Arts*, 12: 115–37.

Ruddock, A.D. (1998c) Scientific criticism? A critical approach to the resistive audience. *New Jersey Journal of Communication*, 6: 59–80.

Ruddock, A.D. (1999) Methodological boundaries and public knowledge: can we measure culture? Paper presented at the Conference on Researching Culture. University of North London, 12 September.

Said, E. (1978) *Orientalism*. New York: Vintage.

Schiller, H. (1996) *Information Inequality: the Deepening Social Crisis in America*. New York: Routledge.

Schlesinger, P., Dobash, R.E., Dobash, R.P. and Weaver, C. (1992) *Women Viewing Violence*. London: British Film Institute.

Schramm, W. (1963) Communication research in the United States. In W. Schramm (ed.), *The Science of Human Communication*. New York: Basic Books. pp. 1–16.

Schudson, M. (1987) The new validation of popular culture: sense and sentimentality in academia. *Critical studies in Mass Communication*, 4: 51–68.

Seale, C. (1998) Statistical reasoning: causal arguments and mulitvariate analysis. In C. Seale (ed.), *Researching Society and Culture*. London: Sage. pp. 180–91.

Seale, C. and Filmer, P. (1998) Doing social surveys. In C. Seale (ed.), *Researching Society and Culture*. London: Sage. pp. 125–45.

Seaman, W. (1992) Active audience theory: pointless populism. *Media, Culture and Society*, 14: 301–12.

Sebastien, R.J., Parke, R.D., Berkowitz, L. and West, S.G. (1978) Film violence and verbal aggression: a naturalistic study. *Journal of Communication*, 28 (3): 164–71.

Seiter, E. (1992) Semiotics, structuralism and television. In R. Allen (ed.), *Channels of Discourse, Reassembled*. London: Routledge. pp. 31–66.

Seiter, E. (1999) *Television and New Media Audiences*. Oxford: Clarendon Press.

Seiter, E., Borchers, H., Kreutzner, G. and Warth, E. (1996) Don't treat us like we're so stupid and naïve: towards an ethnography of soap opera viewers. In H. Baehr and A. Gray (eds), *Turning it On*. London: Arnold. pp. 138–56.

Shapiro, M. and Lang, A. (1991) Making television reality. *Communication Research*, 18: 685–705.

Shields, R. (1992) Spaces for the subject of consumption. In R. Shields (ed.), *Lifestyle Shopping: the Subject of Consumption*. London: Routledge. pp. 1–20.

Shrum, L. (1994) Assessing the social influence of television: a social cognition perspective on cultivation effects. *Communication*, 22: 402–29.

Signorelli, N. (1986) Selective television viewing: a limited possibility. *Journal of Communication*, 36: 64–75.

Silverman, D. (1993) *Interpreting Qualitative Data: Methods for Analysing Talk, Text and Interaction*. London: Sage.

Silverman, D. (1998) Research and social policy. In C. Seale (ed.), *Researching Culture and Society*. London: Sage. pp. 97–110.

Silverstone, R. (1994) *Television and Everyday Life*. London: Routledge.

Silverstone, R. (1996) From audiences to consumers: the household and the consumption of communication and information technologies. In J. Hay, L. Grossberg and E. Wartella (eds), *The Audience and its Landscape*. Boulder, CO: Westview Press. pp. 281–96.

Silverstone, R. and Hirsch, E. (1994) Introduction. In R. Silverstone and E. Hirsch (eds), *Consuming Technologies*. London: Routledge. pp. 1–11.

Silverstone, R., Hirsch, E. and Morley, D. (1994) Information and communication technologies and the moral economy of the household. In R. Silverstone and E. Hirsch (eds), *Consuming Technologies*. London: Routledge. pp. 15–31.

Smart. B. (1993) *Postmodernity*. London: Routledge.

Sokal, A. (1996) Transgressing the boundaries: towards a transformative hermeneutics of quantum gravity. *Social Text*, 46: 217–52.

Spivak, G. (1988) *In Other Worlds: Essays in Cultural Politics*. New York: Routledge.

Stouffer, S. (1950/1953) Some observations on study design. In B. Berelson and M. Janowitz (eds), *Reader in Public Opinion and Communication*. Glencoe, IL: Free Press. pp. 520–4.

Tuchman, G. (1978) *Making News: A Study in the Construction of Reality*. New York: Free Press.

Tudor, A. (1999) *Decoding Culture*. London: Sage.

Turner, G. (1990) *British Cultural Studies*. Boston: Unwin Hyman.

Walkerdine, V. (1993) 'Daddy's gonna buy you a dream to cling to (and mummy's gonna love you just as much as she can)': young girls and popular culture. In D. Buckingham (ed.), *Reading Audiences: Young People and the Media*. Manchester: Manchester University Press. pp. 74–88.

Wallace, M. (1990) Negative images: towards a black feminist criticism. In S. During (ed.), *The Cultural Studies Reader*. London: Routledge. pp. 118–34.

Warde, A. (1994) Consumers, identity and belonging. In R. Keat, N. Whitely and N. Abercrombie (eds), *The Authority of the Consumer*. London: Routledge. pp. 58–74.

Weber, M. (1977) Objectivity in social science and social policy. In F. Dallmayr and T. McCarthy (eds), *Understanding and Social Inquiry*. Notre Dame, IL: University of Notre Dame Press. pp. 24–37

Wertham, F. (1955) *Seduction of the Innocent*. London: Museum Press.

Williams, R. (1960) *The Long Revolution*. London: Chatto and Windus.

Williams, R. (1978) *Keywords*. London: Fontana.

Willis, P. (1998) Notes on a common culture. *European Journal of Cultural Studies*, 1: 163–76.

Wilson, F.G. (1942/1975) *The Federalist* on public opinion. In R. Carlson (ed.), *Communication and Public Opinion: a Public Opinion Quarterly Reader*. New York: Praeger. pp. 500–12.

Winch, P. (1977) The idea of a social science. In F. Dallmayr and T. McCarthy (eds), *Understanding and Social Inquiry*. Notre Dame, IL: University of Notre Dame Press. pp. 142–57.

Winston, B. (1986) Debate has not halted the flow of blood. *The Listener*, 23 January, pp. 9–10.

Winston, B. (1990) How are media born? In J. Downing, A. Mohammadi and A. Sreberney-Mohammadi (eds), *Questioning the Media*. New York: Sage. pp. 55–72.

Winston, B. (1998) *Media, Technology and Society*. London: Routledge.

Wober, J. (1998) Cultural indicators: European reflections on a research paradigm. In R. Dickinson, R. Harindranath and O. Linné (eds), *Approaches to Audiences: A Reader*. London: Arnold. pp. 61–73.

Wolfe, K.M. and Fiske M. (1949) Why read comics? In P. Lazarsfeld and F. Stanton (eds), *Communications Research 1948–9*. New York: Harper. pp. 3–50.

Wren-Lewis, J. (1983) The encoding/decoding model: criticisms and redevelopments for research and decoding. *Media, Culture and Society*, 5: 151–69.

Wright, H. (1998) Dare we decentre Birmingham? *European Journal of Cultural Studies*, 1: 33–56.

Yeo, E.J. (1996) *The Contest for Social Science: Relations and Representations of Gender and Class*. London: Rivers Oram Press.

Zaller, J. (1994) Positive constructs of public opinion. *Critical Studies in Mass Communication*, 11: 276–86.

Index